not ref

DIVIDED LOYALTIES

DIVIDED LOYALTIES

Fort Sanders and the Civil War in East Tennessee

by Digby Gordon Seymour

THE UNIVERSITY OF TENNESSEE PRESS • KNOXVILLE

DEDICATED

TO THE MEMORY OF MY GRANDFATHER

CAPTAIN ARTHUR WILLIS GLOSTER

who with Nathan Bedford Forrest enlisted in White's Tennessee Mounted Rifles, their hands together on the same Bible. Commissioned in the Confederate Engineering Corps, he served at Columbus, Ky., Island 10, Fort Pillow, Shiloh, Tupelo, and Fort Pemberton, and was captured at Vicksburg. After exchange, he commanded the Pontoon Train of the Western Army from Missionary Ridge to Atlanta to the final surrender in North Carolina.

AND WRITTEN AS A CENTENNIAL GIFT FOR MY WIFE

LOIS

AND CHILDREN

JOHNNY, JIMMY, AND TOMMY

Contents

Foreword

FOR too long the Battle of Fort Sanders has been neglected in published histories of the Civil War. In this violent twenty-minute battle, the Confederate army suffered casualties at the rate of forty per minute; and, of even greater significance, the "Arch of the Confederacy" was finally crumbled. Because the victorious Union army was able to hold Knoxville, the line of communication between the Confederate armies in Virginia and Georgia was cut and the South's offense was materially weakened. With East Tennessee in Union hands, the Confederates were forced to detour troops through Middle and West Tennessee and North Carolina over circuitous routes causing much delay.

It is fitting, therefore, that this story be properly recorded and that it be written by one who has more than a passing interest in the Civil War in East Tennessee. Such is the case with Digby G. Seymour, the author of *Divided Loyalties*, whose scholarly approach is warmed by a long-time personal and family involvement in the subject.

Dr. Seymour's father, the late Charles M. Seymour, was a distinguished Knoxville attorney who imparted to his son a deep love of history. His mother, the late Flora Nell Gloster Seymour, was a member of a prominent Tennessee family that played an active role on the side of the Confederacy: her father, Arthur W. Gloster, was an officer in the Confederate army, taking the oath of allegiance along with Nathan Bedford Forrest; her uncle fought and died for the Confederacy at Murfreesboro. But this was a war where even the members of families were divided by their allegiance to the North and to the South. Dr. Seymour's paternal great-grandfather, Charles Seymour, an Englishman who came to this country in 1848, sympathized with the North. A paternal uncle, Major General James H. Wilson, was commander of Sherman's cavalry and aided in the capture of Jefferson Davis.

The Seymour family home was located on Knoxville's Melrose Avenue, where many gun emplacements helped defend the city against the assault of Confederate armies. The residence overlooked the Tennessee River which was always a major consideration in the movement of troops by both the North and the South.

The ability of Dr. Seymour to place the Battle of Fort Sanders in proper perspective is a fine contribution to the history of this unfortunate conflict. In his research on the Civil War campaign up the valley from Chattanooga, he has located many photographs and developed other items of interest which have not heretofore been published. I am sure that the general public as well as students of this period will derive much pleasure and gain valuable information from the historical records assembled and placed in such readable form by Dr. Seymour.

GEORGE R. DEMPSTER
Member of the Board
Knoxville-Knox County
Civil War Centennial Committee
Mayor, City of Knoxville,
1952-1955

Preface

IN HIS headquarters on Kingston Pike just outside of Knoxville, Tennessee, Lee's "War Horse," James Longstreet, commander of First Corps, Army of Northern Virginia, ponders with heavy heart the mission before him. Knoxville is ringed with the flags of Dixie, and General Longstreet means to fly them from the masts of the Courthouse before the week is done.

Nearby, on Cherokee Heights, young Porter Alexander, Longstreet's First Corps colonel of artillery, has his guns trained on the key position of Fort Sanders, the Union earthworks bastion guarding the western approaches to the city.

The First Corps has arrived at Knoxville fresh from a smashing triumph over the Union armies at bloody Chickamauga near Chattanooga. Before that, on the trail that has led them here, Longstreet and his men have come through the strife at Chancellorsville, Fredericksburg, and Gettysburg. . . .

It is now one hundred and forty-nine days after Gettysburg. The fortunes of war have bloodied the fields of East Tennessee. The War Horse chews his cigar relentlessly. Opposing him are twelve thousand Union soldiers from the Army of the Ohio—veterans of Bull Run, Williamsburg, Fair Oaks, Antietam, and Vicksburg. Their leader is Major General Ambrose Burnside. Once the North's hero for his amphibious assault upon the eastern shores of North Carolina and Virginia, the warrior with the long, flowing side whiskers has seen better days. President Abraham Lincoln had personally selected him to succeed George McClellan as the Commander-in-Chief of the Army of the Potomac. But Burnside had recklessly smashed into Lee

and Longstreet at Fredericksburg and was crushed, his casualty list numbering more men than he now commands. This time he is the quarry, not the hunter.

Inside the city of Knoxville are hundreds of loyal citizens eager to help repel the Rebel invader. The Negroes work feverishly to strengthen the earthworks. But also in the town are many hearts anxious for Longstreet to march triumphantly through its ravaged streets, to cleanse the area of the accursed Yankees. This divided and beleaguered city is more than a battleground in the War Between the States. Here there has been true civil war, with neighbor turned against neighbor. Ministers of the Gospel have been beaten and imprisoned for their sympathies. Violence has plagued this land until no house or yard has been free from conflict.

If Longstreet does not have enough to contend with in his immediate task of defeating Burnside and recapturing Knoxville for the Confederacy, he can contemplate with alarm the forces that are moving relentlessly against his rear. General U. S. Grant, now commanding the western theater, has read Lincoln's urgent dispatches to "free" his beloved East Tennesseans and has sent his most trusted and aggressive subordinate to drive Longstreet from Tennessee. General William T. Sherman is literally marching his men out of their shoes to reach Knoxville and Burnside before the Union garrison is starved or beaten into submission.

And so the stage is set. From their fog-shrouded position high on the southwestern banks of the Tennessee River, just below Knoxville, the rifled cannon of Porter Alexander belch

DIVIDED LOYALTIES

forth their angry fury, the signal for the attack on Fort Sanders, November 29, 1863. Once more the long gray line of the Confederate Army will charge headlong into glory and disaster.

Why are these men here? What manner of courage or of madness will hurl the sons of Georgia, of Mississippi, of South Carolina, of Arkansas, and of Texas against an almost impregnable fortress manned by determined volunteers from New York, from Michigan, from Ohio, and from Massachusetts?

In August, 1863, Edward A. Pollard, the great Southern historian, wrote in his *Southern History of the War*:

The Eastern portion of Tennessee abounds in hills, rocks, poverty, and ignorance. But its military situation was one of great importance to the Confederacy. The enemy already held West and Middle Tennessee. It required but to occupy East Tennessee to have entire possession of one of the most valuable States of the Confederacy. They [the Federal troops] also felt bound in honor and duty to render the long-promised assistance to the Unionists of East Tennessee. Tennessee would be more thoroughly theirs than Kentucky, when once they filled this eastern portion of it with their armies. The essential geographical importance of this country to the Confederacy was too obvious to be dwelt upon. It covered Georgia and involved the defences of the cotton region of the South. Through it ran a great continental line of railroad, of which the South could not be deprived without unspeakable detriment. The importance of this road to the supply of our armies was no less considerable than to the supply of our general population.

President Lincoln said that if the Union armies could take East Tennessee he would have "the Rebellion by the throat," and that it "must dwindle and die."

Today in upper and middle East Tennessee there are so very few historical markers and reminders of the Civil War that it is easy to forget that the struggle for this area was a continuing event invoking national attention in the North and South, and that the climax of the campaign, the Battle of Fort Sanders, was initiated at the highest level.

This book was written to commemorate the self-sacrificing gallantry of both the Union and Confederate armies that fought the bloody Battle of Fort Sanders, November 29, 1863. For making this book possible I am indebted to my father, the late Charles M. Seymour, who gave to me a deep love of history; and to my mother, the late Flora Nell Gloster Seymour, who helped preserve our Southern heritage by enrolling her eight children in the Children of the Confederacy before some could stand up and walk.

Special thanks go to Ray Smith of Chicago who graciously provided 244 references from the *Confederate Veteran Magazine*, which he personally indexed as a hobby; to Hirst D. Milhollen of the Library of Congress; and to the General Services Administration of the National Archives for supplying the many photographs of Knoxville and of the fortifications.

I am also indebted to Pollyanna Creekmore of the Lawson McGhee Library; to Carolyn Jakemen of the Houghton Library, Harvard University; to the Massachusetts, Michigan, and Ohio Civil War Centennial Commissions; to Dr. Stanley J. Folmsbee and Dr. Harold S. Fink of the Department of History of the University of Tennessee; to City Editor Dick Evans of the Knoxville *Journal*; and to Dr. Richard Brailey for his maps.

A final word of deep appreciation to two people who need no thanks to realize a sense of fulfillment of a dream—who acted as critics, typists, grammarians, artists, and military consultants, and who spurred the work on from its infancy by words of encouragement and sound advice—my sister Nell Seymour Holloway and her husband, Major Leo Holloway of the United States Air Force, Taranto, Italy.

DIGBY GORDON SEYMOUR

Knoxville, Tennessee
August 15, 1963

DIVIDED LOYALTIES

Gay Street - Knoxville Tenn - (1861). (Drawn from Memory)

Simultaneous recruiting for the Confederate and Union armies on Gay Street, Knoxville, Tennessee, 1861.

1

The Disloyal Unionists

THE people of East Tennessee fondly called their land the "Switzerland of America." A mountainous region of cool climate and small valley farms in contrast to the nearby humid plantation flatlands, East Tennessee lay in, but not entirely of, the South, along the dividing line between two great agricultural regions. To the south were the tropical fruits and cotton fields where a feudal society grew rich but stagnated on the labor of men not dignified with surnames. To the north were the fruits and cereals of the temperate zone where a new civilization grew strong from the power of machines and metals.

Gradually during the westward expansion of the young United States, East Tennessee became isolated from the rest of the nation. At first a crossroads for the pioneers moving westward over the massive Appalachian range, the region was later bypassed for better routes that lay to the north and to the south. In the first half of the nineteenth century, East Tennessee had given to public life a class of men with distinctive physical, intellectual, and moral qualities. They were tall, angular, rawboned; they were alert, positive, and often narrow-minded; they were honest and sincerely patriotic, but vindictive and unrelenting—the truest of friends, the most aggressive and dangerous of foes. Such men had long since subdued the redcoats and the redskins.

As the years passed, isolation and inbreeding forged the bonds of the family clans. Now the people found their pleasure and excitement in political stump-speakings, religious camp meetings, and homemade liquors. Scotch-Irish by birth, they hated the plantation aristocracy of

the coast, had little intercourse with their Indian neighbors, and were indifferent to the Negro slaves.

Within the bounds of this geographical and cultural isolation there erupted the most violent passions of a bloody civil war fought between families and friends while the nation was fighting the greater struggle of North against South. The plight of the loyal Unionists of East Tennessee during the Civil War was to find no parallel in the rest of the states. Later, recounting their miseries in a petition to Congress in 1864, they recalled:

Their arms and ammunition were seized, before they could organize, by the Rebel soldiers; and though the government, which owed them protection, did not protect them, yet their hearts clung to the government and they prayed for the Union. Five thousand of their men have seen the inside walls of Rebel prisons, and hundreds of them, covered with filth, devoured with vermin, famished with hunger, have died martyrs to their country there. Their property has been seized, confiscated; their houses pillaged; their stock driven off; their grain consumed; their substance wasted; their fences burned; their fields laid waste; their farms destroyed by friends as well as foes. The Rebels robbed them; the Federals devoured them; for they had short supplies; and our women broke their last biscuit, and gave them the biggest half, out of the mouths of hungry children. They gave up the last horse, mule, cow, sheep, hog, everything they had to the soldiers that needed them, because they were Union soldiers, or were plundered out of them by the enemy. Their young men have been hunted like wild beasts, by soldiers, by Indians, sometimes by bloodhounds, and when caught, tied two-and-two to long ropes, and driven before cavalry—thin clad, barefooted and bleeding—over frozen roads and icy creeks and rivers. Some have been beaten with ropes, with straps, and with clubs.

Oliver P. Temple. An active Union supporter, he later gave the land for Temple Avenue in Knoxville.

Some have been butchered, others shot down in their own homes or yards—in the highroad, or the fields, or in the forests; others still have been hung up by the neck to the limbs of trees, without judge or jury—there is no single neighborhood within the bounds of East Tennessee, whose green sod has not drunk the blood of citizens murdered.[1]

Although separated from the Northern states except by way of Kentucky, which was bound to the Union against the will of many of its people, most East Tennesseans remained steadfastly loyal to the Union.

Paradoxically, in Knoxville, the dominant commercial and manufacturing town of East Tennessee, many of the leading citizens were sympathetic to the South. As early as 1857, they had promulgated sectional feeling by holding a meeting of one of the "Southern Commercial Conventions," although the commercial vitality of Knoxville was at that time negligible among Southern cities. And in 1860, the great secessionist orator, William L. Yancey of Alabama, was invited to town to speak on "Southern Rights."

The pro-Union loyalties of most East Tennesseans became evident, however, when Yancey started addressing the crowd assembled outdoors. Badgered with jibes from the audience, Yancey challenged his hecklers to join him on the platform for debate. He soon found himself confronted by such prominent community leaders as Judge Samuel Rodgers, Mr. Oliver P. Temple, Mr. John Fleming, Dr. William Rodgers, and the Rev. William G. Brownlow.

"Parson" Brownlow, editor of the Knoxville *Whig* and uncompromisingly Unionist, was a man of strong opinions who neither gave nor sought quarter in theological and political controversy. He was known as an orator all over the South long before the Civil War began. It was said that he was hated by Knoxvillians who favored the Confederacy "the way Irish Catholics hated Cromwell."[2]

Thomas A. R. Nelson, a Tennessee Unionist leader. He later broke with the administration of Abraham Lincoln.

William G. Brownlow, the "Parson." East Tennessee's outstanding
Union supporter, he was the fiery editor of the Knoxville *Whig* and
was Tennessee's first post-Civil War governor.

Brownlow, in his bombastic style, told Yancey and the crowd that not only would he refuse to join any secession or armed opposition to the authority of the national government, but he would unite with thousands of men who would defend the Union in East Tennessee, and "over their dead bodies they who sought to overthrow the Government would have to make their way." Yancey, a considerably calmer orator, replied that, as a loyal son of Alabama, he would abide by the decision of Alabama, and go as it would go. But he then turned toward Brownlow, pointed his finger belligerently, and defiantly thundered: "As for this man who talks of confronting the sons of the South in a contest for their rights, with the armed opposition of East Tennesseans—if [my] State determined upon resistance, [I] would meet Mr. Brownlow in the bloody strife and would give him the bayonet up to the muzzle!" [3]

The violent threats were to portend even more violent deeds; it was folly to think that strife could be avoided. The leading Tennessee historian, Dr. J. G. M. Ramsey, had written in 1858:

I conceal from no one my deep conviction that the days of our present Union are nearly numbered. . . . Our people will never again be a unit. . . . The high toned New-England spirit has degenerated into a clannish feeling of profound Yankeeism. . . . The masses of the North are venal, corrupt, covetous, mean and selfish. . . . We are essentially two people.[4]

Ramsey's "two people," however, lived side by side in Knox County and East Tennessee. No state border, no natural barriers, separated Secessionist from Unionist. In 1860 the population of Knox County was 20,020 white citizens and 2,370 slaves. Knoxville had 3,704 persons. Its corporate limits extended from the Holston River [5] on the south to the Gray Cemetery and tracks of the East Tennessee and Georgia Railroad on the north, and from First Creek on the east to Second Creek on the west. Within these narrow confines, the early skirmishes were verbal battles emphasized by gestures and menacing threats. Union and Confederate rallies were sometimes held at the same time on the same street.

In the early days of 1861, the time for words was drawing to an end; action replaced boasts. In January, Governor Isham G. Harris, an open and avowed Southern supporter, called the Tennessee General Assembly into special session, and an act was passed authorizing the people of Tennessee to vote for calling a convention to secede from the United States. But on February 9, the election day, the convention was defeated by a vote of 69,387 to 57,798. Harris had played his trump card and lost; Tennessee, it seemed, would remain with the Union.[6]

Governor Isham G. Harris. He led Tennessee into the Confederacy.

For a time there remained in Tennessee a hard core of Whig leaders of national prominence who condemned both coercion and secession. While disapproving of military action against the South, they did not believe that their state should side against the government. The most outstanding of the Whig neutralists was John Bell, a native Tennessean who had run for President against Lincoln in 1860 as leader of the Constitutional Union Party. Bell had envisioned Tennessee as "the peacemaker between the states of the South and the general government." But the tide of secession soon swept away sentiments of neutrality, including those of Bell, as the nation took up arms.

On one occasion in February, 1861, Bell was overheard on a train in conversation with Jefferson Davis, who was going to his home in Mississippi by way of the railroad through Virginia and Tennessee. Seated beside him, Davis turned to Bell and asked him what he proposed to do. Bell replied, "Mr. Davis, I am too old for active service in the field, but be assured, sir, if it becomes necessary, I shall take the stump in Tennessee and use all of my power to have my State represented by sixty or eighty thousand soldiers for the South." [7] Bell's Whig friend, Felix K. Zollicoffer of Nashville, joined him in defection, declaring, "Let us emulate the glorious example of our fathers in arms. We must not, can not, stand neutral and see our Southern brothers butchered." [8]

In April, President Lincoln called upon Tennessee, as well as the other states, to provide volunteers to help subdue the Southern Rebellion. This call for troops had a profound effect on the attitudes of many who had previously voted for allegiance. James Otey, Protestant Episcopal Bishop of Tennessee, had earlier declaimed: ". . . the cry, like a death-knell, rings through all our borders. *'The Union is dissolved! and the sun of our glory has gone down!'* Ruin with its wild shriek of despair, spreads its dark wings over all the land, and foreshadows the 'desolation that comes like a whirlwind.' " [9] But now that the sword was drawn, the good Bishop threw off the yoke of despair and assumed the mantle of the proud cavalier of the South. To a friend he now confided:

Your views, like mine, I doubt not, have undergone a great change in regard to the moral aspect of the contest. Since Mr. Lincoln's proclamation, and the attitude assumed, and the purposes proclaimed by the North, I have no sympathy with the U. S. Government—no respect for its rulers—very little regard for the Northern people. Our duty is clearly and unequivocally to repel by force, and to make every sacrifice rather than submit to an administration that tramples down every barrier raised by our Forefathers for the protection of personal, social and public rights. [10]

Popular sentiment in Tennessee generally opposed President Lincoln's call for troops, and Governor Harris was quick to respond. He rejected the President's mandate and entered into a military league with the Confederate States of America, under which troops were enlisted all over the state. Without having seceded or joined the Confederacy, Tennessee was functioning independently in actual rebellion against the United States.

On May 7, 1861, the Tennessee legislature approved the Military League, and the question of separation from the Union was submitted again to the people at a general election, June 8. This time the state went overwhelmingly with the Confederacy by a vote of 104,913 to 47,238. East Tennesseans cast 32,923 of the minority votes, but Knoxville voted 777 to 377 for "separation." [11] Knoxville was to become the focal point of a struggle between the now "disloyal Unionists" and their Confederate rulers. For more than two years, the greater struggle between the North and the South would play a secondary role to the family fight at home.

Tennessee was no longer neutral. The "Volunteer State" lived up to her name as thousands joined the ranks of both armies. Tennessee gave 136,000 troops to the Confederacy, a figure exceeded by no other state. And 31,092 men, mostly from East Tennessee, joined the Union army. Fighting for the North, 8,777 Tennesseans died, the highest percentage of casualties of any state. On the other hand, the 9,414 men killed in the Confederate army placed Tennessee nearest the bottom in this respect. Four hundred and fifty-four battles and skirmishes were fought within her borders, a record exceeded only in Virginia. [12]

Confederate armies would win great victories at Shiloh, Stones River, and Chickamauga, only to retire from the field or lose the campaign by hesitant strategy. In politics, no Tennessean would become a member of the ruling Confederate government, but Andrew Johnson of East Tennessee would become President of the United States. The state blessed with many navigable waters would furnish the Confederacy with no outstanding naval commander, but David Farragut of Knox County would become the highest ranking officer in the United States Navy.[13] No Tennessean would achieve the rank of full general and command an army in the field for the Confederacy. But at Appomattox when Robert E. Lee was asked to name the greatest soldier under his command, he answered, "A man I have never seen, sir. His name is Forrest." [14] Nathan Bedford Forrest of Tennessee, neglected

by his own army, was to the North "the devil" whom Northern soldiers were implored to catch "if it costs ten thousand lives and breaks the treasury," but they did not succeed until a full month after Lee surrendered. Tennessee, the Southern state least affected by the Reconstruction tragedy, would be the birthplace of the Ku Klux Klan, of which Forrest became the head.

Tennessee and her people thus played their parts in a remarkable illustration of the Jominian concept that "war is a great drama, in which a thousand physical or moral causes operate more or less powerfully and which can not be reduced to mathematical calculations." [15]

NOTES

1. Edward Everett, *Account of the Fund for the Relief of East Tennessee*, pp. 6-7.

2. Lyman P. Powell, *Historic Towns of the Southern States*, p. 468.

3. Thomas W. Humes, *The Loyal Mountaineers of Tennessee*, p. 84.

4. J. G. M. Ramsey, in a letter to L. W. Spratt, April 29, 1858. Copy in McClung Collection, Lawson McGhee Library, Knoxville. Published in William B. Hesseltine (ed.), *Dr. J. G. M. Ramsey: Autobiography and Letters*, p. 94.

5. This part of the Holston River, between its confluence with the French Broad River and the mouth of the Little Tennessee River, has, since about 1880, been considered part of the main Tennessee River. See Stanley J. Folmsbee, Robert E. Corlew, and Enoch L. Mitchell, *History of Tennessee*, I, 16-17.

6. Mary Emily Robertson Campbell, *The Attitudes of Tennesseans Toward the Union, 1847-1861*, pp. 288-90.

7. *Confederate Veteran*, XI (March 1903), 116. The letter-writer who reported this conversation added that when the train stopped at Knoxville, Davis went out on the platform and spoke to an assembled crowd.

8. *American Annual Cyclopaedia*, 1861, p. 679.

9. William M. Green, *Memoir of Rt. Rev. James Hervey Otey*, p. 348.

10. James H. Otey to Edward C. Burks, in *American Historical Review*, XXXI (July 17, 1861), 100.

11. Campbell, pp. 291-94.

12. Francis T. Miller, *The Photographic History of the Civil War*, X, 146-48.

13. Although Matthew F. Maury, the great oceanographer, was born in Virginia, he entered the Confederate navy from Tennessee. His primary work was purchasing vessels and naval stores in Europe.

14. Andrew Lytle, *Bedford Forrest and his Critter Company*, p. 357.

15. *The Official Army Information Digest*, XVI, No. 8 (August 1961), 18. Baron Antoine Henry Jomini was a Swiss officer who served with Napoleon. At the time of the Civil War he was the leading theorist and writer of warfare. He emphasized maneuver rather than battle, the capture of places rather than the destruction of armies. Forrest, Sherman, Grant, and Sheridan broke with these concepts to begin modern concepts of total war.

David Glasgow Farragut, first Admiral of the United States Navy. He was born at Lowe's Ferry, in Knox County where a school, a hotel, and a community bear his name.

2

Keystone of the Confederate Arch

TO Abraham Lincoln there was no question that East Tennessee and its people were his main source of strength in the South, and immediately after the disaster that befell his army at Bull Run, he ordered an all-out advance into East Tennessee from the Cincinnati base. There were both military and political reasons for his strategy. Union occupation of the territory would sever the vital railroad line connecting Virginia with the Mississippi Valley, and the area was ablaze with Unionists eager to join his legions.

East Tennessee was even more important to the Confederate States. The Richmond *Enquirer* was quick to point out that within the entire perimeter of the Southern defenses, East Tennessee was the "Keystone of the Confederate Arch." [1] The South moved into action. Even before Tennessee had broken from the Union, companies of Rebel troops were recruited in Knoxville and nearby counties, mustered into service with state militia, and stationed at strategic points. In February, 1861, one such unit was already encamped on College Hill, the home of East Tennessee University, most of whose students had deserted the campus to join the Confederate army.

The first Knoxvillians to enlist in the Rebel ranks were enrolled in the Mitchel Guards, and William G. Swan, former mayor of Knoxville, was named commanding officer. This infantry company, named for John Mitchel, a fiery Irishman who was once a resident of Knoxville, was limited to men of Irish descent. [2] The Mitchel

Andrew Johnson. A United States Senator from Tennessee and a staunch Unionist, he became President of the United States.

Connelly F. Trigg, active East Tennessee Unionist

The death of Charles Douglass, a Unionist who was shot while sitting at his window on Gay Street, Knoxville—sketched in the 1860's

Guards and other companies soon organized trained at the fairgrounds two miles east of Knoxville.[3] By late February about eight hundred soldiers were encamped near Knoxville. They posed a threat to Andrew Johnson and other notable Federal sympathizers who came periodically to plead the Union cause.

On one occasion, as Johnson began to speak from a platform erected on Gay Street, a Confederate band in a hotel across the street burst forth with "Dixie" and "The Bonnie Blue Flag," and armed Confederate troops dispersed the crowd. Bloodshed was prevented only by the entreaties of peaceable men of both sides.

In May, 1861, Unionists held another rally and defiantly raised the American flag to the top of a "tall liberty pole at the corner of Gay and Main," according to a letter of the time.[4] Among those listening to Connelly Trigg's main address at this rally were Major Washington Morgan, of the Military League state troops, and Charles Douglass, a familiar figure around town known for his fondness for homemade liquor.

Douglass was peaceable enough during his sober moments, but these were infrequent. On the day the beginning of the Civil War was announced to the public, Douglass was found sitting on Gay Street in front of the Lamar House, beating a bass drum. "We believed that he'd be the first man killed without ever being in a battle," wrote John Crozier some years later.[5]

During Trigg's address at the May Unionist rally, an argument arose between Major Morgan and Douglass, and Morgan fired at Douglass as he entered a store, wounding him slightly and killing a passerby. This was the first clash of arms in Knoxville, setting the pattern for the bitterness that followed, as neighbor turned upon neighbor. Major Morgan then went to the military camp, gathered several hundred state troops, and marched back up Gay Street. Violent conflict was prevented by Colonel David Cummings —a leading Confederate citizen of Knoxville who originally came from Anderson County— and two Union citizens, Abner Jackson and John Williams, who together persuaded the soldiers to return to camp.

A few days later as Charlie Douglass sat by a window of his house, he was mortally wounded by an unknown person who fired from a hotel window a hundred yards distant. Both Unionists and unfriendly secessionists gathered for the funeral, the angry Unionists determined to make

Saltpeter cave and storage buildings in East Tennessee destroyed by Union cavalry raiders

a martyr of a man who might have passed on unattended in other circumstances. Once again Colonel Cummings, whose military bearing and forcefulness were imposing, intervened, leaping upon his horse to help the minister lead a peaceful procession to the grave of the unfortunate Charlie.[6]

These minor clashes of citizens who had once been friends were of little importance in the history of the long war. But they indicated early and clearly that whoever wanted to control East Tennessee would have to do so by force. The Confederacy could not count on loyalty in this explosive region of one of its states, but its existence was dependent upon the strategic location and the natural resources of East Tennessee.

At Richmond, Virginia, the Confederacy's President Jefferson Davis and his military staff studied their material resources and requirements. It was not a bright picture. But the South was afire with enthusiasm and hope; a way would be found. The staff could count only about 150,000 rifles and muskets in the whole Confederacy, a few boxes of sabers and swords, a few hundred pistols. No ammunition or powder had been manufactured in the South

since the War of 1812; the little stored in depots was left over from the Mexican War. Except at Harpers Ferry Armory, all war materials had been made in the North. Workmen skilled in these arts were few.

Surveying this bleak picture, the Confederate Chief of Ordnance, General Josiah Gorgas, noted one bright spot. In East Tennessee there were metals and tools for war. The area had the only blast furnaces outside of Virginia. Copper, a necessity for field artillery and percussion caps, was beginning to be mined near Ducktown, Tennessee. By 1863, a copper rolling mill nearby was turning out 6,000 pounds a day. When it was destroyed by Federal troops on Christmas Eve, 1863, the Confederacy was so hard pressed that men were sent scurrying into the mountains of East Tennessee, North Carolina, and Virginia to strip moonshine stills of their copper tubing— a most unpopular move at any time.[7]

East Tennessee caves contained an unlimited supply of niter. The Confederacy was laid off in districts, each under an officer, the purpose being to collect nitrous earth found under old houses and barns. By 1864, some 2,800,000 feet of earth in various stages of nitrification were collected, part of which would yield one and one-half pounds of niter per foot. The officers were sometimes called "Iron Agents." In command of Niter and Mining District Number Seven at Knoxville (also called the "Zollicoffer District") was Charles Ducloux, a native of Lucerne, Switzerland, who migrated to Knox County. Ducloux retained this duty until June, 1863, when the first Federal troops raided Knoxville.[8]

Lead was stripped from window sashes of

Charles Ducloux, Confederate niter officer for the Knoxville District. He is pictured here when he represented the Felix Zollicoffer Chapter of the United Confederate Veterans at the funeral of Jefferson Davis.

homes and from sewer conduits. The one-half-inch lead conduit of East Tennessee University's private water supply was carried away.[9] Agents were sent hastily North and to Europe to buy arms and ammunition. In short, the South became a beehive of activity, in marked contrast to the popular conception of it as a land of lazy, indolent people. The scope of the South's transformation from an agrarian society to a formidable military power was a miracle not fully appreciated to this day.

General Gorgas recorded that in April, 1861, the South was without an arsenal, laboratory, powder mill, foundry, or rolling mill, except in Richmond, and that before the end of 1863, the Confederacy supplied them. In detail, he wrote:

During the harassments of war, while holding our own in the field defiantly and successfully against a powerful enemy, crippled by a depreciated currency; throttled with a blockade that deprived us of nearly all the means of getting material or workmen; obliged to send almost every able bodied man to the field; unable to use the slave labor, with which we were abundantly supplied, except in the most unskilled departments of production; hampered by want of transportation even of the commonest supplies of food; with no stock on hand even of articles such as steel, copper, leather, iron, which we must have to build up our establishments—against all these obstacles, in spite of all these deficiencies, we persevered at home, as determinedly as did our troops in the field, against a more tangible opposition; and in that short period created, almost literally out of the ground, foundries and rolling mills at Selma, Richmond, Atlanta, and Macon; smelting works at Petersburg; chemical works at Charlotte; a powder mill far superior to any in the United States and unsurpassed by any across the ocean; and a chain of arsenals, armories, and laboratories equal in their capacity and their improved appointments to the best of those in the United States, stretching link by link from Virginia to Alabama.[10]

Knoxville became a vital link in the chain. Manufacturing plants in Knoxville were expanded. The A. L. Maxwell Machine Shop in North Knoxville, a plant consisting of a fine brick building and a storehouse, was converted into an armory with a blacksmith and carriage-maker's shop attached. Originally, no arms were made at the arsenal, but flintlocks were altered to percussion. Major S. H. Reynolds was put in command of operations. Thomas Riggins, a native of McMinn County, was named gunsmith and superintendent of the arsenal. Locally, he was known as "Armorer for the South."

Armorer Riggins, born in 1821, had been apprenticed to the gun shop of a relative when he was only ten years old. By the time he was twenty-four, he could make a rifle out of raw iron, and many a contestant from East Tennessee won shooting matches with a Riggins rifle. In early 1861, he personally armed the "East Tennessee Squirrel Shooters," a Rebel volunteer cavalry company. He joined the Third Tennessee Infantry Regiment, but the Confederate

Armorer and his handiwork. Thomas Riggins, "Armorer for the South," is shown *at right* when he was ninety, in a 1911 photograph taken at his home. The old Kentucky flintlock rifle *below* was converted to a percussion musket by Riggins at Knoxville's Confederate arsenal, where he worked during the war. Believed to be the only Knoxville-made specimen in existence, the rifle is owned by the Chicago Historical Society. A close-up of the lockplate, *far right,* shows the stamping "Knoxville, C.S.A., 1862."

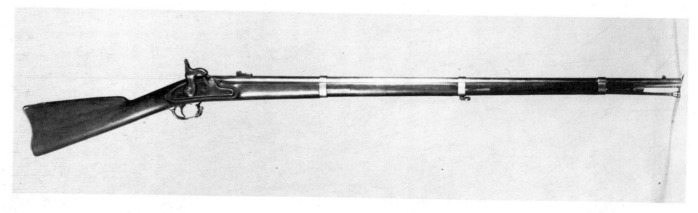

government ordered him to Knoxville to instruct sixty mechanics in converting old fowling pieces into cavalry rifles. Wagonloads of old Kentucky rifles were shipped to Riggins and his men to be converted to percussion lock, large-bore carbines.[11] Later, Parson Brownlow's steam-powered printing plant was conscripted and used for conversion of sporting rifles to cavalry carbines.

The Knoxville Arsenal also obtained arms for the Confederacy from other local manufacturers. At Mossy Creek (Jefferson City), a gun factory and saltpeter works functioned until destroyed by Federal raiders under Colonel William P. Sanders, June 21, 1863. A man named Galyon, of Sevier County, operated a small Confederate gun shop for more than two years. A local citizen developed a method of manufacturing percussion caps, and production of this necessary article was carried out extensively in Knoxville.

By May 30, 1862, the Knoxville Arsenal was producing new rifles; John D. Gray, an arms procurer for the Confederacy, wrote to Captain Richard Cuyler, Commander of the Macon, Georgia, Arsenal: "I have a contract with the Ordnance Department at Knoxville approved by the Department at Richmond, for making 200 rifles and 1,000 carbines to be completed in eight or nine months. . . ."[12]

In September, 1862, command of the Knoxville Arsenal was turned over to Major J. A. Brown, Chief of Ordnance for General Edmund Kirby Smith. Major A. Leyden, commanding the Ninth Georgia Artillery Battalion, succeeded Brown in July, 1863. The Military Storekeeper was Captain P. M. McClung, great-grandson of both William Blount, the Governor of the Tennessee territory prior to statehood, and of James White, the founder of Knoxville. As a member of the Home Guards, Captain McClung was later killed in the first Federal raid into Knoxville by a unit of the Fifth Kentucky Cavalry commanded by Colonel William P. Sanders. Sanders himself later was killed during the Confederate siege of Knoxville.

When the Union troops under General Ambrose Burnside entered Knoxville in September, 1863, they found at the arsenal: 2,000 pikes, 2,500 pounds of crude niter, one steam engine of fifty horsepower with gearing, six iron lathes, four boring machines, and three planing machines.[13] They burned the buildings during the November siege of Knoxville by Confederate units detached from the Army of Northern Virginia. Riggins, the Armorer, served the remainder of the war as a private in the Third Tennessee Infantry Regiment.

Other manufacturing was carried on, also, in spite of the handicaps of geographical isolation and military blockade. In December, 1861, Joseph A. Mabry established a depot of clothing and tents. John S. VanGilder, president of the Knoxville Leather Company, expanded his operations to include the manufacture of military trappings. Charles M. McGhee, operator of a meat-packing plant, was appointed a colonel in the Commissary Department of the Confederate army. Alfred Buffat, a skilled miller, supplied tremendous quantities of refined flour and was exempt from military service by the Confederacy so as to keep up his important work. S. T. Atkin contracted to supply the Confederate government with all the iron he could manufacture at his plant. Mr. Atkin, being a sensible businessman in this time of war, also started a coffin factory. When Federal troops occupied Knoxville in 1863, they put Mr. Atkin in jail.

East Tennessee's wealth of raw and manufactured materials and its livestock and grain production combined to make the region essential to the Confederacy. A history of the war said that, when the Union occupied the area in 1863, the Confederacy "had been deprived of one of the chief sources of its subsistence. [Afterwards] it was forced to mainly depend upon Florida for its meat while its supply of corn was principally derived from the rich valleys of the Alabama and Tombigbee rivers. The Confederate army was already cut off from the immense cattle growing region west of the Mississippi and from the corn and bacon of Tennessee." This book added, in a note:

Says the Knoxville *Register* (published at Atlanta, Georgia, after the Federal occupation of East Tennessee), "If any one doubts the necessity which would compel President Davis to sacrifice Richmond, Charleston, and Mobile, all to reac-

quire East Tennessee, he need only ask the commissary general by what agencies and from what sources the armies of the South have been sustained during the first years of the war. East Tennessee furnished the Confederate States with 25,000,000 pounds of bacon. Last year the State of Tennessee fed the army." The Richmond *Examiner* of October 31st corroborates this testimony

Railroad bridge across the Holston River at Strawberry Plains. This bridge shown guarded by a sentry, was destroyed four times in the war.

in the following terms: "Except what was furtively obtained from Kentucky, the whole army supply of pork came from East Tennessee, and the contiguous counties of the adjoining states. The product of corn in that region was very heavy, and no portion of the Confederacy, equal in extent, afforded as large a supply of forage and winter pasturage."[14]

From Richmond by way of Bristol to Knoxville, a single track of standard uniform gauge ran uninterrupted. Called the East Tennessee and Virginia, this railroad connected at Knoxville with the East Tennessee and Georgia trunk, which went on to Chattanooga. It was the shortest route from the Confederate capital to Chattanooga, was thus the gateway to the entire Mississippi Valley, and was the only such connection west of the Blue Ridge Mountains. Eastward, the railroads of Virginia to Charlotte, Wilmington, Atlanta, and New Orleans were practically worthless. Lines were short, were not always connected, had no bridges across some rivers, and—like many railroads of the era—had different gauges. Sixteen different, interrupted railroad lines were involved in a journey from Richmond to Atlanta and on to Chattanooga.

Lacking men and machines to correct the poor lines, the authorities quickly realized that East Tennessee's railroad must be made secure. Even before hostilities began, guards were stationed at every bridge, every crossing, every tunnel. Only the most loyal Confederate soldiers and citizens were entrusted with this vital mission. The danger had been made very clear. As early as May, 1861, Parson Brownlow openly advocated burning the bridges so that the arch would fall down![15]

NOTES

1. James Welch Patton, *Unionism and Reconstruction in Tennessee,* p. 58.

2. John Mitchel had been the editor of *The Nation,* a seditious publication printed in Dublin. He was deported to Australia by the British, but he escaped and came to New York in 1854. He migrated to East Tennessee and at Knoxville became a fast friend of William Swan. Mitchel published a newspaper in Knoxville called *Southern Citizen,* which advocated reopening the slave trade. At the start of the war Mitchel moved to Richmond, where he edited the Richmond *Examiner.* There is a Tennessee state historical marker (1 E 13) on State Highway 73 in the Coker Hill Chapel area in Blount County indicating where Mitchel first resided in East Tennessee. See Samuel C. Williams, "John Mitchel, the Irish Patriot, Resident of Tennessee," East Tennessee Historical Society's *Publications,* No. 10 (1938), pp. 44-56.

3. Prominent citizens who supported these organizations and believed passionately in the Confederate cause were John Boyd, William G. Churchwell, David H. Cummings, John H. Crozier, Joseph A. Mabry, W. G. McAdoo, Campbell Wallace, Moses White, and Dr. J. G. M. Ramsey, the historian.

4. Charles Ducloux, "Scrapbook" (hereafter cited as Ducloux Scrapbook) in Lawson McGhee Library.

5. John H. Crozier in a letter to the Knoxville *Tribune,* March 22, 1885.

6. Humes, pp. 101-102, 347.

7. William A. Albaugh III and Edward N. Simmons, *Confederate Arms,* p. 209.

8. With about forty other soldiers, Ducloux was attacked by Federal cavalrymen on Kingston Pike and retreated to the main building of the University, from which point he watched the fighting north of the city. Ducloux Scrapbook and miscellaneous unindexed papers at Confederate Memorial Hall, Knoxville.

9. Stanley J. Folmsbee, *East Tennessee University, 1840-1879,* The University of Tennessee *Record,* Vol. 62, No. 3 (May 1959), p. 15.

10. Ben LaBree, *The Confederate Soldier in the Civil War,* p. 329.

11. *Confederate Veteran,* XIX (July 1911), 315.

12. *The War of the Rebellion: A Compilation of the Official Records of the Union and Confederate Armies* (hereafter cited as O.R.), Captured Rebel Records, XXXVI, 4.

13. *Confederate Veteran,* XXXV (February 1927), 51.

14. Alfred H. Guernsey and Henry M. Alden, *Harper's Pictorial History of the Great Rebellion,* p. 569.

15. Knoxville *Whig,* May 25, 1861.

The Considerate Commander

BY THE summer of 1861 the Confederate States of America had assumed all the characteristics of an independent nation: agents of the new nation were in control of the civilian governments, an army was being raised to defend its borders and preserve its independence, and its diplomats were casting about for allies and world recognition. But while some success was achieved in early overtures to England and France, no progress was made in securing the loyalty and support of the mountaineers of East Tennessee and western North Carolina; only the people of the larger cities of Knoxville and Chattanooga had willingly joined the move for Southern independence. To these cities the Confederate government dispatched armies led by its most forceful but tolerant commanders, to insure the integrity of the surrounding territory and the subservience of the populace. It was hoped that, by force of arms and friendly persuasion, the foment incited by active Unionists in East Tennessee could be neutralized, and that subsequent aggression by the Federal government would cause the Unionist leaders to defect to the Southern banners.

In early June the city of Knoxville was still controlled by the Military League troops. Their primary function was to protect the manufacturing facilities and the railroads that were daily transporting soldiers from the Southwestern states through East Tennessee into Virginia.

The Third Alabama Infantry, the first regiment from the southwest to pass through Knoxville, had been greeted with wild cheering and gifts of food and clothing at every stop along the way from its home base—until it reached Knoxville. Here it was greeted with threats from Parson Brownlow himself.[1] As the troops strolled through town, they spotted the United States flag flying from a pole and rushed to pull it to the ground, but their officers quickly prevented the desecration.

The continuous transit of troops was witnessed by people loyal to the Union with feelings of dissatisfaction, which sometimes grew into animated wrath. At Strawberry Plains a regiment of Southern troops, being transported by train, fired on a mass meeting of Unionists as they passed, and the fire was returned. Though no life was lost in the brief encounter, the feelings of hatred were naturally intensified. To prevent further occurrences in the future, President Davis undertook to disarm the population.

Accordingly, on July 26, 1861, the District of East Tennessee of the Confederate Armies was established, and Brigadier General Felix K. Zollicoffer was named first commander. Born in Maury County in 1812, General Zollicoffer as a young man had been a journeyman printer in Knoxville and was widely known and admired. He left Knoxville to serve in the Seminole War. Later he was editor of the Nashville *Banner*, was State Comptroller from 1844 to 1849, and continued his career in the State Senate. He was in the United States Congress from 1853 to 1859 and a delegate to the Peace Conference held at Washington in 1861. Politically, he was a staunch Whig, but he had been stunned by Lincoln's call for troops after the attack on Fort Sumter. He offered his services to Tennessee's Governor Harris and in May, 1861, after Tennessee approved the Military League, was appointed a brigadier general of the Provisional Army. After commanding an instruction camp,

Brigadier General Felix K. Zollicoffer. **He** was the first Confederate commander of the District of East Tennessee, with headquarters at Knoxville. His daughter, Loulie Zollicoffer Sansom, was a founder of Knoxville's Chapter 89, United Daughters of the Confederacy.

he took over the new post, and, although his military knowledge was limited, his political fame gave importance to the position.

At this early point in the war, the South felt it had little to fear from the overwhelming numerical superiority of the North. The belief that one Southerner was worth ten Yankees was seriously entertained by some fanatics, possibly with some hint of justification. Since Revolutionary days, the Southern people had borne the brunt of military duties. In the War of 1812, the North furnished only 58,552 soldiers, the South 96,812. In the Mexican War the little state of South Carolina furnished 5,696, while Massachusetts supplied only 1,047. The total number of troops contributed by the North to the Mexican War was 23,054, whereas the South contributed 43,-

630—nearly double, and, in proportion to her population, four times as many.[2]

But no fight brings out more violence and passion than a family fight. New England, which had been lax in defending the national honor in the war with the British in 1812, poured out almost her entire qualified population to aid in the subjugation of the South. The Midwest, particularly Illinois, was seething with the fervor of mobilization. The Chicago *Tribune* insisted on its demand that the new West be allowed to fight the battle alone. "Let the East," cried this valiant sheet, "get out of the way; this is a war of the West. We can fight the battle, and successfully, within two or three months at the furthest. Illinois can whip the South by herself. We insist on the matter being turned over to us."[3]

Nonetheless, Zollicoffer believed he had little to fear from these impetuous Northerners, for he was separated from the Ohio River by Kentucky, whose governor had wired Lincoln that the state would "furnish no troops for the wicked purpose of subduing her sister Southern States." Establishing his headquarters in Knoxville, Zollicoffer picked General William R. Caswell, commander of the Tennessee Provisional soldiers, as his aide and Major F. B. Fogg, only son of the ardent Unionist lawyer, Francis B. Fogg of Nashville, as his adjutant. No immediate plans were developed for offensive action, so the Confederate military set about accomplishing their first task, which was to convert or disarm the disloyal population. Zollicoffer seemed disposed to exercise authority with a lenient hand and to abstain from needless severities.

The first rumblings of discontent came from his supporters. The Knoxville *Register,* a small daily newspaper, accused him in its editorials of too little use of his power. There were complaints that Zollicoffer, a Whig, allowed too many Democrats to be appointed to offices in the new government, although this was a natural course because the Democrats were known as the party of strongest sympathy with secession. Zollicoffer was so lenient as to tolerate the continued existence of the *Whig,* the weekly newspaper edited by William G. Brownlow, despite its editor's printed statement: "We can never live in a Southern Confederacy and be made hewers of wood and drawers of water for a set of aristocrats and overbearing tyrants." [4] Brownlow peppered the occupying authorities with words only a brave or impudent man would publish. "Aye, we say put down the rebellion, and force rebels to lay down their arms, if, in so doing, we have to exterminate from God's green earth every living human being south of the Mason and Dixon Line." [5]

Zollicoffer made an initial but reluctant move against Brownlow by arraigning the editor's son, John Bell Brownlow, before him upon the accusation of General W. P. Lane of McMinn County. The son was accused of circulating a copy of *Impending Crisis of the South,* a book not considered favorable to the South and so controversial that it had precipitated a crisis in the United States Congress following its publication. In a personal hearing before the Confederate commander, Brownlow was freed of charges against the military forces, but he was immediately rearrested and jailed on the same charge under an order, previously issued, concerning civilians. He was again acquitted and released, although he refused to take the oath of allegiance to the Confederate States. Instead, he joined the Union army and became a lieutenant colonel, commanding the Ninth Regiment of Tennessee cavalry. John's brother, James P. Brownlow, by 1865 a brigadier general in the First Tennessee Volunteer Cavalry Regiment, was also a thorn in the Confederate side. [6] James P. threatened to kill the enemy rather than take prisoners, and General Forrest, the Southern cavalry leader, was anxious to settle with him for this breach of military custom in a sometimes chivalric war. [7]

Zollicoffer moved hesitantly, but did forbid flying the United States flag from public poles. A few defiant citizens continued to display the colors from windows of their houses. But in August he took sterner measures and dispatched cavalry units to disarm Union men in Anderson, Campbell, Scott, and Fentress counties. The campaign went on through November with varying degrees of success. Brownlow was forced to stop publication of the *Whig* on October 24, fled Knoxville, and went into hiding in Tuckaleechee Cove, Blount County, until arrested on December 6.

The office of Brownlow's Knoxville Whig. Brownlow's steam-powered printing plant was adapted by the Confederates for the conversion of sporting rifles to cavalry carbines.

Tennessee riflemen on their way to join the Virginia army

NOTES

1. *Confederate Veteran,* VII (January 1899), 6.

2. Edward A. Pollard, *Southern History of the War,* I, 48.

3. Pollard, I, 61.

4. Knoxville *Whig,* January 26, 1861.

5. *Ibid.,* August 10, 1864. This editorial, although written after the end of Confederate occupation in East Tennessee, indicates the general tone of Brownlow's writings and his dislike for the idea of secession. Mr. Brownlow, who was a Methodist minister as well as a newspaper editor, was East Tennessee's outstanding citizen of the Civil War era. He became the state's first governor upon its readmission to the Union, and later a United States Senator. An excellent account of his career may be found in Betsey B. Creekmore, *Knoxville.* See also E. Merton Coulter, *William G. Brownlow: Fighting Parson of the Southern Highlands* (Chapel Hill: 1937).

6. William F. Amann, *Personnel of the Civil War,* II, 59. Colonel Brownlow of the 1st Regiment, Tennessee Volunteer Cavalry, received the brevet rank of brigadier general, March 13, 1865.

7. O. R., Ser. I, XXXI, Part I, 591. It is interesting that the Brownlows, East Tennessee's outstanding Unionists, were pitted against Bedford Forrest, the Confederate cavalryman from West Tennessee whom General Sherman called "the most remarkable man our Civil War produced on either side."

4

Revolt in the Ballot Box

WHILE the Southern states busily plotted their defensive strategy, the North, in determining to crush resistance, was forced to aggression. General Winfield Scott, commander of all Union forces, was old and now too fat to mount his horse. But old "Fuss and Feathers" was not too senile to serve his country with his brain.[1] In his fertile mind the aims and the strategy to follow were quite clear. On paper he sketched a general outline for conduct of the war. Although the popular cry was "On to Richmond," Scott realized, as few did then, that the war would be long, protracted, and won by attrition and not by tactical maneuvers. He called for immediate blockading of the Southern coasts by the navy. The army would drive down the Mississippi to the Gulf, splitting the Western states from the Confederacy and holding the valley to complete the blockage. With rebellions isolated, they could be crushed in pockets one at a time. The principal thrusts would be through Virginia and simultaneously into the heart of the Confederacy, using the waters of the Tennessee and Cumberland rivers. Scott's plan, when leaked to the press, was unpopular. The emotional fever that gripped the North demanded spirit and fanatic drive. His plan was jeered at and nicknamed "Anaconda." Unfavorably regarded as it was at the time, however, "Anaconda" proved to be the ultimate strategy which led to Appomattox.

Still, it was a leisurely plan in conception, and East Tennesseans were loath to wait for "liberation," as General Zollicoffer found to his dismay. In August, 1861, he very persuasively promised that "the military authorities are not here to offend or injure the people, but to insure peace to their homes, by repelling invasion and preventing the horrors of civil war. Treason to the state government cannot, will not, be tolerated. But perfect freedom of the ballot box has and will be accorded and no man's rights, property, or privileges shall be disturbed."[2]

Despite his protestations of moderation, Zollicoffer found himself surrounded by multiple pockets of resistance as the mountaineers gathered all available weapons and met in secret rendezvous to plan their own private revolution. In August, at the time of the usual biennial Tennessee elections, they brazenly exercised their freedom at the ballot box by electing Union

Horace Maynard, successful Union candidate for the United States Congress in 1862 from the Knoxville District

23

John Baxter, Union sympathizer. Defeated in the race for the Confederate Congress from Knoxville, he later defended "bridge burners" and the "train stealers."

candidates overwhelmingly in the congressional districts around Knoxville. The winners quickly departed for Washington in fear of their lives, presumably leaving vacant four seats in the Confederate Congress at Richmond which East Tennessee was entitled to fill. The Confederate Constitution provided that states should have as many delegates in the Confederate Congress as they were entitled to in Washington. Delegates would be elected from the congressional districts then established by law in the same manner as for election of members of the United States Congress.[3]

Of the Union candidates elected, Horace Maynard, from the Second or Knoxville District, was a native of Massachusetts and graduate of Amherst who had moved to Knoxville in 1837 to become Professor of Mathematics at East Tennessee University. To avoid arrest, Maynard fled Knoxville and was already on the way from

his home to the Kentucky border at the time of the election and was soon safely beyond it.[4]

The successful Unionist candidate from the First District, Thomas A. R. Nelson, was the acknowledged leader of the old Whig Party in East Tennessee. He gained international renown for a speech in the United States Congress against secession, an oration hailed by the London *Times* as a masterpiece. Mr. Nelson left his home in Jonesboro and traveled towards Cumberland Gap, by then already occupied by Confederate troops. On the road at night, he was seized by soldiers and taken as a prisoner of war to Richmond, Virginia. Shortly afterward, he took the oath of allegiance to the Confederate government and was set free to go home. For a time he remained an impassive spectator to the political changes evolving during the war. But when Lincoln suspended the writ of *habeas corpus,* Nelson began to have misgivings about the rights of citizens and the purposes of the war and, after the Emancipation Proclamation, turned his back on his past, declaring that the last link was broken that bound him to the Federal government for which his ancestors had fought.[5]

In the Third or Athens District, election was claimed by both the Confederate and Union candidates, and each took his seat in his respective legislature. But George Bridges, the Union choice, was seized while traveling through Kentucky and returned to Knoxville under arms. There he signed an oath of submission to the Confederacy. He later escaped by means of the underground railway and took his seat in Congress on February 23, 1863, nine days before the adjournment of the session.

Dr. A. J. Clements of the Fourth District claimed election and was seated in the United States Congress, January 13, 1862.

The Tennessee General Assembly in October, 1861, divided the state into eleven districts, and congressmen were elected for all eleven in November. William G. Swan of Knoxville, commander of the Mitchel Guards, defeated John

Wartime sketch of Cumberland Gap, held by Confederate troops,
through which Unionists attempted to escape from East Tennessee

Baxter to represent the Second District in the Confederate Congress.[6]

In Washington, Representative Maynard teamed with Andrew Johnson, the Democratic Senator who had retained his seat in the Senate of the United States in the face of the secession of Tennessee. Together they moved within the highest circles of the Federal government, constantly pressing, continually urging a Union advance into East Tennessee.

NOTES

1. General Scott had achieved fame in the Mexican War upon the capture of Vera Cruz. He was the first general-in-chief of the United States Army during the Civil War. He was then nearly seventy-five years old and too feeble for active service. He retired November 1, 1861, and was succeeded by George McClellan.

2. "Address of General Felix Zollicoffer to the Citizens of East Tennessee," in the Knoxville *Whig*, August 10, 1861.

3. *House Journal*, 1861, 2 extra sess., p. 56.

4. Horace Maynard was appointed Attorney-General of Tennessee in 1862 by Andrew Johnson, the Military Governor. He later served twelve years in the United States Congress. He was appointed U.S. Minister to Turkey in 1875 by President Grant. In 1880 he was made Postmaster-General by President Hayes.

5. O. R., Ser. I, XVI, Part II, 909-11. Thomas A. R. Nelson was one of President Andrew Johnson's counsels in the impeachment trial of 1868. See Thomas B. Alexander, *Thomas A. R. Nelson of East Tennessee* (Nashville: 1956).

6. Philip M. Hamer, *Tennessee: A History*, I, 554.

5

Bushwhackers and Vigilantes

THE Confederate government was well aware that any Federal move into East Tennessee would have to come through southeastern Kentucky, following the route of the forbidding, ancient Wilderness Trail which passed through Cumberland Gap, a narrow and easily defended pass located sixty miles north of Knoxville. Charged with the defense of the Gap and the entire Western Territory was General Albert Sidney Johnston, a man President Davis considered the ablest soldier in the entire Confederacy.[1] With only 20,000 men, half of whom were armed with flintlocks, he was ordered to defend the line stretching from Virginia across the width of Tennessee and Missouri to the Kansas border. Johnston was also empowered by Davis to decide whether or not Kentucky was to be occupied by Confederate troops. On his journey from Richmond to West Tennessee, the General stopped in Knoxville to confer with General Zollicoffer, commanding his eastern anchor. The two quickly agreed that the natural defense of East Tennessee began at Cumberland Gap, and Johnston ordered that it be occupied immediately.[2]

Zollicoffer, reluctant to perform any overt act of aggression against a state which had declared its neutrality, notified Kentucky's Governor Magoffin that, "the safety of Tennessee requiring," he was occupying Cumberland Gap and the neighboring mountains. He took pains to . point out that "Tennessee feels and has ever felt towards Kentucky as a twin sister; their people are one people in kindred sympathy, valor, and patriotism; we have felt and still feel a religious respect for Kentucky's neutrality. We will respect it as long as our safety will permit. If the

Federal forces will now withdraw from their menacing position, the force under my command shall be immediately withdrawn." [3] After fortifying the Gap, Zollicoffer moved the rest of his command westward to a point where he could protect the Jamestown and Jacksboro roads and prevent ingress from central Kentucky to both East Tennessee and Nashville.

Opposing the Confederates, forty miles north of the Gap at Camp Andrew Johnson, near Barbourville, Kentucky, was an unlikely group of refugees from East Tennessee, most without any war equipment, calling themselves the First and Second Tennessee Volunteers, United States Army. Samuel P. Carter, their organizing and commanding officer, was a native Tennessean recently recalled from duty in Brazil as a lieutenant in the United States Navy upon the specific request of President Lincoln. Ordered to Cincinnati, on July 23, 1861, he met secretly there with Lieutenant William Nelson, also detached from naval duty, who had been assigned to provide secret arms for the loyal home guards of Kentucky.

Carter and Nelson were detailed to recruit men from Tennessee, Kentucky, and North Carolina into the Union army and to get them into shape to operate behind the Confederate lines. Their objective was the seizure of bridges and railroads into East Tennessee, thereby severing the Holston Valley from Virginia. Nelson began recruiting in Kentucky for a drive down the Wilderness Trail. Carter hurried to his home, Carter County, Tennessee, to rally men in rebellion against the Confederate government, but much to his surprise, he found no easy way to organize resistance forces. It was at this time

Southern Unionists fleeing to the North through the hidden mountain trails, as pictured in 1863

that he retreated into Kentucky to establish Camp Andrew Johnson, from which he dispatched agents to beg Tennessee Union sympathizers to join him.[4]

Kentucky's governor protested to Lincoln against recruiting in his state, but both sides moved fast to occupy the state that had announced its "neutrality." On September 5, General Leonidas Polk marched his Confederate troops into Hickman, Kentucky.[5] General U. S. Grant retaliated by crossing the Ohio River into Paducah. President Davis ordered Zollicoffer to shift his troops from Knoxville and Cumberland Gap and seize Camp Johnson as well as Camp Robinson, which was commanded by

Lieutenant Samuel P. Carter, U. S. Navy. President Lincoln chose him to head a secret army of loyal East Tennesseans.

Camp Dick Robinson, rendezvous point

Lieutenant Nelson. Zollicoffer took three regiments, brushed aside the Kentucky home guards, and established Camp Buckner at Cumberland Ford. He captured the saltworks at Manchester, took the salt and wagons, sent them on to Knoxville, and defeated the home guard at Barbourville. Then, believing that he had more to fear from revolt at home, he left General William Churchwell in command at Cumberland Gap and went back to East Tennessee.

During Zollicoffer's absence, Colonel William B. Wood was made commander at Knoxville. Being less patient than his predecessor, he periodically marched his troops through town to maintain discipline and authority. Many Unionists who had been disgruntled, but who had respected the sincerity of General Zollicoffer, openly defied Colonel Wood. The Reverend Thomas Humes, the rector of St. John's Episcopal Church, resigned rather than offer prayers

Lieutenant William Nelson, U. S. Navy. He was detailed to supply arms to loyal Kentucky volunteers.

ently recruited loyal East Tennesseans

Thomas W. Humes. Rector of St. John's Episcopal Church and later president of East Tennessee University, Humes defied the Confederate government but respected the officers in charge at Knoxville.

for Jefferson Davis and the Confederate armies. The Colonel, fearing that he could not cope with the situation, on November 1 wrote to Secretary of War Judah P. Benjamin at Richmond:

There can be no doubt of the fact that large parties, numbering from twenty to a hundred, are every day passing the narrow and unfrequented gaps of the mountains into Kentucky to join the army. My courier, just in from Jamestown, informs me that a few nights since, one hundred and seventy men passed from Roane County into Kentucky. I do not believe that the Unionists are in the least reconciled to the (C. S.) Government, but on the contrary are as hostile to it as the people of Ohio, and will be ready to take up arms as soon as they believe the Lincoln forces are near enough to sustain them.[6]

Operating out of Knoxville, the Confederates then began a more potent campaign to wipe out resistance. Vigilance committees were dispersed all around East Tennessee with the authority to arrest persons on suspicion of hostility.

Rev. William Duggan's "march"

The Reverend William Duggan, a Methodist, was arrested and marched fifty miles on foot, accused of praying for the Union. To retaliate, the Unionists organized "bushwhacking" societies to harass Confederate troops and destroy property of Southern sympathizers. In very short order, the first inklings of the horrors of true civil war were visited upon the citizens of East Tennessee.[7] There was no discipline by commanders nor restraint imposed by the codes of war to alleviate the bitter hatreds that swept over the land. But in spite of guerrillas, bushwhackers, and vigilantes, possibly for lack of a plan and a leader, there had been no overt act of violence against the government of the Confederate States of America.

NOTES

1. A. S. Johnston was the ranking general officer in active service following Adjutant General Samuel Cooper. He was followed in rank by Robert E. Lee, Joseph E. Johnston, and P. G. T. Beauregard. His full title was "General Commanding the Western Department of the Army of the Confederate States of America."

2. Stanley F. Horn, *The Army of Tennessee*, p. 55.

3. W. J. McMurray, *History of the Twentieth Tennessee Regiment, Volunteer Infantry, C.S.A.*, pp. 384-85.

4. Robert U. Johnson and Clarence C. Buel (eds.), *Battles and Leaders of the Civil War* (hereafter cited as *Battles and Leaders*), I, 373-74.

5. Lieutenant General Leonidas Polk was a West Point graduate who had left the army for the church and eventually became the first Protestant Episcopal Bishop of Louisiana in 1841. He commanded the First Division of A. S. Johnston's army. Polk fought at Belmont, Shiloh, Perryville, Murfreesboro, and Chickamauga. After Chickamauga he was suspended by Bragg, but the charges against him were dismissed. He was killed near Marietta, Georgia, in 1864, opposing Sherman. As an Episcopal Bishop he was the principal founder of the University of the South at Sewanee, Tennessee. A recent biography of Polk is Joseph H. Parks, *General Leonidas Polk, C.S.A.: The Fighting Bishop* (Southern Biography Series [Baton Rouge: 1962]).

East Tennessee Union men in secret meeting swearing allegiance to the Union, as seen by an artist of the times.

6

The Bridge Burners

THE Reverend William Blount Carter, a Presbyterian minister of Elizabethton and brother of the Union commander of Camp Johnson, had for months seriously considered William Brownlow's scheme to burn the East Tennessee bridges. In September he made his way to his brother's camp and revealed his plans, which were forwarded to General George Thomas, Union commander in Southeastern Kentucky, who in turn relayed them to Washington. President Lincoln and General George McClellan approved the scheme and sent $1,000.[1]

The plan called for groups of men to burn, on the same night, nine wooden railroad bridges between Bristol, Virginia, and Stevenson, Alabama, thus blocking the use of 250 miles of railway and impeding the progress of men and provisions to the Army of Northern Virginia. On the night of November 8, 1861, the burners struck, destroying the two bridges between Knoxville and Bristol, one between Knoxville and Chattanooga, two south of Chattanooga, and lesser bridges over the Hiwassee River and Lick Creek. The bridge over the Holston River at Strawberry Plains in Jefferson County was saved by the vigilance and bravery of the watchman, Edward Keelan, who was the sole guard that night. He fought off twelve men, wounding several and killing one. Keelan was wounded and, believing himself dying, declared: "They have killed me, but I saved the bridge."[2]

The bridge-burning, serious as it was in severing railroad connections, had an even more startling psychological effect. The Confederate government assumed that the deed was a signal to light flames of revolt all over East Tennessee and that an invasion by Union soldiers from Kentucky was imminent. People gathered in the towns and cities to hear the news as it spread with the speed of uncontrolled fire. Confederate commanders in the villages began seeing Union invaders at every crossroad. Telegrams and letters poured into Knoxville and Richmond, increasing the alarm. The major in command at Loudon wrote: "The Union feeling in this county is exceedingly bitter, and all they want, in my opinion, to induce a general uprising is encouragement from the Lincoln armies. They have a great many arms, and are actually manufacturing Union flags to receive the refugee Tennesseans when they return. They are getting bold enough."[3]

On November 11, Colonel Wood at Knoxville wrote to Richmond: "The whole country is now in a state of rebellion. A thousand men are within six miles of Strawberry Plains and an attack is contemplated tomorrow."[4] Knoxville was immediately placed under martial law. All weapons of citizens were seized, and no one was allowed to enter or leave town without a permit signed by a committee of three Confederate citizens, headed by Austin Sperry, editor of the Knoxville *Register*. General Zollicoffer wrote from his headquarters at Jacksboro to Colonel Wood: "I will to-morrow send dispatches to the forces near Jamestown, the cavalry near Huntsville, that near Oliver's, and start out the cavalry here, to commence simultaneously disarming the Union population. You will please simultaneously send orders to all detachments under your command to inaugurate the same movement at the same

East Tennessee railroad bridges. Some were destroyed by both the Confederate and Union troops during the war.

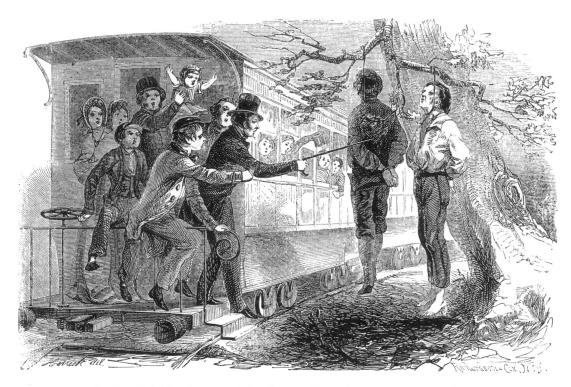

Bodies of bridge burners being beaten by train passengers near Greene-ville. The men were hanged by order of a Maine colonel serving with the Confederacy.

time in their various localities. Their leaders should be seized and held as prisoners. The leniency shown them has been unavailing. They have acted with duplicity and should no longer be trusted." [5]

Everyone suspected of complicity in the bridge-burning was arrested. Others who were known Union sympathizers, including Parson Brownlow, were jailed. The county jail, known as "Castle Fox," which stood near the present courthouse, soon overflowed, and a temporary prison was set up in a house at the northeast corner of Main and Prince (Market) streets. During the remainder of November and in December, as many as fifteen to sixty prisoners a day were locked in the Knoxville jails. Colonel Wood wrote to Secretary of War Benjamin for instructions on November 20.

SIR: The rebellion in East Tennessee has been put down in some of the counties, and will be effectually suppressed in less than two weeks in all the counties. Their camps in Sevier and Hamilton counties have been broken up and a large number of them made prisoners. Some are confined in this place and others sent to Nashville. In a former communication I inquired of the Department what I should do. It is a mere farce to arrest them and turn them over to the Courts. Instead of having the desired effect to intimidate them, it really gives them encouragement and emboldens them in their traitorous conduct. . . .

They really deserve the gallows, and if consistent with the laws, ought speedily to receive their deserts. But there is such a gentle spirit of conciliation in the South, and especially here, that I have no idea that one of them will receive such a sentence at the hands of any jury. I have been here at this station for three months, half of the time in command of this Post, and I [have] had a good opportunity of learning the feeling pervading this country. It is hostile to the Confederate Government. They will take the oath of allegiance with no intention to observe it. They are the slaves of Johnson and Maynard and never intend to be otherwise. . . . To convict them before a Court is next

William Brownlow in the Knoxville jail, being greeted by fellow political prisoners

to an impossibility. . . . The bridge burners and spies ought to be tried at once.

The reply from the Confederate War Department came within the week:

COL. W. B. WOOD:

SIR—Your report of the 20th instant is received, and I now proceed to give you the desired instruction in relation to the prisoners of war taken by you among the traitors of East Tennessee.

First. All such as can be identified in having been engaged in bridge-burning are to be tried summarily by drum-head court-martial, and, if found guilty, executed on the spot by hanging. It would be well to leave their bodies hanging in the vicinity of the burned bridges.

Second. . . . In no case is one of the men, known to have been up in arms against the Government to be released on any pledge or oath of allegiance. The time for such measures is past. . . .

Your vigilant execution of these orders is earnestly urged by the Government.[6]

Major Robert B. Reynolds was thereupon ap-

pointed commissioner of the Confederate States District Court in charge of the trials at Knoxville.[7] Named as successor to Colonel Wood at Knoxville, General W. H. Carroll organized the trials for the bridge-burning suspects. During December three prisoners were convicted by the military tribunals and executed. A fourth, Harrison Self, was spared by Jefferson Davis following a telegram his daughter sent to the President pleading for her father's life.[8]

At Greeneville, two suspects named Hensie and Fry were convicted and sentenced to immediate execution by Colonel Ledbetter, the post commander. According to instructions, their bodies were left suspended four days near the railroad track.[9] Southern sympathizers riding by in the trains reached out and beat the bodies with sticks. Soon the decomposition of the corpses forced authorities to cut down the bodies, and no further exhibitions of the sort occurred.

True civil war as citizens assault Union sympathizers

But the gallows at Knoxville remained standing as a mute deterrent to all who might contemplate further action against the Confederate government.

General Zollicoffer now came back to Knoxville and, confident that resistance was quelled, relieved the city of martial law. As the soldiers who had guarded the city withdrew, Unionists, numbering among them Connelly Trigg, left for Kentucky. But the worst thorn in the Confederate side, Parson Brownlow, still remained. Ever since October he had been hiding in the Smoky Mountains, where he encamped with friends. General Carroll and his successor, General George Crittenden, persuaded Brownlow to return to Knoxville to surrender and promised that no bodily harm would befall him. Brownlow was instructed on December 4 by A. S. Cunningham, acting adjutant general at Knox-

ville, to report to headquarters to pick up a passport which would entitle him to safe conduct into Kentucky. However, before the passport could be issued, Brownlow was arrested by order of Commissioner Reynolds, upon the affidavit of District Attorney John C. Ramsey that Brownlow was a traitor to the Confederacy. He was jailed for a few weeks and released upon the advice of a physician. Imprisoned in his own home until March, 1862, he was then escorted by a Confederate military force to Nashville and turned over to Federal authorities. He was warmly welcomed by his old compatriots, Horace Maynard, Connelly Trigg, and Andrew Johnson, who was then military governor of the state.

In Tennessee the bridge-burning did not produce the massive uprising that was feared. But in Kentucky, General Samuel Carter and his

Brigadier General William H. Carroll. He was Confederate brigade commander in the Department of East Tennessee, in command at Knoxville, December, 1861.

loyal Tennessee regiments, supported by General George Thomas and his troops from Indiana and Ohio, received the news with feelings of great satisfaction. Destruction of the railroads had been their first objective. Now they could proceed with phase two of their plan, the invasion of East Tennessee. They struck camp and were about to march towards Cumberland Gap when an unexpected order from General William T. Sherman, commander of all Union forces in Kentucky, stopped them. Sherman feared that the Union troops were too widely scattered and that large Confederate forces were concentrated at Bowling Green, Columbus, and Cumberland Gap. Detaining Carter and Thomas, he wired Washington for more men and supplies.

Sherman's fears were not entirely groundless. General Leonidas Polk occupied Columbus, a rail terminus on the Mississippi River south of Paducah. General Simon Bolivar Buckner, a native Kentuckian, had moved from Camp Boone to occupy Bowling Green and sent an advance detachment to Elizabethton, only thirty-three miles from Louisville. Zollicoffer moved his army through Cumberland Gap and announced that he would take Louisville. To oppose these Confederate troops, General Sherman had a motley crew of non-uniformed Kentucky home guards and hastily recruited, untrained volunteers from Indiana and Ohio. His main force consisted of the loyal Unionists from Tennessee at Camps Johnson and Robinson. General Thomas, commanding at Robinson, was not impressed with his troops at hand. Accustomed to the discipline of the regular army, Thomas had little confidence in the raw recruits, who seemed more moved by speeches of politicians than commands of officers. The camp had become a rendezvous for Horace Maynard and other politicians, more impetuous than wise in military affairs.

As Thomas prepared for an offensive, Zollicoffer made demonstrations against him at Wild Cat Mountain, just beyond Rockcastle River. Thomas sent General A. A. Schoepf and the 33rd Indiana Regiment to meet the assault. Zollicoffer's men were repulsed, and the Union commander dispatched General Carter and the East Tennesseans in pursuit. They were stopped at London, Kentucky, by Sherman's order. Carter's troops threw down their rifles in disgust and many left. Some pleaded, some wept, and they shouted abuse against Sherman for halting their return to their native East Tennessee and their families. Andrew Johnson was furious. It required all the restraint General Thomas could muster to keep himself from arresting Johnson for inciting the troops. Johnson and Maynard immediately left for Washington to plead their case with Abraham Lincoln.

The Secretary of War hurried down to Louisville to confer with Sherman, and, as a result, the latter was removed from command and General Don Carlos Buell placed in charge of Union hopes in Kentucky.[10]

NOTES

1. Carter eventually received $20,000 for his activity in organizing the clandestine work force. Patton, pp. 60-61.

2. O. R., Ser. I, IV, Part I, 231. Also see Ducloux Scrapbook, p. 247.

3. Humes, p. 135.

4. *Ibid.*

5. *Ibid.*, p. 139.

6. *Ibid.*, pp. 139-41.

7. Major Robert Bannon Reynolds served in the Mexican War. While he was in service his home was built on the high hill in Bearden just west of Knoxville. The house, called Knollwood Hall, is at 6411 Kingston Pike and is in use today. In 1863 it served as General Longstreet's first headquarters during the siege of Knoxville. Reynolds has two children living today.

8. Humes, p. 150.

"KNOXVILLE, DEC. 27, 1861"

"HON. JEFFERSON DAVIS:

"My father, Harrison Self, is sentenced to hang at four o'clock this evening, on a charge of bridge-burning. As he remains my earthly all and all my hopes of happiness centre in him, I implore you to pardon him.

"ELIZABETH SELF."

9. Colonel Ledbetter was a native of Maine serving in the Confederate army. Ledbetter had married a Southern lady and was probably trying to show his loyalty to his adopted land. He should not be confused with Danville Leadbetter, the Confederate officer who served in Knoxville in 1862-63.

10. William T. Sherman had many Southern friends and was distrusted by some Federal authorities. Early in the war a Cincinnati newspaper declared him to be insane (see Earl S. Miers, *The General Who Marched To Hell* [New York: 1951], p. 17). Sherman was saved from military obscurity by General Grant, who requested his services in the West. See also Jesse Burt, "East Tennessee, Lincoln, and Sherman," East Tennessee Historical Society's *Publications*, No. 34 (1962), pp. 3-25.

The First to Die

WITH headquarters at Louisville, General Buell on December 2, 1861, issued orders creating the Army of the Ohio, consisting of six divisions. The Federal War Department simultaneously created the Department of the Ohio "to consist of the States of Ohio, Michigan, Indiana, that portion of Kentucky east of the Cumberland River, and the State of Tennessee."[1] Thus Buell had troops and the resources of several states, an advantage not enjoyed by his predecessors. He began at once his task of forging an army out of raw material, organizing brigades and regiments and introducing drill and discipline. He agreed with Sherman that his troops were not in shape to invade East Tennessee. Carter and Thomas pleaded with Buell to no avail. Carter then wrote to Congressman Maynard, requesting the government at Washington to order the invasion, and Maynard delivered the letters to Lincoln. Obviously, Lincoln was sympathetic, but he had not yet gained control over his generals. He merely endorsed the letters and sent them to General McClellan with the penciled notations: "Please read and consider."[2]

Buell had come with instructions from Secretary of War Cameron to divide the Union forces in Kentucky, with one unit operating from Cincinnati against Knoxville and the other from Louisville against Nashville. Knoxville was to be the first objective. McClellan wrote to Buell, urging him to seize the East Tennessee and Virginia Railroad to cut off supplies to Lee's army in Virginia.[3] But Buell had plans of his own and was not inclined to listen to advice from those far removed from the scene. As did Sherman

before him, he wished to build an army to sweep south on the Cumberland and Tennessee rivers and open up the entire Mississippi Valley to the Union forces; East Tennessee seemed to him a lesser objective which would serve only to help the Army of the Potomac. He considered his strategy more important to the grand scheme of conquering the entire South.[4]

But Buell had not reckoned with the political pressure the Unionists from East Tennessee would place on President Lincoln. Representative Maynard and Senator Johnson went to the President and obtained his promise that an advance toward Knoxville would be made immediately. In his annual message to Congress, Lincoln stated: "I deem it of importance that the loyal regions of east Tennessee and western North Carolina should be connected with Kentucky and other faithful parts of the Union by railroad. I therefore recommend, as a military measure, that Congress provide for the construction of such road as speedily as possible."[5] Congress took no action on this request, so Maynard wrote Buell a curt letter intending to prod him into action.

Buell paid no attention to the politicians and kept his forces idle. He conferred frequently with General Thomas at Lebanon and in January advised Thomas that Zollicoffer was advancing from Cumberland Gap toward Mill Springs, a few miles southwest of Somerset, Kentucky. President Lincoln became impatient and telegraphed to ask, "Have arms gone forward to East Tennessee. Please tell me the progress and condition of the movement in that direction. Answer!"[6] Buell stubbornly replied that he could

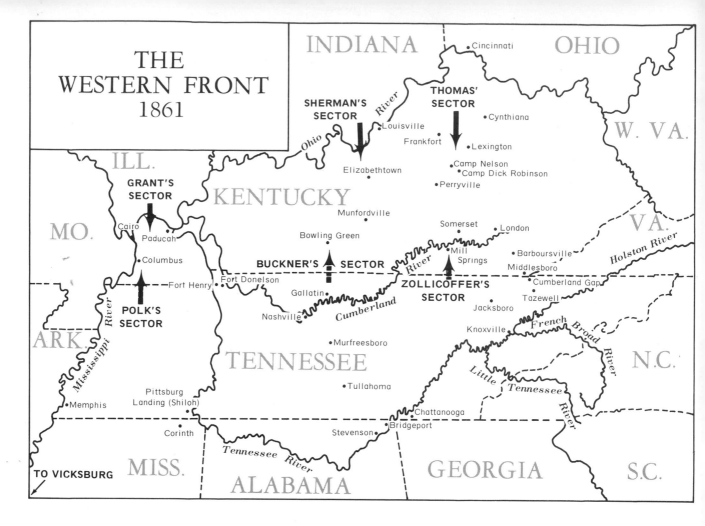

THE
WESTERN FRONT
1861

not make a significant advance with the force at hand. Chagrined, Lincoln tried another approach and wrote Buell a letter explaining his concern.

Your dispatch of yesterday has been received, and it disappoints and distresses me. I have shown it to General McClellan who says he will write you today. Again, I cannot see why the movement on East Tennessee would not be a diversion in your favor, rather than a disadvantage, assuming that a movement towards Nashville is the main object.

But my distress is that our friends in East Tennessee are being hanged and driven to despair, and even now I fear, are thinking of taking rebel arms for the sake of personal protection. In this we lost the most valuable stake we have in the South. My dispatch to which yours is an answer, was sent with the knowledge of Senator Johnson and Representative Maynard of East Tennessee, and they will be upon me to know the answer, which I cannot safely show them. They would despair, possibly resign to go and save their families somehow, or die with them.

I do not intend this to be an order in any sense, but merely, as intimated before, to show you the grounds of my anxiety.[7]

But the Federal forces made no forward movement. Buell did write to his President that any thrusts made in this direction would be done "more by my sympathy for the people of East Tennessee and the anxiety with which you and the general-in-chief have desired it than by my opinion of its wisdom." [8]

But if the Union forces would not advance by design they were soon forced into a sideline offensive by the mistakes of their adversaries. Abraham Lincoln was not alone in having troubles with generals.

For some time, Jefferson Davis and his War Department at Richmond had had doubts about the military abilities of General Zollicoffer. Consequently, they assigned Major General George B. Crittenden to take over the District of East Tennessee. A native Kentuckian, brother of General Thomas L. Crittenden of the Union army and son of United States Senator John J. Crittenden, the new commander was a West Point graduate who had been a lieutenant colonel in

General George Crittenden. He succeeded Zollicoffer as Confederate commander at Knoxville.

the United States Army. He established his supreme headquarters at Knoxville on November 24, remained a month, and then set off to have a look at his forces and the enemy confronting them.

In the over-all situation, the supreme Confederate commander in the West, General Albert Sidney Johnston, was threatened by General Henry Halleck in the West [9] and by General Buell in Kentucky. Halleck, with armies at Cairo and Paducah under Grant and C. F. Smith, menaced Columbus, the key of the lower Mississippi River, and Forts Donelson and Henry, which defended the waterways of the Cumberland and the Tennessee. Buell's right wing also confronted Donelson and Henry, his center was thrust towards Bowling Green, and his left was advancing under General Thomas against Zollicoffer at Mill Springs on the upper Cumberland. Crittenden realized that, if Mill Springs were

taken by Union forces, the way was open for them, by the Jacksboro and Jamestown roads, either to East Tennessee on the one hand or to Nashville on the other.

He thereupon ordered Zollicoffer to remain behind the Cumberland River and to observe the movements of the enemy. However, Zollicoffer chose to disobey and crossed to Camp Beech Grove on the right bank, fortifying this position with earthworks. He placed there five regiments of infantry, twelve pieces of artillery, and several hundred cavalry; at Mill Springs he put two infantry regiments and several hundred more cavalry in reserve. The position at Beech Grove had no military advantages. The river lay to the rear, and in front the terrain was not suitable for artillery fire. Provisions and forage were scanty, and the men subsisted mostly on bread alone. Only small quantities of corn could be found for the horses and mules. The region had been stripped bare, and the condition of the roads and the poverty of the intervening countryside made it impossible to transport supplies from Knoxville, one hundred and thirty miles to the south.

Back in Knoxville, Crittenden received word from Zollicoffer announcing the crossing of the Cumberland. The courier was ordered to return to Zollicoffer at once and instruct him to recross the river and resume his position on the left bank. Early in January, General Crittenden traveled to Mill Springs and found the Confederates still on the north bank. Zollicoffer apologized, but explained that the messenger had been delayed in the return trip, and that meanwhile the river had risen too high to cross and he had no means of ferrying his artillery and wagons back to the left bank. Crittenden accepted the excuse. He detailed men to build flatboats to transport the wagons, but steady rainfall and lack of skilled engineers and carpenters slowed the work. On January 18 he learned that General Thomas was approaching with a considerable force, producing the situation that the order to Zollicoffer had intended to prevent. He also had reports that General Schoepf was moving from Columbia, Kentucky, to unite with Thomas. As the rains continued to fall, it occurred to Crittenden that the two Union armies would be traveling very slowly. His only hope lay in striking Thomas by surprise before the forces merged. At midnight he ordered the attack on Thomas, who was encamped only six miles away.[10]

The brigade of General Zollicoffer's Tennesseans led the advance. All night long the men plodded in a turmoil of mud, rain, and darkness. At dawn the cavalry encountered the first Union pickets two miles from their camp. Then the Tennessee troops discovered that the rain had rendered their flintlocks useless, and the Tennesseans were dispatched to the rear. The 15th Mississippi Regiment advanced to the front, and nearly half fell in the action. The battle was fought in wood lots and meadows along Fishing Creek by troops who had never known battle before. When one Confederate line instinctively took cover in a ravine, an enraged Union officer climbed a fence and challenged the Rebels to stand up and fight.

The surprise attack had failed, but the Confederates pushed on forward, ascending the last hill to its crest, where the heaviest fighting raged. Zollicoffer ordered General Carroll ahead with reinforcements. At this moment there occurred a little lull in the fighting, and Colonel Speed Fry, a Kentucky Union officer, rode a short distance to the right to get a better view of the Rebels in that direction. At the same moment General Zollicoffer, being in the rear of the 19th Tennessee Regiment of his command, mistakenly thought that Fry's Fourth Kentucky Regiment was part of his own brigade. He therefore ordered his troops to cease firing, because they were shooting their own men, and went forward to the front. His uniform covered by a white waterproof coat, Zollicoffer rode through the smoke and haze until his knees touched Fry. "We must not fire on our own men," the Confederate leader told Fry and, nodding his head to the left,

Colonel Speed Fry, Kentucky Union officer. He is credited with the slaying of General Zollicoffer at the Battle of Mill Springs.

said, "These are our men." Fry replied that he would not fire on them intentionally and began to move back toward his regiment.[11]

Suddenly another Confederate officer, not as nearsighted as his commander rushed towards Fry, who, quickly perceiving the mistake, fired on the onrusher and Zollicoffer. The Confederate general fell to the ground, struck by Fry's pistol shot in his breast and by two musket balls fired by nearby soldiers. Although Colonel Fry received credit for the killing, the Headquarters Company of the Tenth Indiana Regiment reported by letter to *Harper's Weekly* that the fatal shot was fired by Corporal James Swan, an expert marksman from Company H.[12]

The battle was virtually over. Crittenden attempted a rally by ordering up General Carroll's Tennesseans, but they were thrown into confusion by artillery fire from the Union batteries and the advance of General Carter's East Tennessee Unionists on the right. Crittenden was compelled to withdraw. The Confederate army broke apart during the retreat, many men de-

Death of General Felix Zollicoffer at Mill Springs, Kentucky

serted to go to their homes, and the countryside swarmed with fugitives.

The Battle of Mill Springs, sometimes called the Battle of Fishing Creek, was fought on a small scale, neither side having more than 4,000 men engaged. But it had far-reaching significance and outcomes. In at least one quarter, it was credited with being a crisis. *Harper's Weekly* in an editorial February 8, 1862, declared:

This victory inaugurates the close of the rebellion, and may be not inappropriately termed "the beginning of the end." . . . Treason draws a great deal of its sustenance from Kentucky and Tennessee, and will not readily surrender these states. In the Border States are their greatest forces and their greatest moral strength. Conquer the Border States, and the rebellion is mortally wounded. Our generals know this. The rebel generals know this.

At Knoxville the news of the defeat and the loss of Zollicoffer caused great consternation. It was the first fight of importance near the town, and most of the Confederate chieftains had been stationed near the scene at different times. Zollicoffer's death was a grievous blow, as he was the most popular Confederate leader in Tennessee, and it was mourned as a personal bereavement. The first Confederate general killed in the Civil War, he had exemplified firmness of will, genuine courage, and some military talent. When his body fell into the hands of the enemy, General Thomas had it prepared for burial and sent through the lines to the family in Nashville. An elegy written by a Southern poet, Henry L. Flash, was a favorite poem in the South for many years afterwards.

ZOLLICOFFER

First in the fight, and first in the arms
    Of the white-winged angel of glory,
With the heart of the South at the feet of God
    And his wounds to tell the story.

For the blood that flowed from his hero's heart
    On the spot where he nobly perished
Was drunk by the earth as a sacrament
    In the holy cause he cherished.

In heaven a home with the brave and the blest
    And for his soul's sustaining
The apocalyptic smile of Christ
    And nothing on earth remaining,

But a handful of dust in the land of his choice
    And a name in song and story,
And fame to shout with brazen voice:
    "He died on the field of glory." [13]

Following the retreat, as the defeated Confederate soldiers streamed into Knoxville, quarters were made for the wounded. The buildings of East Tennessee University were taken over for emergency hospitals. Dr. Francis A. Ramsey and Dr. Richard O. Currey were appointed surgeons in the Confederate army and took command of the emergency hospitals, as well as those that had been established earlier in the Deaf and Dumb Asylum (now City Hall) and the Courthouse. Dr. Ramsey induced Dr. Fielding P. Sloan of the Fifth Tennessee Cavalry to transfer to the college hospital to assist the wounded. [14]

Now, for the first time, it dawned upon the people of Knoxville that there was a possible fighting chance for the North. Maybe one Rebel soldier was not necessarily superior to five Yankees. Confederate panic was widespread. Blame for the defeat was leveled at General Crittenden and General Carroll, who were even accused of being drunk on the eve of the battle. Such accusations were proved false, and President Davis was quick to exonerate his commanders. The defeat, he stated, was due to the antiquated equipment with which the men were trying to defend their homelands and the death in battle of their beloved leader, Zollicoffer. [15]

With victory at Mill Springs, the way to East Tennessee was again wide open to Union invasion. But General Buell still would not take it. Instead, he pressed Grant into moving on the Confederate center and capturing Fort Henry and Fort Donelson, with help of the United States Navy; and the Confederates gave up Nashville. All of these developments made General Albert Sidney Johnston's position at Bowling Green precarious, and he retreated toward Mississippi. Westward, more Confederate disasters befell, as Columbus, Kentucky, was abandoned and Madrid Bend and Island No. 10 fell to Union troops. Then, on April 7, the Confederates received their bloodiest repulse in the war so far on the second day of the Battle of Shiloh. General Johnston was mortally wounded. General Pierre G. T. Beauregard assumed command of the shattered Southern forces, and slowly they evacuated Tennessee and retreated into Mississippi.

General Buell's strategy had paid dividends, up to a point. Tennessee was swept away from Confederate control, except the vitally important East, the only area, paradoxically, supporting the Union. President Lincoln, on March 4, 1862, appointed Tennessee Senator Andrew Johnson as military governor of the state, a position not sanctioned by law nor precedent in American history. Governor Harris was forced to flee southward with the Army of Tennessee.

Thus far, the North appeared to be far ahead in its pursuit of the war; Union armies had won battles and conquered territory. But they had not destroyed a Confederate army nor effectively blocked the South's capacity to continue the fight. The South's finest troops and leaders were still fighting in Virginia. And, as a result of Buell's hesitancy to obey Lincoln's pleas, the supply lines through East Tennessee remained intact.

NOTES

1. Jefferson Davis, *The Rise and Fall of the Confederate Government,* II, 18.

2. Robert L. Kincaid, *The Wilderness Road,* p. 233.

3. *Battles and Leaders,* III, 34.

4. General Buell was a disciple of Jomini, believing campaigns could be won as easily by movement as by battles.

5. Abraham Lincoln, Annual Message to Congress, December 3, 1861, in James D. Richardson (comp.), *A Compilation of the Messages and Papers of the Presidents, 1789-1902* (Washington, D.C.: 1903), VI, 46.

6. Telegram to General D. C. Buell, January 4, 1862, in O.R., Ser. I, VII, Part I, 468.

7. Telegram to General D. C. Buell, January 6, 1862, in O.R., Ser. I, VII, Part I, 530-31.

8. O. R., Ser. I, VII, Part I, 530-31.

9. Major General Henry Halleck commanded the Department of the Mississippi from November, 1861, to July, 1862, when he became general-in-chief of all Union armies. Grant succeeded him as general-in-chief in 1864.

10. Davis, II, 18-19.

11. *Battles and Leaders,* I, 387-92.

12. *Harper's Weekly,* March 8, 1862.

13. McMurray, p. 385.

14. *Confederate Veteran,* VIII (February 1900), 84.

15. Davis, II, 19. General Zollicoffer's daughter, Loulie Zollicoffer Sansom, became a resident of Knoxville and one of the founders of Chapter 89 of the United Daughters of the Confederacy. Parson Brownlow, who knew Zollicoffer intimately for twenty-five years, said: "He was a man who never wronged an individual out of a cent in his life; never told a lie in his life; as brave a man personally as Andrew Jackson ever was; and the only mean thing I ever knew him to do was to join the Southern Confederacy." Frank Moore, *The Civil War in Song and Story,* p. 464.

8

A Debtor's Paradise

THE spring of 1862 witnessed a falling-off of acts of violence within East Tennessee. In March, the Second Regiment of East Tennessee Infantry and a unit of Kentucky cavalrymen under Colonel J. P. T. Carter did venture down through Big Creek Gap in the Cumberland Mountains into Campbell County. At Jacksboro, Confederates drove them back toward Kentucky.

Knoxvillians found it increasingly difficult to buy food and manufactured goods. Prices rose as a result of speculation, profiteering, and genuine scarcities. Coffee and salt became the most wanted items. Gold and silver disappeared from circulation. Next, the various bank notes of the state-chartered banks disappeared. Hoarded for emergencies, these notes, even though their value was depreciated, were worth 25 per cent more than Confederate notes. Banks passed out Confederate paper and gradually withdraw their own notes from circulation.[1]

Debtors had a windfall, as they could pay in depreciated bank notes or, better still, Confederate notes. The creditor was in an uneasy position, for if he refused Confederate currency he was subject to suspicion and abuse. In April, 1862, the military authorities held that any persons refusing to accept these notes would be guilty of political offense and punished accordingly. This threat was apparently effective, because no arrest for refusing to accept Confederate currency was recorded.[2]

To add to the money woes of Southern authorities, the Federal government circulated counterfeit Confederate money printed near Richmond, Kentucky, and smuggled it through

Two Confederate postal stamps issued at Knoxville under Postmaster C. W. Charlton. Note the misprint of Charlton's middle initial.

Dr. J. G. M. Ramsey, historian and Confederate sympathizer. He became the custodian of Confederate funds at Knoxville.

Cumberland Gap. John W. Faxon, a Chattanooga banker, was assigned to report on this problem in Knoxville to Dr. J. G. M. Ramsey, who was officially titled "Depository of the Government." On one occasion Faxon delivered to Ramsey $10,000 in counterfeit Confederate bills which a hotel-keeper named Patterson had smuggled in a coffee sack from the Gap.[3]

Meanwhile, regular Confederate postal service was established. Knoxville was one of sixteen Southern cities which are known to have printed stamps for the Confederate States of America.[4]

Five-dollar note of the Bank of East Tennessee countersigned by General Churchwell, Confederate provost marshal at Knoxville

Monroe County scrip, 1863

Cleveland, Tennessee, scrip, 1862

Fourth Tennessee Regiment scrip, good at the commissary

NOTES

1. Humes, pp. 176-78.
2. *Ibid.*
3. *Confederate Veteran,* VII (August 1899), 339.
4. *Ibid.,* II (March 1894), 78.

9

Kindly Yet Firmly

AT KNOXVILLE on March 8, 1862, Major General Edmund Kirby Smith succeeded General Crittenden as Confederate commander of the District of East Tennessee, which was soon reorganized as the Department of East Tennessee. The new commander took an immediate liking to the mountainous country and its people and established his headquarters in the home of James Cowan, where he was daily served "the finest coffee in the world."

General Kirby Smith was reputed to have "firmness, decision of will and other qualities of character required by his office, and also of as great humanity and kindness as consist with the vigorous conduct of war. A marked contrast in his favor was observed between his general bearing at the town [Knoxville] and that of some Confederate officers who had chief command there. In scholarly attainments he surpassed them all, in personal morals he was without reproach, and his manners were quiet and unpretentious." [1]

He was born in St. Augustine, Florida, May 16, 1824, served in the Mexican War, and was a professor of mathematics at West Point. In April, 1861, he resigned his commission as captain to join the Confederacy and was made a brigadier general in June. He served as commander of a brigade and chief-of-staff to General Joseph E. Johnston, predecessor to General Robert E. Lee as commander of the Army of Northern Virginia. Kirby Smith was wounded at the First Battle of Bull Run, after which he was promoted to major general.

He brought with him to Knoxville the divisions under General William B. Bate and General John C. Vaughn, along with Captain Frank Maney's Tennessee Artillery Battery. [2] He found some 2,000 troops at Knoxville, 4,000 at Cumberland Gap, and various small units scattered throughout East Tennessee. No one had been in command since the departure of General Crittenden to the Battle of Mill Springs in January.

Kirby Smith's first task upon assuming command at Knoxville was to muster sufficient forces for adequate defense of East Tennessee. However, he had no more success than Zollicoffer in obtaining the cooperation of East Tennesseans. In April he wrote to the Adjutant General in Richmond: "Every effort made by the State authorities to call out the militia of East Tennessee has proved unavailing. The county officers chosen in the recent State elections are generally open advocates of the Federal Government. The people only await the appearance of a Northern army to range themselves under their banner." [3]

In the same month the Confederate Congress passed the Conscription Law, requiring every male citizen between eighteen and thirty-five to serve. But the stubborn East Tennesseans refused to attend muster at their regimental parade grounds, and it was not long before many sought refuge in Kentucky. Starting at night in bands of ten to a hundred, they journeyed under cover of darkness to the border. One body of refugees, numbering six or seven hundred, was seized by Confederate cavalry at Blaine's Cross Roads, Grainger County, and marched under guard through Knoxville on the way to prisons in the South. [4]

Kirby Smith was urged by his government and by Confederate sympathizers in Knoxville

General William B. Bate, above left, brigade commander at Knoxville under Kirby Smith

General John C. Vaughn, above right, who was brought from Virginia to Knoxville by Kirby Smith. His cavalry frequently chased Unionists into their mountain hideouts.

Major General Edmund Kirby Smith. He succeeded Crittenden as commander of Confederate forces in East Tennessee with headquarters at Knoxville.

to use severe measures in crushing Union resistance in East Tennessee, but he was not inclined to do so. In his memoirs, written much later, he stated that "with the sense of justice and regard for law, by which I faithfully endeavored to direct every act of administration during the war, I determined to deal kindly, yet firmly, with the Union element, and if possible, to win it over to the side where it rightly belonged." [5]

He had President Davis' permission to reestablish martial law and to dispense with civilian courts. On April 18, he issued the following proclamation:

The Major General commanding this Department, charged with the enforcement of martial law, believing that many of its citizens have been misled into the commission of treasonable acts through ignorance of their duties and obligations to their State, and that many have actually fled across the mountains and joined our enemies under the persuasion and misguidance of supposed friends, but designing enemies, hereby proclaims:

First. That no person so misled, who comes forward, declares his error, and takes the oath to support the Constitution of the State and of the Confederate States, shall be molested or punished on account of past acts or words.

Second. That no person so persuaded and misguided as to leave his home and join the enemy, who shall return within thirty days of the date of this proclamation, acknowledge his error, and take an oath to support the Constitution of the State and of the Confederate States, shall be molested or punished on account of past acts or words.

After thus announcing his disposition to treat with the utmost clemency those who have been led away from the true path of patriotic duty, the Major General commanding furthermore declares his determination henceforth to employ all the elements at his disposal for the protection of the lives and property of the citizens of East Tennessee—whether from the incursions of the enemy or the irregularity of his own troops—and for the suppression of all treasonable practices.

He assures all citizens engaged in cultivating their farms that he will protect them in their rights, and that he will suspend the militia draft under the State laws, that they may raise crops for consumption in the coming year. He invokes the zealous cooperation of the authorities and of all good people, to aid him in his endeavors.

The courts of criminal jurisdiction will continue to exercise their functions, save the issuance of writs of *habeas corpus.* Their writs will be served

Volunteers to the Confederate army. Those from Knoxville included representatives of some of the most prominent families: (1) Moses White, (2) Frank A. Moses, (3) Reps Jones, (4) Stuart McMullen, (5) S. A. McDermott, (6) S. B. Boyd, (7) Judge William T. Newman, (8) Colonel Henry Ashby and Charles Coffin, (9) Abner Baker, (10) Hugh White, (11) Rev. John Bryson, (12) Hector Coffin, (13) James Coffin, (14) Dr. John M. Boyd, (15) Insley Deadrick, (16) Dr. Newton McNutt, (17) John M. Brooks, (18) Rev. Polk Gammon, (19) Gideon Hazen, (20) Fred Ault, (21) Dr. John M. Kennedy. Each filled his life with adventure and color, but some of the more interesting facts include the tragic fate of Abner Baker (9), who was hanged, and on whose monument is inscribed, "the coward dies many times, the brave but once." A veteran's camp was named after Fred Ault (20), and W. T. Newman (7) later became a Federal judge. S. B. Boyd (6) was imprisoned in Camp Chase and refused to come out at the end of the war, because he would not swear allegiance to the United States. He remained firm in his purpose and was only released when a friend took the oath for him. The youngest-appearing of this brave band is Gideon Hazen (19). For more information about him, see chapter 10, note 4.

Company A, Fifth Georgia Infantry. These "Clinch Rifles" were the Confederate garrison troops in Knoxville in the spring of 1862.

and their decrees executed by aid of the military, when necessary.

When the courts fail to preserve the peace or punish offenders against the laws, those objects will be attained through the action of military tribunals and the exercise of the force of his command.

(Signed) E. KIRBY SMITH
Maj. Gen. Comm'dg Dep't E. T.[6]

Doubtless, no one paid much heed to the proclamation, for five days later a second was published.

To THE DISAFFECTED PEOPLE OF EAST
TENNESSEE
HEADQUARTERS DEPARTMENT OF EAST TENN.
Office Provost Marshal, April 23, 1862
The undersigned, in executing martial law in this Department, assures those interested who have fled to the enemy's lines, and who are actually in their army, that he will welcome their return to their homes and their families; they are offered amnesty and protection, if they come to lay down their arms and act as loyal citizens, within the thirty days given them by Major General E. Kirby Smith to do so.

At the end of that time, those failing to return to their homes and accept the amnesty thus offered, and provide for and protect their wives and children in East Tennessee, will have them sent to their care in Kentucky, or beyond the Confederate States' line at their own expense.

All that leave after this date, with a knowledge of the above acts, their families will be sent after them.

The women and children must be taken care of by husbands and fathers, either in East Tennessee or in the Lincoln Government.

(Signed) W. M. CHURCHWELL,
Col. and Provost Marshal [7]

It is not certain that General Kirby Smith approved general application of the drastic proposal in this second proclamation. He did, however, authorize the compulsory removal from Knoxville to Virginia, thence beyond the Confederate lines, of the wives and families of Representative Horace Maynard and the Reverend William G. Brownlow.

In spite of widespread resistance in East Tennessee to the Confederate Conscription Law, Confederate recruiting there was not a total failure. In addition to the Mitchel Guards recruited earlier, Company E of the 19th Tennessee Infantry was organized at the fairgrounds on June 10, with D. H. Cummings appointed as colonel in command. The Fourth Infantry Regiment was recruited under Colonel W. M. Churchwell, and a flag was presented to the

Fourth by a delegation of Confederate ladies of Knoxville at the Lamar House.[8] Some Knoxvillians joined the 31st Tennessee under Colonel William Bradford, and Captain A. A. Blair recruited sufficient men to make up Company D of the 65th Tennessee Infantry. Lieutenant Colonel William Brazelton organized Brazelton's Battalion, consisting of seven companies of men from Knox County; this unit merged with the First Tennessee Infantry, and its Company E was to take part in the siege of Knoxville. Captain N. C. Langford raised Company I which joined the Second Tennessee Cavalry. The 37th under Moses White enrolled 771 men, but could find weapons for only 200.

The first artillery battery to train in the Knoxville area had been the Rutledge Rifles, which was stationed at Camp Cummings in August,

Officers of the "Rutledge Rifles." Recruited in Nashville and trained at Camp Cummings in Knoxville in August, 1861, this Confederate light artillery battery fought at Shiloh and Mill Springs.

1861. Later four batteries of light artillery were organized locally, each battery having four smoothbore six-pounders and two twelve-pound howitzers. H. L. McClung, W. H. Burroughs, W. C. Kain, and G. A. Huwald commanded these units.[9]

Most of the units of East Tennesseans recruited in the Union army were assembled in Kentucky, for they could not very well organize at home. Company C of the First Tennessee Cavalry, U. S. Volunteers, was composed of men from Knox County, with Captain James P. Brownlow as commander; the Second, Third, Fourth, and Ninth cavalry regiments had many men from Knox County, and the First, Second, Third, Sixth, and Eighth infantry regiments had a large number of East Tennesseans who fled from the Confederate Conscription Law.

Kirby Smith asked the War Department to transfer his East Tennessee soldiers away from regions close to Kentucky, fearing that they might desert for political beliefs or monetary inducements. For weeks the Fifth Georgia Infantry, known as the "Clinch Rifles," was the only garrison unit stationed at Knoxville. But soon the War Department sent three definitely loyal Confederate Tennessee regiments from Joe Johnston's Virginia army to replace the men sent away. By June, Kirby Smith's forces had swelled to 18,000, as Generals Henry Heth and John P. McCown arrived at Chattanooga and General Carter L. Stevenson at Clinton.

NOTES

1. Humes, p. 170. A recent biography of Kirby Smith is Joseph H. Parks, *General E. Kirby Smith, C.S.A.* (Baton Rouge: 1962).

2. General W. B. Bate, a native of Gallatin, Tennessee, had commanded an Alabama brigade in Virginia and became famous as a cavalry brigade leader. He was governor of Tennessee, 1883-87. At the close of his last term he was elected to the United States Senate, and, by re-election, he held that office until his death in 1905. Senator Bate delivered the dedicatory address at the unveiling of the Confederate Monument in Knoxville. J. C. Vaughn, another Tennessee cavalryman, had been on duty patrolling the upper East Tennessee and Virginia supply lines.

3. O. R., Ser. I, X, Part I, 385-86.

4. Humes, pp. 165-66.

5. A. H. Noll, *General Kirby Smith*, p. 202.

6. Humes, pp. 172-73.

7. *Ibid.*, p. 173.

8. *Confederate Veteran*, IX (April 1901), 173.

9. Information supplied by Mrs. Charles Wayland of Knoxville from personal records and files of the U.D.C.

10

A Panic in Kentucky

BY EARLY June, 1862, Confederates in East Tennessee were threatened with encirclement by Federal forces occupying Kentucky, western and central Tennessee, and northern Mississippi and Alabama.

On June 6, Federal Major General George Morgan started southward toward Cumberland Gap with his Seventh Division of the Army of the Ohio, composed of men from Wisconsin, Michigan, Ohio, Indiana, Illinois, Kentucky, and Tennessee.[1] Kirby Smith's Confederates left the Gap in haste, abandoning tents, ammunition, and food. They spiked five large guns and pitched one nicknamed "Long Tom" over a cliff to a ledge two hundred feet below. The Union forces hauled "Long Tom" back up and incorporated it into their own fortification of the Gap. Morgan wired Washington for reinforcements so he could push farther into East Tennessee, but the War Department, deeply involved with the campaigns of Halleck, Grant, and Buell in the West, ignored his request.

On the Confederate side, General Braxton Bragg of North Carolina assumed command in the West, replacing the ailing Beauregard shortly after the Confederate evacuation of Corinth, Mississippi. Bragg's immediate task was to attempt to turn the tide of disaster. He decided upon a rapid march to Chattanooga, in order to protect Georgia from invasion and to prevent further Federal incursions into East Tennessee. By this move, he might also unite with Kirby Smith at Knoxville.

To mislead the enemy he first made feints with cavalry under Colonel Joseph Wheeler and General Frank C. Armstrong toward West Tennessee and northern Alabama.[2] And he sent word to Kirby Smith to dispatch Colonel John Hunt Morgan to Kentucky to pave the way for invasion. Morgan, the dashing cavalry leader, thus set out on the raids that were to attract the concern of President Lincoln.

The thirty-six-year-old John Morgan, a native of Huntsville, Alabama, joined the Confederate army as commander of the Lexington Rifles of Kentucky. He scouted and, as a colonel, organized Morgan's Squadron, originally consisting of three cavalry companies, which operated in Tennessee and Kentucky and distinguished itself at the Battle of Shiloh. Early in June, 1862, he established headquarters in Knoxville across the street from the Bell House and recruited two companies of East Tennesseans into his raiding band.

Morgan's raiders included colorful units, such as Captain R. M. Gano's Texas Squadron, the "Partisan Rangers" from Georgia, and Colonel Basil Duke's Battalion, as well as an English soldier of fortune, George St. Leger Grenfell, who brought a letter of introduction from General Lee. Grenfell signed up as Morgan's adjutant and drilled the men in the French cavalry technique he had learned as a veteran of Crimean and North African campaigns. Twice a day he held a dress parade, which was an odd sight to Knoxvillians who watched. Only a few of the seasoned troops had uniforms, some of them being of Union vintage. Most of the recruits wore blue jeans. Those who did not own a rifle or revolver were issued clubs for the coming raid into Kentucky. Morgan assured them that they would get all the arms they needed from the

General John Hunt Morgan, C.S.A., and his wife. Morgan operated
out of Knoxville in the summer of 1862, making raids into Kentucky.

Yankees. Within a few weeks, Grenfell had the troops in fighting shape. Morgan left Knoxville on the fourth of July with nine hundred men, soon picked up three hundred more, and sped to Kentucky. Two hundred of the band had neither rifle nor pistol.[3]

The Rebel raiders overcame a battalion of Pennsylvania cavalry at Tompkinsville, captured the commander, and went on to Glasgow. They then penetrated all the way to Cynthiana, about forty miles south of the Ohio River, capturing seventeen towns, a numerically superior Federal force, and 3,000 rifles at Lebanon, and destroying military stores, railroad bridges, and other property valued at $10,000,000. Colonel Morgan accomplished all of this with a loss of not more than ninety of his own men killed, wounded, and missing.[4] He marched more than a thousand

General Basil Duke, regimental commander under Morgan

RICHARD MORGAN

CHARLTON MORGAN

CALVIN MORGAN

THOMAS MORGAN

John Hunt Morgan's four brothers. They learned French cavalry technics at Knoxville.

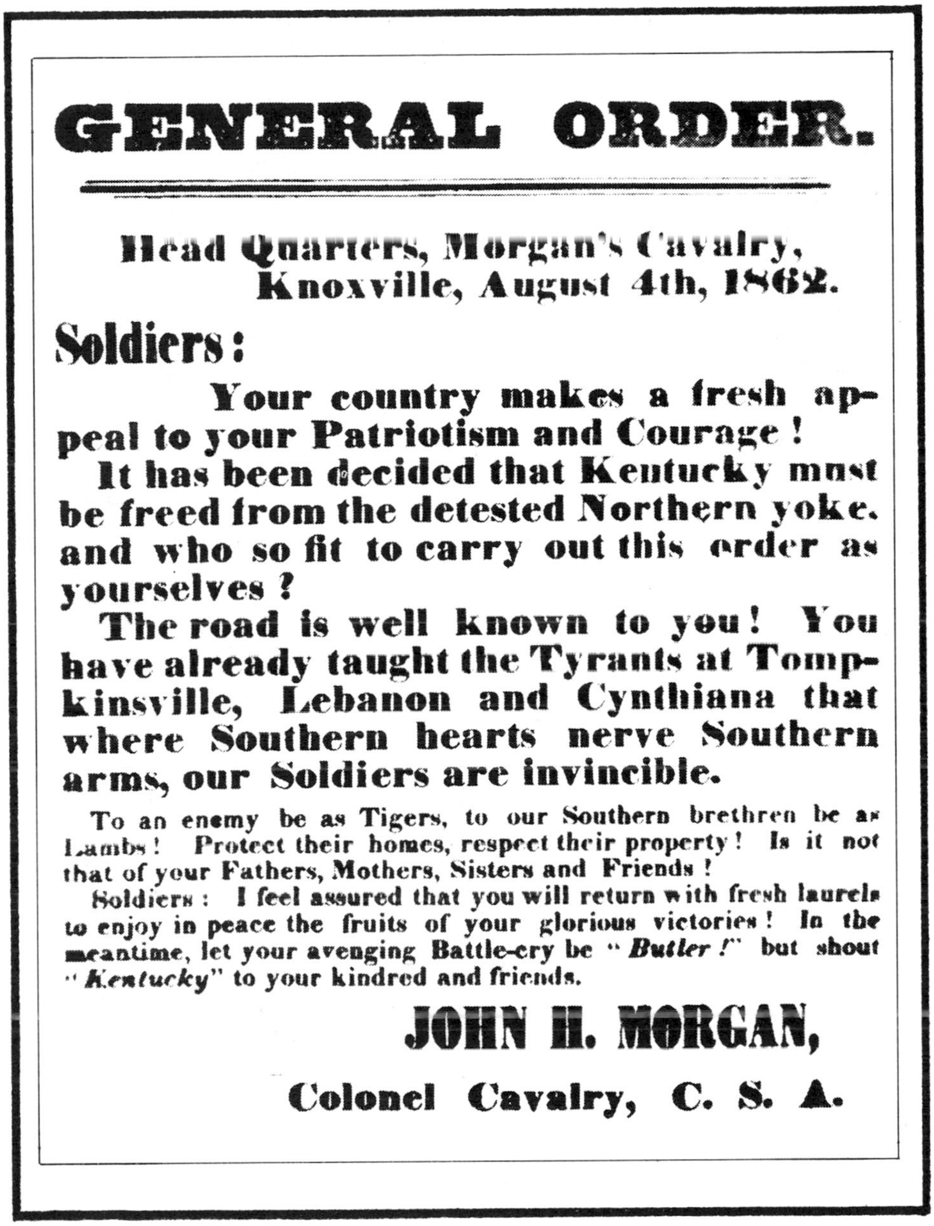

GENERAL ORDER.

Head Quarters, Morgan's Cavalry,
Knoxville, August 4th, 1862.

Soldiers:

Your country makes a fresh appeal to your Patriotism and Courage!

It has been decided that Kentucky must be freed from the detested Northern yoke, and who so fit to carry out this order as yourselves?

The road is well known to you! You have already taught the Tyrants at Tompkinsville, Lebanon and Cynthiana that where Southern hearts nerve Southern arms, our Soldiers are invincible.

To an enemy be as Tigers, to our Southern brethren be as Lambs! Protect their homes, respect their property! Is it not that of your Fathers, Mothers, Sisters and Friends!

Soldiers: I feel assured that you will return with fresh laurels to enjoy in peace the fruits of your glorious victories! In the meantime, let your avenging Battle-cry be "*Butler!*" but shout "*Kentucky*" to your kindred and friends.

JOHN H. MORGAN,

Colonel Cavalry, C. S. A.

Order issued before Confederate invasion of Kentucky

miles in twenty-four days and took at least 1,200 prisoners. Besides, he put the people of Cincinnati into a state described by one of their newspapers as "bordering on frenzy." An aroused Abraham Lincoln wired to General Halleck in Corinth, Mississippi: "They are having a panic in Kentucky. Please look to it." [5]

Morgan retreated from Kentucky when he learned that a superior Federal detachment was out to capture him. But at Somerset he stopped long enough to take possession of the telegraph office and calmly countermand all of the previous orders to pursue him that had been wired by the Union commander at Louisville. [6]

In August he was on the rampage again, after issuing a general order from his Knoxville headquarters:

SOLDIERS:

Your country makes a fresh appeal to your Patriotism and Courage! It has been decided that Kentucky must be freed from the detested Northern yoke, and who so fit to carry out this order as yourselves?

The road is well known to you! You have already taught the Tyrants at Tompkinsville, Lebanon and Cynthiana that where Southern hearts nerve Southern arms, our Soldiers are invincible.

To an enemy be as Tigers, to our Southern brethren be as Lambs! Protect their homes, respect their property! Is it not that of your Fathers, Mothers, Sisters, and Friends!

Soldiers: I feel assured that you will return with fresh laurels to enjoy in peace the fruits of your glorious victories! In the meantime, let your avenging Battle Cry be "Butler" but shout "Kentucky" to your kindred and friends.

JOHN H. MORGAN
Colonel Cavalry, C. S. A.[7]

The colonel then moved swiftly to capture Gallatin, north of Nashville, and the Federal garrison. He personally captured the railroad station, passing himself off as a Federal officer pursuing "John Hunt Morgan." The station master, armed with a revolver, boldly spoke out: "I wish I could meet the damned guerrilla." Morgan formally introduced himself and disarmed the astounded agent. At Hartsville, the Rebel raider was intercepted by a cavalry detachment which General Buell had sent up to drive him out of Middle Tennessee, but Morgan adroitly turned the tables and captured the Federal leader, General R. L. Johnson, and seventy-five of his men. Receiving this news at his Union occupation center in northern Alabama, General Buell was oppressed with gloomy forebodings about his long, vulnerable supply line from Kentucky—the Louisville and Nashville Railroad.

NOTES

1. George W. Morgan had been a lawyer and U.S. Minister to Portugal. Ill health forced his resignation from the army in 1863. For a discussion of the Cumberland Gap campaigns, see General Morgan's account in *Battles and Leaders,* Vol. III, and Robert L. Kincaid, *The Wilderness Road,* Chap. 17.

2. Joseph Wheeler was one of the ablest of the Confederate cavalry chieftains, first as a raider, then as commander of a corps of 12,000 men. Late in 1862 he was made a brigadier general. Frank Armstrong became famous as the commander of a brigade in Forrest's cavalry.

3. LaBree, pp. 101-103.

4. One Knoxvillian, Gideon Hazen, who went with Morgan on the first raid into Kentucky, was captured and died in the Dry Tortugas Prison. His mother never believed he was dead; and every night for twenty years until her death she kept a light burning in a window to welcome him home. Knoxville *Journal,* April 26, 1936. Gideon Hazen's father and Captain Marcus Bearden owned a paper mill located west of Knoxville from which the name of Paper Mill Road is derived.

5. Horn, p. 161.

6. *Confederate Veteran,* XXXVI (July 1928), 256.

7. From the Williamson Papers now housed at the University of North Carolina. Morgan often printed his orders and staff reports, employing a professional printer from Canada who had enlisted in his command. There are many excellent accounts of Morgan's career. The most detailed account of his stay in East Tennessee is in *The Bold Cavaliers, Morgan's 2nd Kentucky Cavalry Raiders,* by Dee Alexander Brown.

11

The Locomotive Chase

ALTHOUGH General Buell was considered a conservative warrior who preferred to fight battles with maps, marching, and strategy rather than men and guns, he inadvertently became a party to one of the most striking and novel events of the entire Civil War.

In his employ was a spy, James J. Andrews. In March, 1862, Buell had sent Andrews and eight other men to burn the bridges west of Chattanooga, but the plan failed. Nevertheless, Andrews made considerable reconnaissance, journeying as far south as Atlanta.

The spy then submitted a plan to General O. M. Mitchel of Buell's army for a raid in which he would take twenty-four men into Confederate territory and by capturing a train would burn the bridges on the northern part of the Georgia State Railroad (the Western and Atlantic), as well as one on the East Tennessee and Georgia Railroad where it approached the Georgia line. If the plan worked, Chattanooga, which was virtually unguarded by Confederate troops, would be isolated. The raiders selected were all soldiers from three Ohio regiments. They exchanged their uniforms for Southern civilian dress. Splitting into small groups, they journeyed southward, and finally twenty of them rendezvoused with their leader, Andrews, at Marietta, Georgia—two hundred miles from their starting point.

On Saturday, April 12, the raiders boarded a train as ordinary passengers at Marietta and traveled eight miles to Big Shanty (Kennesaw Station), where the conductor, engineer, and many of the passengers hurried to breakfast, leaving the train unattended. The disguised soldiers seized control of the train, detached and used the locomotive, tender, and three box cars. The throttle was pulled open, and the locomotive known as "The General" jerked northward with a roar.

As the "General" darted away triumphantly, the Confederate camp and station were in the wildest uproar. But out of the confusion at Big Shanty two men emerged who were determined to foil the unknown captors of their train.

There was no telegraph station and no other locomotive on hand to use in pursuit, so the conductor of the train, W. A. Fuller, and Anthony Murphy, foreman of the Atlanta railway machine shops, started on foot as fast as they could

James J. Andrews, leader of the raid

Throwing ties on the tracks to obstruct pursuing train

Andrews' raiders abandoning the locomotive

run. Shortly they found a handcar, which they pumped as far as Etowah, Georgia. There they pressed into service the locomotive "Yonah," and, after loading it with nearby Confederate soldiers, they started north.

While Fuller was waging his desperate pursuit, Andrews and his raiding party were experiencing the thrill of passing enemy towns and country unmolested. Frequently they stopped to cut telegraph wires and load on cross-ties to be used in burning bridges, and at one point they tore up the track behind them. Wood and water were obtained at the way-stations with no difficulty; Andrews told the station-tenders that he was an agent of General Beauregard running an

impressed powder train through to the troops at Corinth, Mississippi.

At Etowah Station, Andrews had seen the "Yonah" standing on a side track with steam up but, not wishing to alarm the guards, left it unharmed. Here also the raiders waited for more than an hour to let three southbound trains pass. Andrews kept up a bold front and stayed near the telegraph office to prevent any warning from reaching the station-master. The Federals remained concealed in tightly-shut boxcars, hearing sounds outside, but unable to distinguish words.

Finally, as the "General" moved back onto the main track from the siding at Etowah Station, Andrews was startled to hear the shrill cry of the "Yonah." Fuller and the pursuing party were only four minutes behind, but the three southbound trains also delayed them. Fuller and Murphy therefore abandoned the "Yonah" and ran across to another side track, where they uncoupled the engine and one car of the "William R. Smith." With forty armed men they renewed the chase.

Near Adairsville, the raiders had cut the rails, and the pursuers were again forced to abandon their train. Next, they commandeered "The Texas," which had been forced to a siding at Adairsville by the bold Andrews. But every trick of Andrews to throw off his relentless pursuers failed. Mile after mile, around curves and past stations, the chase continued. Andrews dropped his boxcars one by one and threw all of his cross-ties onto the tracks, attempting to slow Fuller's party. Finally Andrews had no car left and no fuel; the last had been thrown upon a burning car in the vain hope of stopping pursuit.

Three miles above Ringgold, Andrews ordered his men to jump from the train and scatter into the woods, each man for himself. Several of the men were captured that very day, and all but two within a week. These last two were caught just before entering northern lines. The raiders, wearing civilian clothes and within enemy lines, were held as spies at Chattanooga.[1]

The Knoxville jail and courthouse

COURT HOUSE AND YANKEE BULL PEN

Trial of the train stealers in courthouse at Knoxville. Private George
D. Wilson, Second Ohio Volunteers, is on the stand.

Andrews and seven of his men were tried, condemned, and executed. But Union forces came so close to the city before the others could be tried that General Kirby Smith ordered them transferred to the larger and stronger jail at Knoxville. The spies were given in custody at Chattanooga to a detachment of John Morgan's guerrilla fighters. Morgan's men, who for the most part raided in their civilian dress, were sympathetic to the Union soldiers, raiders like themselves, who were suffering the indignity of leg irons. They demanded respect and courtesy for their prisoners.

At Knoxville the captives were thrown into the massive, square building which served as the Knoxville military jail. It was filled with dirty, ragged Union prisoners and Southern deserters.

General Kirby Smith assigned Colonel Joseph Bibb of the 23rd Alabama Infantry to preside over the military trial of the remaining twelve Union spies.[2] Captain Leander V. Crook, the local judge advocate, visited them and informed them that they could have counsel if they could find anyone who would serve. The prisoners got word to Judge Oliver Temple, a known Unionist, who agreed to defend them, and Colonel John Baxter also came forward with an offer to help.[3] Temple and Baxter were more judicially learned than the other court members, but less knowledgeable in military law. Conductor Fuller came in person to testify for the prosecution. By an order dated June 14, 1862, at Knoxville, General Kirby Smith approved the military court's decision to execute Private George D. Wilson of Company B, Second Ohio, the only raider tried. The court was disbanded as word spread of Union raids in upper East Tennessee, and the remaining eleven prisoners were transferred to the Atlanta prison. All of them later escaped or were exchanged.

Except for the excitement of the locomotive chase and the trials and talk about John Morgan's raids, the ordinary routine of life in Knoxville was placid in the summer of 1862. An interesting incident did occur in July when forty Union soldiers who had been captured by Bedford Forrest at Murfreesboro were marched down Gay Street with the horses and wagons seized in the raid. The captives were sent on to prison in Georgia, but their personal letters were distributed among Confederate soldiers and citizens, who read them publicly on the streets.[4]

NOTES

1. For detailed information on the famous locomotive chase, see O. R., Ser. I, X, Part I, 630-39; *Battles and Leaders,* II, 709-16; William Pittenger, *The Great Locomotive Chase.* It was an eighty-seven-mile chase. The captured engine, the "General," has recently toured the country in observance of the Civil War Centennial and is at present in Union Station, Chattanooga. The "Texas" remained in service until 1907. In 1911 it was moved to Grant Park, Atlanta, where it is housed in the Cyclorama.

2. *Confederate Veteran,* XI (September 1903), 398.

3. *Ibid.* John Baxter was known to the raiders for his defense of bridge burners and other Unionists previously tried in the military courts at Knoxville. Baxter, a slaveholder, was nonetheless opposed to secession.

4. Humes, pp. 186-87.

12

Wither the Bright Hopes

IN THE second quarter of 1862, notable changes occurred in the Federal commands. Halleck was summoned to Washington to become supreme Federal commander; General John Pope was sent to Virginia to try his skill against Lee; and Grant and Buell were restored to independent commands in the West. Grant remained in Mississippi and Buell was ordered to cross the Tennessee River and occupy East Tennessee.

After some delay, General Buell moved across northern Alabama toward Chattanooga in mid-July. General Kirby Smith at Knoxville was convinced that the Rebel Morgan's cavalry raids had disrupted Buell's supply and communications lines and on July 20 he telegraphed his superior officer, General Braxton Bragg, at Tupelo, Mississippi: "It is time to strike Buell's rear." [1]

Bragg's army began a secret move to Chattanooga, with the ultimate purpose of uniting with Kirby Smith for an invasion of Kentucky. Kirby Smith's part was to march through Cumberland Gap, Tennessee, and on to the Ohio River. [2]

By a successful invasion of Kentucky, the Confederates hoped to gain the active support of a large part of the Kentucky population. And if, instead of making a frontal assault on Buell in Middle Tennessee, Bragg should move north secretly from Chattanooga and Knoxville and then sweep westward through Kentucky, he could destroy Buell's supply lines and isolate him deep in hostile territory, either forcing Buell to retreat across the Ohio or giving Bragg a tremendous advantage should they meet in battle. If this move were successful, it would strain the supply lines of Grant in Mississippi, possibly cause him to withdraw also, and completely reverse the tide of Southern disaster.

To start the invasion, Bragg ordered 34,000 men under General William Hardee to Chattanooga, screened by cavalry of Generals Joe Wheeler and Frank Armstrong. General McCown marched his troops from Chattanooga to Knoxville, and Bragg sent the brigades of Generals Patrick Cleburne and T. J. Churchill, some 6,000 strong, to join Kirby Smith. On August 14 Kirby Smith and his forces left Knoxville. General Henry Heth, with 4,000, was ordered to march to Barbourville, preceded by Colonel John S. Scott's 900 cavalrymen. General C. L. Stevenson, with 9,000, was ordered to surround Cumberland Gap and Federal General George Morgan's fort there.

General Morgan's position was so formidable that the Confederates skirted it and, advancing rapidly, outmarched their own supply wagons. Foraging corn and apples and capturing salt, they jokingly decided that C. S. A. stood for "Corn, Salt and Apples." [3] They skirmished with a Federal force under General William Nelson at Richmond, killing 206, wounding 844, capturing 4,303, destroying a Union wagon train, and capturing nine pieces of artillery and 10,000 rifles. Confederate losses were 78 killed and 372 wounded. The same day, the news came that, in Virginia, General Lee decisively defeated General Pope at the Second Battle of Bull Run and was probably going to cross the Potomac and attack Washington.

Kirby Smith swept through Richmond, Kentucky, then seized Frankfort and twenty more

General Braxton Bragg, Commander of the Western Armies of the Confederacy

KENTUCKY INVASION

Legend:
1 General Buell
2 General Bragg, August 28
3 General C. L. Stevenson
4 General Morgan at Cumberland Gap
5 General Kirby Smith (August 14) with Generals Churchill and Cleburne

guns. By September 4, Cleburne, Churchill, Heth, and John Morgan's raiders had pushed through and marched triumphantly through the streets of Lexington. The cavalry roamed as far north as Covington. Just across the Ohio River, Cincinnati was placed under martial law, business was suspended, and citizens were ordered to build breastworks to defend the city.

General Bragg was delayed at Chattanooga awaiting his baggage trains, but finally on August 28 he crossed the Tennessee River and started northward up the Sequatchie Valley through Pikeville to Sparta, then on to Gainesboro on the Cumberland River. He wrote to Kirby Smith to join him at Glasgow, Kentucky, forty miles east of Bowling Green. He reached Glasgow on September 13 and three days later captured Munfordville without a fight seizing 5,000 rifles, the artillery, and the entire garrison.

Acting on advice from President Davis, General Bragg issued a proclamation:

Kentuckians, I have entered your state with the Confederate Army of the West, and offer you an opportunity to free yourselves from the tyranny of a despotic ruler. . . . We come to guarantee to all the sanctity of their homes and altars. . . . I shall enforce a rigid discipline and shall protect all in their persons and property. . . [4]

Bragg, the sternest of disciplinarians, meant what he said. One Confederate soldier who had taken a few apples from an orchard outside of Glasgow was executed on the spot, in front of shocked and horrified soldiers and citizens.[5]

On September 16, the same day that Bragg took Munfordville, Union General George Morgan began retreating north from Cumberland Gap through the Yellow Creek Valley. His Tennessee troops marched out with tears in their eyes, as they turned away once again from the land they had sworn to "liberate." As they left, the Union men gave old "Long Tom" his second shove over the cliff and blew up their fortress. The shells continued to explode for eighteen hours, delaying General Stevenson's pursuit. Morgan's retreat from Cumberland Gap to the Ohio River was memorialized in a ballad composed at the time by an unknown mountaineer minstrel.

CUMBERLAND GAP

*Each first line is repeated
three times*

The first white man in Cumberland Gap,
Was Doctor Walker, an English chap.

Chorus
Lay down, boys, and take a little nap,
Fourteen miles to Cumberland Gap.

Daniel Boone on the Pinnacle Rock,
He killed Indians with an old flintlock.
(Chorus)

Cumberland Gap is a noted place,
Three kinds of water to wash your face.
(Chorus)

Cumberland Gap with its cliff and rocks,
Home of the panther, bear, and fox.
(Chorus)

September mornin' in sixty-two,
Morgan's Yankees all withdrew.
(Chorus)

They spiked Long Tom on the mountain top,
And over the cliffs they let him drop.
(Chorus)

They burned the hay, the meal and the meat,
And left the Rebels nothing to eat.
(Chorus)

Braxton Bragg with his Rebel band,
He run George Morgan to the bluegrass land.
(Chorus)

Me and my wife and my wife's grand'pap,
All raise Hell in Cumberland Gap.
(Chorus)[6]

General Bragg's strategy had worked well. He had marched his men six hundred miles, captured a Union position, and impaired Buell's lines of communication. To complete the campaign, he now needed only to unite with Kirby Smith and strike Buell, who had rushed from Alabama to Nashville and was now coming fast toward Louisville and his supplies.

The South was on the offensive everywhere except in northern Mississippi. Lee and Stonewall Jackson were probing into Maryland against McClellan. General Humphrey Marshall with 3,000 Southern troops was moving into Kentucky from Virginia near Pound Gap to intercept the fleeing George Morgan. Confederate General John Breckinridge, former Vice-President of the United States, reached Knoxville with 2,500 men from the Trans-Mississippi Army and joined them to the 4,000 troops and 2,000 exchanged prisoners occupying the city.

Now a victory by Bragg over Buell would force Grant to ease his threat against Vicksburg. Confederate hopes for independence seemed brighter at this moment than they ever would again.

Southern fortunes soon began to fade, when Bragg, apparently assailed by doubt and lack of self-confidence, lost the initiative. Perhaps his attitude was influenced by the unenthusiastic reception he received in Kentucky. He had hoped to recruit a large number of Kentuckians into his army, but was soon disillusioned. Kirby Smith wrote to him on September 18 that "the Kentuckians are slow and backward in rallying to our standard. Their hearts are evidently with us, but their bluegrass and fatback are against us." And on September 25, Bragg wrote to his War Department: "I regret to say we are sadly disappointed in the want of action by our friends in Kentucky. We have so far received no accession to this army. General Smith has secured about a brigade—not half our losses by casualties of different kinds. Unless a change occurs soon, we must abandon the garden spot of Kentucky." [7]

Now, when the situation demanded continued bold action, Bragg became hesitant and passive. General Basil Duke later described him as a man of "strange contrast exhibited by the nerve and purpose of his plan and the timidity and the vacillation of his conduct." In Kentucky, as Duke expressed it, the Confederate commander displayed "that fatal irresolution which was to wither the bright hopes his promises and his previous action had aroused." [8]

General Patrick Cleburne, Confederate brigade. commander in the Kentucky invasion

Braxton Bragg delayed too long, and Buell slipped right by him into Louisville, where he received reinforcements. Kirby Smith was ordered to remain around Lexington, and the two invading armies did not unite while on the offensive.

On October 8, Bragg and 15,000 troops ran head on into a force three times their number at Doctor's Creek near Perryville, Kentucky. General Benjamin Cheatham's Tennesseans charged into the Federals under George Thomas and Philip Sheridan. Neither Union nor Confederate commanders showed much skill or insight into the others' plans; but the Rebels, though terribly outnumbered, drove their enemy

General Henry Heth, brigade commander under Kirby Smith

back two miles from the first line of battle and captured fifteen pieces of artillery.

Perryville was a standoff in that the Confederates won the field but failed to pursue their advantage. It is probable that Bragg had it in his power here, by concentrating his troops, to crush the Union strength in Kentucky, but he was deceived as to the disposition of the forces against him, and he scattered his own. Had he fallen on the Federals at Perryville with his whole available strength of 40,000 men, he might have dispersed the Union army and given it such a blow that it could not have made a stand south of the Ohio River. But, fearing that the Federals were receiving heavy reinforcements, he ordered a withdrawal on October 10 and was at Camp Breckinridge (Camp Dick Robinson) two days later.

That night Kirby Smith began his evacuation of Lexington. The town was looted, and everything that could not be carried off was burned. An immense cavalcade of wagon trains, filled with ammunition, and batteries of captured artillery headed the procession southward. Then followed trains of merchandise, provision trains of army stores, trains containing 20,000 captured rifles, escorts of cavalry, and artillery drawn by oxen. Farther behind came private trains of refugees, fleeing with their families and servants, women and children, in carriages, stagecoaches, express wagons, ambulances, and every available vehicle at hand. Finally came the brigades of Rebel soldiers, thousands of head of cattle, horses, and mules, and 4,000 shiny new United States wagons. The procession was forty miles long! General Joe Wheeler's cavalry covered the retreat.[9]

Bragg and Kirby Smith finally united at Harrodsburg, with Buell in pursuit not far behind. Kirby Smith, angered because of his own inactivity and the indecision of his commander, demanded: "For God's sake, General, let us fight Buell here." Bragg replied, "I will do it, sir." But once more he failed to seize his advantage.[10] General C. C. Gilbert, commander of Buell's Third Corps, recorded that "it was a piece of very good fortune for the Union side that the Confederates did not return to renew the battle, for they would have had such an advantage in numbers and in the character of their troops that the Army of the Ohio would have been placed in great peril."[11]

On October 13, the two Southern leaders began evacuating Kentucky by way of Crab Orchard, London, and Barbourville to Cumberland Gap. Buell gave up the chase at London, and the Confederates proceeded to Morristown and Knoxville. Bragg had a fairly easy time of it across the Wilderness Road, but Kirby Smith had trouble maintaining formation. Hundreds of horses fell, and wagons broke down on the rocky road and the steep slopes. Three thousand men were left to hold Cumberland Gap. By October 23 the two armies were back in Knoxville, where 15,000 men required medical treatment.[12] They had marched one thousand miles, had fought a battle, and were back where they had started two months before. They brought back with them 15,000 horses and mules, 8,000 cattle, 50,000 barrels of pork, 10,000 hogs, 20,000 rifles, 1,000,000 yards of Kentucky cloth, and vast stores of artillery, powder, and ammunition, besides the new wagons.[13] The campaign had been conducted over more territory than any other of the entire war, but the results amounted to nothing of strategic significance.

General Carter L. Stevenson, brigade commander under Kirby Smith. He commanded at Clinton, Tennessee.

General John P. McCown, Confederate commander at Knoxville, December, 1862

On the night that Bragg's army straggled into Knoxville, three inches of snow fell; the men were "grateful" to the Yankee army for the blue wool blankets they had captured in Kentucky.[14] Samuel R. Watkins, of Maury's Grays of the First Tennessee Regiment, said that he and a comrade, strolling along Gay Street, were "the lousiest, dirtiest, raggeditest looking Rebels you ever saw." As the buddies strolled, they spied two pretty girls, who greeted them, saying, "Gentlemen, there is supper for the soldiers at the Ladies Association rooms, and we are sent to bring in all the soldiers we can find." Sam wrote later that he always remembered the odd sight of the two pretty girls walking arm in arm down Gay Street with those "raggeditest" soldiers.[15]

President Davis summoned Bragg to Richmond, Virginia, to make an oral report of the Kentucky campaign. Kirby Smith sent a request to Davis to be relieved of further duty under Bragg. Davis, who was particularly fond of Bragg, declined, but did allow Kirby Smith a leave of absence. The post at Knoxville then came under command successively of General J. P. McCown, General Samuel Jones, and General Dabney H. Maury. The next February, Davis promoted Kirby Smith to full general and transferred him to command the Trans-Mississippi Department at Alexandria, Louisiana.

Meanwhile Lee's offensive in the East had also failed. His detailed plans to invade the North fell into the hands of McClellan, and at Antietam Creek near Sharpsburg, Maryland, September 17, 1862, Lee and McClellan fought the bloodiest one-day battle in the history of American warfare. Even then, Lee was able to fight to a draw, but his invasion plans were thwarted and he retreated into Virginia.

In Richmond, Bragg was warmly received by President Davis, despite his failure to mount an offensive under advantageous conditions at Perryville; for his army had captured the largest booty in modern warfare and seemed to have staved off the Union threat against the Confederate arsenals of East Tennessee and Georgia.

On the Union side, Buell was replaced by General William S. Rosecrans, the Union hero of Corinth, while in Virginia McClellan lost his command to Major General Ambrose Burnside.

Thus, while the South hailed one general for not attacking at all, the North replaced two for not attacking enough. The North was shedding its leaders who fought with maneuvers and maps and substituting hard-hitting infighters like Grant, Sheridan, and Sherman. The South held on to its leaders toward whom its President was obstinately biased.

In the battles of Perryville and Antietam, neither side won a decisive victory, and 31,000 men fell to no apparent avail. Nevertheless, Perryville and Antietam were significant milestones. Afterwards, the North would be on the defensive only once, briefly, during Lee's spectacular invasion of Pennsylvania.

The Confederate invasion of Kentucky launched from Chattanooga and Knoxville had failed to turn the tide of the war in favor of the South; the people of Kentucky did not rally to the Southern standard; and the rich Bluegrass Country once more served as a staging area for a Union drive into East Tennessee. Nevertheless, Bragg's and Kirby Smith's combined operations had produced some positive results for the South. The enormous amount of captured booty was invaluable to the Confederate armies; the gateway to Georgia at Chattanooga was relieved from jeopardy; and East Tennessee and the valuable rail lines which ran through Knoxville were secured for the South for months to come.

NOTES

1. Horn, p. 159.

2. For detailed accounts of the Confederate invasion of Kentucky, consult: Horn, *The Army of Tennessee*; *Battles and Leaders*, III, 1-61; E. A. Pollard, *Southern History of the War*, Vol. II; Kincaid, *The Wilderness Road*, pp. 245-54.

3. Edwin L. Drake (ed.), *The Annals of the Army of Tennessee, An Early Western History* (Nashville: 1878), I, 197.

4. O. R., Ser. I, XVI, Part II, 822.

5. Don C. Seitz, *Braxton Bragg, General of the Confederacy*, p. 174.

6. Irving Silber (ed.), *Songs of the Civil War* (New York: 1960), pp. 227-28. Some artillery shells thought to be suitable for "Long Tom" are on display at Confederate Memorial Hall in Knoxville.

7. *Battles and Leaders*, III, 11.

8. *The Southern Bivouac*, I, 167.

9. *Battles and Leaders*, III, 25; Pollard, II, 144.

10. Noll, p. 219. General Buell acknowledged that Bragg was ready for battle at this point if he could have his own terms, but "the general who offers battle is he who stays to give or receive it." *Battles and Leaders*, III, 31-51.

11. *The Southern Bivouac*, I, 551.

12. Kincaid, p. 254.

13. John B. Jones, *A Rebel War Clerk's Diary*, p. 161.

14. *Confederate Veteran*, XVII (September 1909), 449.

15. Samuel R. Watkins, *Company "Aytch"—First Tennessee Regiment*, p. 61.

13

The Yankees Pay a Visit

FROM Richmond, General Bragg ordered General Polk to move the Army of Tennessee from Knoxville to Murfreesboro by train. Bragg followed shortly and on December 31, 1862, fought Rosecrans in a fierce but inconclusive battle at nearby Stones River. Bragg retired to Tullahoma, leaving the Federals at Murfreesboro, and both armies remained idle until the following June.

Bragg's Army of Tennessee had won many a fight but never a real victory, and the troops were not hesitant to place the blame upon Bragg himself. When they retreated, his men were greatly downcast, insisting that they were not whipped. "It is bad enough," said one bitter Rebel, "to run when we are whipped, but damn this way of beating the Yankees and then running away from them!" One of them was asked where they were retreating to. "To Cuba," he replied angrily, "if old Bragg can get a bridge built across from Florida." [1]

Rosecrans was anxious to learn if Bragg intended to remain in Tennessee or to send troops to strengthen the garrison at Vicksburg. Lacking skillful cavalry (which his Rebel foes always seemed to have), the Union commander's only method of getting such information seemed to be by tapping telegraph wires along the East Tennessee and Georgia Railroad near Knoxville.

Two telegraphers volunteered. F. S. Van Valkenberg and Patrick Mullarkey, accompanied by four East Tennesseans, crossed the Cumberland Mountains, slipped past Confederate guards at Kingston, got about fifteen miles from Knoxville, and for a week listened to all passing dispatches. When they heard a message ordering

the scouring of the region to find Union spies, they decamped and, with capture and death a daily risk, finally reached Union pickets in Kentucky. They had been inside the Confederate lines for thirty-three days, eavesdropping on Rebel secrets between Richmond, Chattanooga, and Knoxville. [2]

New Year's Day, 1863, saw the North committed not to fighting to preserve the Union but, by Lincoln's Emancipation Proclamation, to extinction of slavery by force. The war would end only when the armies and civilians of either North or South were beaten into submission.

In January, General Ambrose Burnside arrived in Kentucky as the new Federal commander of the Army of the Ohio, and General Joe Hooker replaced him as commander of the Army of the Potomac.

Born in Indiana, Burnside was a West Point graduate who had been a professional soldier and then a businessman, manufacturing the Burnside breech-loading rifle which he invented. At the start of the Civil War, he was an official of the Illinois Central Railroad. After fighting at the First Battle of Bull Run, he organized and in July, 1862, became the head of the Ninth Corps, which fought with McClelland at South Mountain and Antietam. [3] In the latter, "Burnside's Bridge" was a focal point on the left wing of the Union assault. He relieved McClellan as commander of the Army of the Potomac November 7, 1862, holding that command just long enough to suffer a terrible repulse by Longstreet under Lee, at Fredericksburg, Virginia, on December 13. At that battle, the carnage among the Union troops attempting to storm Marye's

Major General Ambrose E. Burnside, commander of the
Army of the Potomac facing Lee at Fredericksburg

Heights was so bloody that Burnside and Lincoln both wept, and Robert E. Lee murmured to an aide, "It is well that war is so terrible   we should grow too fond of it." [4]

And now Lincoln, believing that Burnside was a better general than this one battle had shown, was quickly giving him another chance. Burnside arrived in Kentucky, bringing his Ninth Corps as a nucleus for his army, with Lincoln's order to enter East Tennessee at the earliest practical moment.

Meanwhile, General Joseph E. Johnston had been appointed the supreme Confederate commander in the West. [5] In his new command, he was directing the armies of General Bragg in Middle Tennessee, General J. C. Pemberton at Vicksburg, and the forces in East Tennessee.

In the early spring of 1863, General Johnston stopped off at Knoxville on an inspection trip, and the weight of his new responsibilities must have been reflected in his face during an incident that occurred there. One evening in his quarters at the Lamar House, he was host to a roomful of high-ranking Rebel officers dressed in glittering uniforms. A knock was heard, and one of his guests, an officer resplendent with gold lace and stars, opened the door to find an aged Negro standing there, wearing a sunbonnet and carrying a cotton umbrella tucked under her arm.

"Is this Mr. Johnston's room?" she asked. "Mr. Joe Johnston's room? I wants to see him."

In she marched and tapped the chieftain on his shoulder. The General turned and clasped her hand.

"Mr. Joe," she said softly, "you is getting old."

As the General in the splendid gray and gold uniform held her hand and answered her inquiries, tears brimmed his eyes. The spry but gentle old woman who made the Confederate commander weep was Judy, who "toted" Joe in her arms when he was a baby. [6]

At this moment Joe's chief worry was Vicksburg, where General Grant was slowly closing the ring around the South's last hold on the Mississippi River. Another cause for anxiety was the presence of Rosecrans' Federal army at Murfreesboro. A Union flanking movement from the east by Burnside might put Chattanooga in a squeeze. Therefore, in April, 1863, General Johnston recommended to the War Department at Richmond that the East Tennessee forces be strengthened.

As the first step in the reorganization, Major General Simon Bolivar Buckner was named commander of the Confederate Department of East Tennessee. Buckner established his headquarters in Knoxville on April 27. An observer of the time said that Buckner's personal bearing fulfilled the popular notion of a grand army officer. "The attention of citizens was attracted and their criticism challenged by his imposing appearance, as he rode without escort upon a splendid charger through the principal street. His reputation was that of a true gentleman and a soldier of superior merit." [7] Born in Kentucky in 1823, Buckner was a West Point graduate and instructor who chose Confederate service. He had surrendered Fort Donelson to General Grant on February 16, 1862, and was a prisoner at Fort Warren. Following his exchange in August, he had reported for duty as a brigade commander under Bragg.

Buckner gave to Brigadier General Danville Leadbetter, who had helped engineer the fortification around Richmond, Virginia, the task of constructing the Knoxville fortification. Leadbetter had commanded the Knoxville post a short time in 1862 and so was familiar with the terrain. He built defensive works around the railroad depot on the north side of town and commenced an earthwork fort on a hill northwest of the University.

The Confederates called this hilltop stronghold Fort Loudon. Within a few months it would be in Federal hands and renamed in honor of a new Union hero.

By June, 1863, General Grant had called on Burnside's command in Kentucky for help at Vicksburg. Burnside sent the First and Second Divisions of the Ninth Corps, under Major General John G. Parke, and artillery units, under the twenty-four-year-old Lieutenant Samuel N. Benjamin, to join the Union Army of the Tennessee surrounding Vicksburg.

The transfer of some of his men to Vicksburg unnerved Burnside so much that he postponed the expedition into East Tennessee. To compound his difficulties, he was busy protecting his rear from the Rebel raider John Hunt Morgan who this time had passed through Kentucky and was raising a rumpus in Ohio and Indiana.

Burnside would not move forward without his favorite troops of the Ninth Corps, but he set about organizing the various units around him in Kentucky into the 23rd Army Corps, under Major General George L. Hartsuff of New York.

In early June, President Lincoln telegraphed Rosecrans that if Chattanooga and East Tennes-

Major General William Rosecrans, commander of the Army of the Cumberland, driving toward Chattanooga

Major General Simon Bolivar Buckner, commander of Confederate forces at Knoxville in the spring of 1863

see could be taken and held by Federal forces, "I think the rebellion must dwindle and die. I think you and Burnside can do this." [8]

To pave the way for the invasion of East Tennessee upon the return of the Ninth Corps from Vicksburg, Burnside sent Colonel William P. Sanders to lead a cavalry raid on Confederate lines south of Cumberland Gap to tear up bridges and communications. A Kentucky native and West Point graduate, the twenty-eight-year-old Sanders had begun his Civil War service as a captain in the United States Cavalry defending Washington, D. C., had served in the early Peninsular Campaign under McClellan, and three months before had been promoted to colonel in command of the Fifth Kentucky Cavalry.

By General Burnside's order, young Colonel Sanders departed from Mount Vernon, Kentucky, with his band—700 men of the First East Tennessee Mounted Infantry under Colonel R. K. Byrd, 200 men of the 44th Ohio, 200 of the 112th Illinois, 150 of the Seventh Ohio, 150 of the Second Ohio, 100 of the First Kentucky Volunteers, and some from the First Regiment Ohio Artillery Volunteers. They rode to Williamsburg, Kentucky, followed a route known as Marsh Creek Road to near Huntsville, Tennessee, and on to Wartburg, where they captured the Confederate garrison. They met Confederate pickets at Kingston, who alerted the commands at Loudon, Lenoir's Station (Lenoir City), and Knoxville to their approach. At Lenoir's Station, they took the artillery garrison, burned the depot and a cotton factory, and crippled telegraph wires and part of the railroad to Knoxville.

The night of June 19, Colonel Sanders ran into the Confederate pickets outside of Knoxville. He left some of the First Kentucky men to deal with them and rode the rest of his band around to the north. On the 20th, he was moving toward the center of Knoxville on the Tazewell Road. War had come to Knoxville.

By word from Kingston, the Confederates in Knoxville knew that a Union raid on the city was a certainty. General Buckner was off on a march toward Big Creek Gap with most of the post's troops. Colonel Trigg was in temporary command. He had about 1,000 good soldiers in his 51st Virginia Regiment and Colonel J. J. Finley's Seventh Florida Regiment. The Acting Chief of Staff, Major Von Sheliha, ordered Lieutenant Colonel Milton A. Haynes to take charge of the artillery defense of the city and to get men from the convalescents in the hospitals, as well as volunteer citizens. Major S. H. Reynolds, Chief of Ordnance, was ordered to issue to Haynes as many fieldpieces as could be readied in a few hours and 100 rounds of ammunition.

The call went out for Knoxville citizens to report to Colonel Haynes and to Colonel E. D. Blake to help defend their city and brace the garrison, which had only thirty-seven cavalrymen on duty. By nightfall, two hundred citizens and convalescent soldiers reported for duty; and the batteries were manned, one at College Hill, one at Summit Hill, and one at McGhee's Hill, the last-named under Captain Hugh L. Mc-Clung. During the night, Baker's battery at College Hill was moved to a place near the Asylum Hospital (now City Hall). Streets were barricaded with cotton bales.[9]

Major Victor Von Sheliha was quite certain that the city's defenses were in good order. Colonel Haynes then disguised himself as a farmer and ventured out toward the Union lines. Making contact with the Federals, Haynes assured them that he was a loyal Unionist and informed them that they could easily move into the city without much of a fight. Haynes then returned to the city and prepared his make-shift command of convalescents, citizens, and the remaining garrison troops for battle.[10]

Colonel Sanders and his raiders galloped into Knoxville after dark. Approaching the city from the north, the cavalrymen dismounted behind the Confederate Armory buildings, pushed their artillery to the point where Fifth Avenue crosses Gay and Henley, and opened fire.

The skirmish, which was mainly an artillery duel, lasted little more than an hour. Two Confederate officers and an enlisted man lost their lives. When it appeared that the Federal skirmishers were advancing, the gunner of the 12th Confederate howitzer battery complained to Haynes: "Colonel, I can't hit them fellows. Please get down and try it yourself." Colonel Haynes dismounted, ordered the howitzer loaded with canister, and with one well-aimed shot dispersed the raiders.

Colonel Sanders sent a message to Colonel Haynes by a paroled prisoner: "I send you my compliments, and say that but for the admirable manner with which you managed your artillery, I would have taken Knoxville today." [11]

The next morning's Knoxville *Register* had as its banner headline, "Last night the Yankees paid a visit." [12]

Most of Colonel Sanders' shells flew over

Major General John G. Parke, U.S.A., second in command to Burnside

Knoxville harmlessly enough, only frightening the women and children. But one deadly shell wounded a volunteer citizen, killed a sergeant who was lying on the ground, and in its final explosion killed a lieutenant, who was sitting on a fence at the Asylum to see the fight. Then Captain McClung, seeing his men duck for cover at the flash of the Union guns, cried out: "Don't be afraid—there's no danger!" He was instantly hit. As he lay dying, he prayed for "forgiveness to those who killed me." [13]

The Federals outnumbered the defenders but could not have held the town for long. Their primary mission was to destroy communication lines. Sanders captured thirty-one prisoners, eighty horses, and two fieldpieces. He left Knoxville, went to Strawberry Plains, destroyed a bridge at Flat Creek and a 1,600-foot bridge over the Holston River. Destroying everything he could in his way, he was in Boston, Kentucky, on June 24, having sustained loss of only two killed, four wounded, and thirteen missing.

Reporting back to his general, Burnside, Colonel Sanders was immediately dispatched northward to try to catch John Hunt Morgan, the Rebel raider. Spreading devastation in Kentucky, Morgan dashed across the Ohio River and up into Ohio and Indiana, almost reaching Pennsylvania before Federals caught him on July 26.[14]

NOTES

1. Rossiter Johnson, *Campfires and Battlefields,* p. 499.

2. F. T. Miller, VII, 361-62.

3. Burnside was then thirty-nine years old. The grandson of a South Carolina planter, with two cousins in Lee's army, Burnside is remembered for his distinctive sideburn whiskers, which took their name from his.

4. Six separate Federal assaults against Lee failed. During the night Longstreet's men captured a document from Burnside indicating that another assault would be made on the 14th. When Lee read the message he turned to Longstreet and said, "General, I am losing confidence in your friend General Burnside." *Battles and Leaders,* III, 82.

5. General Joseph E. Johnston had commanded the Army of Northern Virginia until wounded at Fair Oaks. He was replaced by Lee. In November, 1862, he was named Chief of the Department of Tennessee, having nominal command of the armies of Bragg in Tennessee, J. C. Pemberton at Vicksburg, Franklin Gardner at Port Hutson, and all forces in East Tennessee.

6. *Confederate Veteran,* XI (February 1903), 60.

7. Humes, p. 208.

8. James R. Sullivan, *Chickamauga and Chattanooga Battlefields* ("National Park Service Historical Handbook Series," No. 25 [Washington, D.C.: 1956]), p. 2.

9. O. R., Ser. I, XXIII, Part I, 385-87, 390-93.

10. O. R., Ser. I, XXIII, Part I, 390-93.

11. *Ibid.*

12. Knoxville *Daily Register,* June 21, 1863. A reproduction of this paper is on display at the Frank H. McClung Museum, Circle Park, Knoxville.

13. Among the prominent Knoxvillians who manned the guns June 20 were Senator Landon C. Haynes, William H. Sneed, John H. Crozier, Rev. Joseph Martin, and Rev. Mr. Woolfolk. Landon C. Haynes was a Senator from Tennessee in the Confederate Congress. Other citizens did not wish their names mentioned in the official report for fear of reprisals. O. R., Ser. I, XXIII, Part I, 393.

14. Morgan and six fellow prisoners escaped from the Ohio Penitentiary at Columbus on November 27 and re-entered Confederate lines near Knoxville. On September 4, 1864, he was killed in attempting to escape capture near Greeneville, Tennessee.

14

The Dreaded Foe So Long Expected

FROM the beginning, the Confederacy had carried on the war by putting several independent armies in the field, each acting without reference to the others except in rare instances. This policy caused the Confederates to be outnumbered in almost every battle, preventing them from seizing the advantage on many occasions when poor tactics of Northern generals gave the South the opportunity to gain numerical superiority by a quick concentration of small armies.

At least one prominent Confederate general opposed the policy of command separation, advocating that the armies support each other by use of the interior railroad lines running from Virginia to Tennessee. In April, 1863, while passing through Richmond, Lieutenant General James Longstreet called on President Jefferson Davis and Secretary of War James Seddon to impress upon them his concept of mobility. He suggested that the only way to relieve Grant's pressure on Vicksburg was to reinforce Generals Johnston and Bragg with units from Virginia sent by the railroad through Knoxville and Chattanooga, overcome Rosecrans, drive to the Ohio River, break Grant's line of communication, and force his recall.[1]

Davis dismissed Longstreet's suggestion, preferring to rely on foreign intervention to solve the South's dilemma, and Secretary Seddon insisted that Grant could be dislodged only by direct attack.

Longstreet did not pursue the subject further with the Richmond authorities, but in May, when he rejoined Lee at his headquarters at Fredericksburg, he restated his plan to send part of the Virginia army through East Tennessee to join Bragg. Lee admitted the logic of the proposition but stated that he was planning a campaign into Maryland and Pennsylvania to achieve the same object. For such an undertaking, Lee would definitely need Longstreet's First Corps.

Lee defeated Hooker at Chancellorsville in May, 1863, but in doing so he suffered the bitter loss of Stonewall Jackson. He reorganized his army into three infantry corps under James Longstreet, A. P. Hill, and R. S. Ewell, with a cavalry division under J. E. B. Stuart, and moved on June 3 to invade Pennsylvania and destroy the bridge over the Susquehanna River at Harrisburg.

General George Meade relieved Hooker as head of the Federal Army of the Potomac and moved north, keeping his troops between the Confederates and Washington. By June 29, the two armies were getting close to each other near Gettysburg, Pennsylvania.

At Murfreesboro, Rosecrans was mounting an offensive toward Bragg at Tullahoma. In Vicksburg, the besieged Confederate soldiers were receiving daily rations of parched corn, counted out by the kernel.

On July 1, Lee drove the Federal forces back through the streets of Gettysburg to Cemetery Hill. Longstreet's corps acted as Lee's right wing. The two generals met at the summit of Seminary Ridge and watched the Union forces concentrating on Cemetery Ridge, some 1,400 yards away. After observing the positions, Longstreet turned to Lee and said: "If we could have chosen a point to meet our plans of operation,

General Burnside's triumphant march into Knoxville, from Harpers' Weekly

Lieutenant General James Longstreet, commander of the First Corps, Army of Northern Virginia

I do not think we could have found a better one than that upon which they are now concentrating. All we have to do is to throw our army around by their left, and we shall interpose between the Federal army and Washington. . . . When they attack, we shall beat them, as we proposed to do before we left Fredericksburg, and the probabilities are that the fruits of our success will be great." [2]

"No," said General Lee. "The enemy is there, and I am going to attack him there. . . . I am going to whip them or they are going to whip me." [3]

From this moment to the bitter conclusion, Longstreet's heart was not in the battle. He

doubted Lee's strategy, and his impatience was obvious. He was further annoyed when shown the plan of battle. As he surveyed the field across which he must order General George Pickett to charge, he sensed the hopelessness of the attack and the cruel slaughter it would cause.

On July 3, 1863, notwithstanding his misgivings, Longstreet ordered his artillery, commanded by young Colonel E. Porter Alexander, to begin the artillery fire. For more than an hour the cannonade rocked the Pennsylvania countryside, but the Northern guns were not subdued. Longstreet turned to his young Virginia subordinate and said: "Pickett, I am being crucified at the thought of the sacrifice of life this attack will make. I have instructed Alexander to watch the effect of our fire upon the enemy, and when it begins to tell, he must take the responsibility to give you your orders, for I can't." [4]

As the general finished, a courier rode up with a note from Alexander, saying, "If you are coming at all you must come at once or I cannot give you proper support." Pickett read the note to Longstreet. "General, shall I advance?" There was no reply from the bowed head of the commander, so bravely Pickett announced, "I am going to move forward, sir."[5]

The magnificent but futile charge of Major General Pickett's division of the First Corps of the Army of Northern Virginia was bloodily repulsed, the South lost the Battle of Gettys-

Colonel E. Porter Alexander, Confederate artillery commander at Gettysburg and Knoxville

burg, and the dream of a Confederate invasion of the North ended.

On the following day, July 4, Vicksburg surrendered, giving the Union control of the entire Mississippi River and releasing the forces of Grant and Sherman to rush to the aid of Rosecrans and Burnside. Grant then returned the Ninth Corps to Burnside in Kentucky. The Corps had earned the nickname "the Wandering Corps," having fought in seven states.

By July 4, Bragg, falling back from Tullahoma and Rosecrans' advance, had his entire army near Chattanooga. In the middle of August, Rosecrans, moved his Army of the Cumberland against Chattanooga from his base at Bridgeport, Alabama, through an open valley. At the same time, Burnside started moving south toward Knoxville.

Bragg retreated toward La Fayette, Georgia, sending orders for Buckner to evacuate Knoxville and join him against Rosecrans. Except for Buckner, the only sizable Rebel force between Burnside in Kentucky and Rosecrans near Chattanooga was a garrison numbering 2,500 at Cumberland Gap under General Frazer.

At long last, Burnside finally complied with Lincoln's order that he enter East Tennessee. On August 16 with the 23rd Corps, about 15,000 men, he left the base at Camp Nelson, fifteen miles south of Nicholasville, and traveled about 220 miles across the desolate Kentucky mountains. An eyewitness to the journey noted that "in many cases the horses utterly failed to drag the guns up the precipitous sides of the ascents, and then the worn and struggling animals gave place to men, who, with hands and shoulders to the wheels and limber, hoisted guns and caissons from height to height. The fearful wayside was strewn with broken wheels and vehicles, and with horses and mules, dying exhausted on the march. Baggage-animals, mules, and drivers, in several instances, made missteps and rolled down precipices. Nothing but the indomitable courage and hardihood of Burnside, nothing less lofty than the heroism that possessed his army, could have ever seen such an undertaking accomplished." [6]

The soldiers carried from sixty to eighty pounds on their backs, and by the time they emerged from the mountains into the valleys of East Tennessee they had thrown away most of their equipment that was not edible. Looking back on the long, terrible hike, one soldier wrote home: "If this is the kind of country we are fighting for, I am in favor of letting the Rebs take their land . . . and go to hell for I wouldn't give a bit an acre for all the land I have seen in the last four days."[7]

The Cumberland Gap garrison was bypassed by the Federal columns that moved down from Kentucky.

The moment General Buckner pulled his Confederate troops out of Knoxville to join Bragg in Georgia, one of the roving, lawless bands which the war had spawned made a raid into town, and steps were taken to organize temporary citizen defenses. Before adequate measures could be agreed upon, an Indiana cavalry detachment, Burnside's advance guard, under Colonel John W. Foster, suddenly dashed into the streets of Knoxville.

They spied Peter Staub, a Swiss immigrant who had become the town's leading tailor, and chased him down the street into the house of a staunch Union supporter. Staub was a Southerner in spirit, but his friend pacified the soldiers, who then moved on into the center of town where they were stopped by a citizen sentry.[8]

A group of women who were standing on the street near the sentry cursed the Yankee invaders, and the next day one wrote in her diary: "Yesterday was the first day of September 1863. Long shall it be remembered among us. It was the day when we beheld for the first time our most dreaded foe, the Yankees, so long expected throughout East Tennessee."[9]

The Federal soldiers could not distinguish between "good and bad Rebels." One soldier from Ohio who was quartered in the home of Mrs.

Blanton, whose sympathies were with the South, attempted to be friendly and reached down to pat the head of her little daughter. The little girl, Martha, quickly and defiantly bit the soldier in the hand.[10] Some Southern sympathizers were arrested and their property seized. Charles Baum, a railroad employee, was one of a number jailed. His house was burned to the ground.[11] Armorer Riggins, Postmaster Charlton, and other Confederates in important posts fled southward.

The loyal Unionist population exploded with joy. Senator Harris of New York received a letter from his son, vividly describing the tumultuous reception which stunned and overwhelmed the Yankee soldiers.

HEADQUARTERS, ARMY OF THE OHIO, KNOXVILLE
Sunday, September 6, 1863

MY DEAR FATHER,

Our troops entered this place without opposition on the part of the rebels, who fled at our approach. A rapid march of 250 miles over mountain roads, made with artillery, infantry, and cavalry was deemed next to impossible by the rebel General Buckner, and before he was aware of it our columns were precipitating themselves down the southern slopes of the mountains with trains of supplies following almost at a trot. It was the most beautiful march of the war. We were surprised at it—the rebels more so—they did not know where to look for us, and as we came upon them by several different roads, they overestimated our force, magnifying it to an army of from 60,000 to 100,000 men, and, without the slightest attempt at resistance, retreated southward, crossed the Holston River, and burned the Loudon bridge, 1,800 feet long, to prevent pursuit.

From time to time during our march, I have written you about our ride through Kentucky, but it was not to be compared in interest to that which we made through East Tennessee. The country is wild and unsettled until you approach Knoxville. We marched from 25 to 30 miles a day, and slept at night sometimes under a tent, sometimes under a fly, and once we bivouacked in a rain that wet us all through. General Burnside had not so much as an overcoat, but with his saddle for a pillow he lay down and we followed suit.

As we approached the settled part of the country we were greeted everywhere with shouts for the Union, cheers for the old flag, and the most unmistakable signs of loyalty. At every house the entire family would appear, often with buckets of fresh water and fruit for the welcome Yankees, and some of the people would scarcely ask for pay for the forage which we had seized to feed our animals, although the corn we had taken was all they had to look to for their winter's food. Sometimes the Stars and Stripes would be carried out to the gate of the dooryard by one of the girls, and the General and Staff would take off their hats, while the escort following gave three cheers. Old gray-haired men would come out and seize the General's hand, bidding him Godspeed, and men would flock in at every halt to be armed and join us. The sufferings of these people have been terrible.

"Glory be to God, the Yankees have come!" "The Flag's come back to Tennessee!" Such were the welcomes all along the road, and as we entered Knoxville, it was past all description. The people seemed frantic with joy. I never knew what the *Love of Liberty* was before. The old flag has been hidden in mattresses and under carpets. It now floats to the breeze at every staff in East Tennessee. Ladies wear it—carry it—wave it! Little children clap their hands and kiss it.

Can you imagine the effect of this on me? My heart is so full and I am so thankful to Almighty God for this bloodless and yet glorious victory, that I will not attempt to say any more on the subject.[12]

By September 3, when Burnside with his main force arrived in Knoxville from Kingston, crowds lined the streets to cheer the Union army. The country people, in particular, were thrilled at the sight of the Stars and Stripes, once again flying from the poles from which they had been pulled down two years before.[13]

The people showered the Union troops with gifts of pie, cake, meat, and bread. But they could not furnish clothing, medical supplies, and ammunition, and Burnside's supply line ran from Cumberland Gap; the route was so long and tortuous that it was in effect worthless. He could not expect help from Rosecrans, operating near Chattanooga, because the latter's base was Nashville, and Bragg was still unconquered. Supplies must come from Chattanooga, but none could until Bragg was driven away.

Burnside's men were exhausted from the perilous march into Tennessee, and the general himself, feeling the effects of the journey, tendered his resignation the day after he arrived in Knox-ville. But President Lincoln wired him on September 10: "A thousand thanks for the late success you have given us. We cannot allow you to resign until things shall be a little more settled in East Tennessee."[14]

The Union commander then established his Knoxville headquarters in the home of John H. Crozier, which stood on the northeast corner of Gay Street and Clinch Avenue (site of the present-day Farragut Hotel).[15] He made several friendly speeches to the townspeople from the balcony of the mansion and treated former disloyal citizens with kindness and impartiality.

During the march from Kentucky, after Burnside had reached Tennessee, he was approached by a group of mountaineer Unionists. A spokesman stepped forward and respectfully said, "General, we want you to give us authority to go down here into the valley and carry off the hogs and cattle we find there." The request was denied. Then the spokesman said that they would make no mistake and would carry off only the cattle and hogs of the Rebels. Burnside replied, "That is not my way of carrying on war," and the mountaineers moved away disappointed.[16]

Immediately after his arrival in Knoxville, Burnside sent a written invitation to the Reverend Thomas Humes to resume his duties as Rector of St. John's Episcopal Church, the only time in the entire war that a commanding general made such a request. On Sunday, September 6, Dr. Humes resumed services. He recorded that he was surprised and impressed by the appropriateness of the Psalm prescribed by the Episcopal Book of Common Prayer for the sixth day of the month, which is the thirtieth Psalm, the beginning words being: "I will magnify thee, O Lord; for thou hast set me up, and not made my foes to triumph over me."[17]

General Burnside himself was a deeply devout Christian. At Camp Nelson on August 14, just before his invasion of East Tennessee, he issued the following order to the Army of the Ohio: "Whenever regimental evening dress parades

Burnside's headquarters in Knoxville, the John Crozier
House at Gay Street and Clinch Avenue

are held, it shall be the duty of the commanding officer to see that the chaplain, or some proper person, in his absence, holds some short religious service, such as the reading of a portion of the Scripture, with appropriate prayer for the protection and assistance of Divine Providence." [18]

After setting up his base camp in Knoxville, Burnside immediately made preparations to secure the remainder of the French Broad–Holston country. On September 9, he forced the surrender of Frazer and his command at Cumberland Gap. Next day he received a dispatch from General T. L. Crittenden indicating that he had been sent by Rosecrans to occupy Chattanooga and that he was "in full possession of this place." Burnside was requested to send his cavalry southward to connect with the Union forces in Chattanooga, but he failed to comply with this order. Instead, he set about to occupy all the important points above Knoxville, leaving sufficient forces at Kingston and Loudon. Units were also sent to occupy Athens and, if possible, Cleveland.

Burnside felt secure in the knowledge that Rosecrans had now occupied Chattanooga. It seemed only a matter of time until the two Union generals could unite and either defeat Bragg decisively or drive him back into Georgia. With all of Tennessee now in Union hands, a rapid thrust toward Atlanta would probably end the war before Christmas. But what Burnside and Rosecrans did not know was that, at this moment in the war, the Confederate government had decided for the first time to use its natural advantage of interior communications and railroads to reinforce Bragg sufficiently to overwhelm them and had conceived a strategy designed to drive them back into Ohio.

NOTES

1. James Longstreet, *From Manassas to Appomattox,* p. 433.

2. *Battles and Leaders,* III, 339.

3. *Ibid.,* pp. 339-40.

4. James S. Montgomery, *The Shaping of a Battle: Gettysburg,* p. 119.

5. *Battles and Leaders,* III, 364-65.

6. Ben Perley Poore, *The Life and Public Services of Ambrose E. Burnside, Soldier—Citizen—Statesman,* p. 215.

7. Bruce Catton, *This Hallowed Ground,* p. 290.

8. Humes, p. 210. Staub, like most Knoxville Swiss immigrants, was a staunch Southerner. After the war he established the famous Staub Theater and was elected mayor of Knoxville in 1881. Staub School, named for him, was consolidated with Van Gilder into Fort Sanders Elementary School.

9. Elisa Buffat, "Some Recollections of My Childhood Days" (unpublished manuscript in McClung Collection, Lawson McGhee Library), p. 23.

In 1893, Captain H. S. Chamberlain of the Second Ohio Cavalry, whom Burnside had appointed quartermaster of the army when he entered East Tennessee, remembered particularly the difficult crossing of the mountains. "Why," he said, "a six mule team would not have been able to haul more from Somerset to Knoxville, than the forage necessary to the subsistence of the mules while making the march."

Chamberlain entered Knoxville September 4, 1863. He spent the night on West Church Street and the next day was accosted by one of Knoxville's best-known citizens, who introduced himself. He was General Joseph A. Mabry, who had been a very pronounced supporter of the Confederacy. General Mabry said; "I am a notorious rebel, these people will all tell you that. I at one time proposed to be one of ten men to contribute one hundred thousand dollars each to the Confederate treasury. I equipped an entire company of soldiers for the Confederacy at my own expense and ran an establishment here that furnished thousands of dollars worth of clothing for the Southern soldiers. I have nothing to conceal concerning my attitude or what I have done, but I am here to tell you that whatever I have that will be of use to your army, you can have it and I shall attempt to conceal nothing." It was a frank statement which made a distinct impression on the Union officer. Chamberlain returned to Knoxville after the war and with L. C. Shepard established the Knoxville Iron Company. Knoxville *Journal,* May 7, 1893.

10. Personal communication from William Marks, Knoxville, Tenn., January 3, 1963.

11. Charles Baum, grandfather of Karl Baum, Knoxville florist, was placed in the stockade on Main Street. Luckily he was wearing his Masonic pin. One of his guards was a colored soldier, also a Mason, though Baum did not recognize the legitimacy of his colored brethren's lodge. One day, the soldier stepped up to Baum and said, "All right, Mr. Baum, you're a Mason and I'm a Mason. I'm going to walk up to the other end of the stockade and turn my back. When I do you're a free man." Baum escaped and was never retaken by Federal authorities. After the war he pressed his claim against the government for destroying his private property. When the judge asked Baum which side he favored in the war, Mr. Baum, then quite elderly, straightened up and cried out, "For the South, Sir!" That outburst ended the case. Interview with Karl Baum, November, 1962.

12. *Harper's Weekly,* October 24, 1863.

13. William D. Hamilton, *Recollections of a Cavalryman of the Civil War After 50 Years,* p. 50. Hamilton says the bashful daughters of the mountains came out to see the blue uniforms and exclaimed: "La, there they come! H'aint they purty. Land sakes, h'aint they a sight of 'em!"

14. Poore, p. 217.

15. Mary U. Rothrock (ed.), *The French Broad-Holston Country,* p. 138. An eyewitness said that "One of the most thrilling scenes I ever had the pleasure to witness, occurred on our arrival here. Generals Burnside, Carter, and Shackelford took up their quarters at the fine house of a noted Rebel who had left the place, and were followed there by an immense concourse of citizens clamorous for a speech. General Carter was first called out, he being an East Tennessean. He was followed by Generals Burnside and Shackelford, and the excitement and enthusiasm of the crowd gained with every word. Meanwhile I had taken my way around to the rear of the house and had got upon the roof of the balcony, and as General Shackelford finished his speech, I unfurled our large garrison flag, and threw it over the balcony. It was caught by the breeze, and as its beautiful folds streamed out upon the air, the people could no longer contain themselves. Shout after shout rent the air. I looked into the house and saw Generals Burnside, Carter, and Shackelford shaking hands, while tears rolled down their cheeks. Some one sang out, 'Get under it, get under it,'— and it seemed as if the

crowd would trample each other under foot in their wild endeavor to do so. I never saw anything like it in my life. You may think from the way I write there are no rebels here. There are a few, but they look as if they enjoyed poor health." Frank Moore, *The Civil War in Song and Story*, p. 396.

16. Humes, p. 229.
17. *Ibid.*, pp. 232-33.
18. Poore, p. 218.

The Flood of the Mighty Gray River

SOON after Gettysburg, General James Longstreet, Lee's most trusted corps commander, again urged President Davis and General Lee to send him and his First Corps by rail from Virginia through Knoxville to join Bragg. Together Longstreet and Bragg would drive Rosecrans out of Tennessee and all the way to the Ohio River, if possible. Lee would remain on the defensive behind the Rapidan River with the two other corps of the Army of Northern Virginia. After several conferences, Longstreet's plan was adopted with one exception. Only two divisions of the First Corps would travel west. Pickett's division would remain with Lee.

Longstreet pressed for an early departure, but it was not until September 9 that the first train came to Orange Court, Virginia, to start south with its load of troops. By this time, Burnside had occupied Knoxville and closed the short interior lines of communication from Virginia to Tennessee. The longer and less favorable route via Wilmington and Augusta was the only way the Virginia troops could reach the vicinity of Chattanooga.

Lee and Longstreet completed their arrangements for transferring the corps. As Longstreet was mounting his horse to ride to the railroad station, Lee strolled out from his tent and said: "Now, General, you must beat those people out in the West." Withdrawing his foot from the stirrup and assuming a respectful position, Longstreet promised: "If I live, but I would not give a single man of my command for a fruitless victory." [1]

After brilliantly maneuvering the Union Army of the Cumberland from Nashville to Chatta-

nooga, between August 16 and September 9, without fighting a pitched battle, General William Rosecrans found himself being compared to Napoleon. Now, logic seemed to dictate that he pause at Chattanooga to rest his weary troops and wait for help from Burnside. The combined Union armies could confront Bragg with a vastly superior force.

On September 13, General Halleck in Washington wired Burnside at Knoxville: "It is important that all available forces at your command be pushed forward into East Tennessee; all your scattered forces should be concentrated there; move down your infantry as rapidly as

Lieutenant Colonel G. Moxley Sorrel, Longstreet's adjutant

possible towards Chattanooga to connect with Rosecrans." [2]

Burnside ordered the Ninth Corps to leave its Kentucky camps and join him in Knoxville as soon as possible. In Chattanooga, however, Rosecrans was not waiting for Burnside. Flushed with success and sensing a quick knockout of Bragg, Rosecrans was pressing southward in three distinct columns, his flanks more than forty miles apart. By September 13 his scouts reported a large Confederate concentration at La Fayette, Georgia. It was Bragg's army, not disorganized and in full flight, as Rosecrans thought, but fully intact and confidently awaiting reinforcements coming from three directions. [3]

Simon Buckner had moved south from Knoxville with his corps of 8,000 before Burnside's arrival and joined Bragg the day he evacuated Chattanooga. General Joe Johnston was sending 11,500 men from his Army of Mississippi. And from Virginia, Longstreet was en route to "beat those people in the West."

Longstreet's move to Georgia was the most outstanding logistical achievement of the Confederacy during the entire war. The railroad through Knoxville had been cut by Burnside, so a journey that should have taken five days required nine, because the First Corps was routed by way of Wilmington and Charlotte to Augusta and then by single track to Atlanta and Ringgold. Colonel Moxley Sorrel, Longstreet's adjutant, said that "Never before were so many troops moved over such worn-out railways. . . . Never before were such crazy cars—passenger, baggage, mail, coal, box, platform, all and every sort, wobbling on the jumping strap iron—used for hauling good soldiers. But we got there, nevertheless." [4]

Garbed in fresh butternut and gray summer uniforms generously donated by the Governor of North Carolina, the troops were full of confidence. They were veterans of the fighting at Manassas, Williamsburg, Fair Oaks, Malvern Hill, Second Manassas, Antietam, Fredericksburg, and Gettysburg. Even when forced to withdraw, as at Gettysburg, they had never considered themselves "beaten."

The First Corps, strengthened after the losses at Gettysburg, consisted of nine infantry brigades and six artillery batteries and represented the best striking power of Lee's army. Major Generals Lafayette McLaws and John B. Hood commanded the infantry divisions. The brigade commanders were men known throughout the world wherever war was discussed. Joseph Kershaw of South Carolina, William Wofford of Georgia, Benjamin Humphreys of Mississippi, Goode Bryan of Georgia, E. McIver Law of Alabama, Micah Jenkins of South Carolina, J. B. Robertson of Texas, George Anderson and Henry Benning of Georgia were famous heroes toasted in every Southern home. E. Porter Alexander, commander of the artillery, not only was

Major General Lafayette McLaws, division commander under Longstreet at Gettysburg, Chickamauga, and Knoxville

an excellent gunner but at the First Manassas had developed a system of telegraphy which helped turn the tide of battle.

Everywhere the troops stopped they were greeted with food and clothing, and "kisses and tokens of love and admiration for these war-worn heroes were ungrudgingly passed around."

The Federals sensed that something was occurring on Lee's Virginia front, because scouts reported unusual activity on the railroads. It finally dawned on Halleck where the troops were going, but by this time there was nothing he could do to help Rosecrans. The nearest Union troops were at Knoxville, and Burnside was moving in every direction out of Knoxville except down the road to Chattanooga. He was loath to abandon his recent conquests and was, perhaps, reveling in his role as savior of the loyal Unionists of East Tennessee.[5]

Early on the morning of September 19, Rosecrans' Army of the Cumberland and Bragg's Army of Tennessee faced each other some twelve miles south of Chattanooga, near Chickamauga Creek, just across the Georgia line. A major battle developed before either commander had prepared a plan. By nightfall little progress had been made by either side, although casualties were heavy. During the night, Longstreet arrived with five of his nine brigades from Virginia, and his corps was assigned to the Confederate right wing.

On the 20th, the battle resumed at daybreak, and neither side made progress; they were almost evenly matched. About eleven o'clock, Longstreet found a breach in the Federal lines and broke through to the rear of the demoralized Federal brigades. As Longstreet's men poured through the gap, sweeping forward like the flood of a mighty river, the entire Union line crumbled. General Gates P. Thruston, a Federal eyewitness, declared: "All became confusion. No order could be heard above the tempest of battle. With a wild yell the Confederates swept on. . . . They seemed everywhere victorious. Rosecrans was borne back in the retreat. Fugitives,

wounded, caissons, escort ambulances thronged the narrow pathways."[6]

Confederate General Bushrod Johnson, whose division had surged through the gap like a tidal wave, was overcome by the magnitude of the furious assault. "The scene now presented was unspeakably grand. The resolute and impetuous charge, the rush of our heavy columns sweeping out from the shadows of the gloom of the forest into the open fields flooded with sunlight, the glitter of arms, the onward dash of artillery and unmounted men, the retreat of the foe, the shout of hosts of our army, the dust, the smoke, the noise of firearms—of whistling balls and grapeshot and of bursting shell—made up a battle scene of unsurpassed grandeur."[7]

As Simon Buckner's Confederate division reached the Chattanooga road and saw General Leonidas Polk's men on the other side, a mighty roar swelled across the countryside. The whole Federal line was taken. "The Army of Tennessee knew how to enjoy its first great victory," said Longstreet. "The two lines, nearing as they advanced, joined their continuous shouts in increasing volume, not as the burstings from the cannon's mouth, but in a tremendous swell of heroic harmony that seemed almost to lift from their roots the great trees of the forest."[8]

Rosecrans' headquarters was overrun, and he fled to Chattanooga. About four o'clock in the afternoon, he rode to the door of the adjutant general's office in Chattanooga, faint and ill. John Fiske reported that "the officers who helped him into the house did not soon forget the terrible look of the brave man stunned by sudden calamity."[9] Only the isolated but stubborn resistance of the corps of George Thomas, a Virginian fighting for the North, prevented the complete destruction of the Federal army. Ever afterwards, Thomas was known as "the Rock of Chickamauga."

Charles A. Dana, Assistant Secretary of War, who was with Rosecrans on the 20th, said: "Bull Run had nothing more terrible than the rout and flight of these veteran soldiers."[10]

Brigadier General Micah Jenkins of South Carolina, who assumed command of Hood's Division, Longstreet's First Corps

Brigadier General E. McIver Law, who was prominent at Gettysburg and Campbell's Station

Brigadier General Joseph B. Kershaw, Confederate brigade commander from South Carolina

Longstreet, who had won the day for Bragg, saw that by a forward movement of the whole army Rosecrans' entire disordered force could be captured in twenty-four hours, leaving no obstacle between Chattanooga and the Ohio River but Burnside, who was still at Knoxville. He ordered the cavalry under General Joseph Wheeler to dash forward between Chattanooga and the fleeing Federals to cut them to pieces, but no sooner had Wheeler started on this movement than he was halted by an order from Bragg, who directed him to pick up arms and stragglers. Longstreet asked for permission to advance. He was refused.[11]

General Nathan Bedford Forrest, who had climbed a tree and was observing the disorganized masses swarming over the fields, though no one was in pursuit, shouted to an aide: "Tell General Bragg to advance the whole army; the enemy is ours." [12]

But the obstinate Confederate commander halted his army. He seemed to be the only man who did not know a great victory had been won. Stunned by his own staggering losses and fearful of "the darkness of the night and the density of the forest," Bragg ordered the army to bivouac on the "ground it had so gallantly won." [13]

Even the next day, Bragg did not pursue, but simply sent out detachments to the battle area

Brigadier General Goode Bryan of Georgia, brigade commander at Gettysburg and Knoxville

Brigadier General G. T. Anderson of Georgia, who served under General Longstreet in Pennsylvania and Tennessee

to gather up arms and captured banners, while others counted prisoners and sent them to the rear.

Rosecrans, now given time to regroup his forces, wired Burnside that "We have met with a severe disaster" and urged him to bring assistance from Knoxville.[14] From Washington, General Halleck sent fifteen telegrams to Burnside urging him to assist Rosecrans, all to no avail. At one juncture, Burnside wired back to Washington that he was moving to Jonesboro. "Damn Jonesboro!" shouted Abraham Lincoln, a man who rarely cursed. In anger, he dictated a reply to his stubborn general: "Yours of the 23rd is just received and it makes me doubt whether I am awake or dreaming. I have been struggling for ten days to get you to go to assist General Rosecrans in an extremity, and you have repeatedly declared you would do it, and yet you steadily move the contrary way."[15]

Down in Mississippi, General William T. Sherman analyzed the catastrophe that befell the Army of the Cumberland. "The whole country seemed paralyzed by this unhappy event; and the authorities in Washington were thoroughly stampeded. . . . Bragg had completely driven

Rosecrans' army into Chattanooga; the latter was in actual danger of starvation, and the railroad to his rear seemed inadequate to his supply. . . . The first intimation which I got of this disaster was on the 22nd of September, by an order from General Grant to dispatch one of my divisions immediately . . . to go towards Chattanooga."[16]

As a result of the Union disaster at Chickamauga, on October 18 General Grant was made commander of the newly formed Military Division of the Mississippi, to include the Departments and Armies of the Cumberland, the Tennessee, and the Ohio. George Thomas replaced Rosecrans in command of the Army of the Cumberland. General William T. Sherman replaced Grant in command of the Army of the Tennessee. Burnside retained command of the Army of the Ohio.

Grant at once began steps to rescue Thomas' troops trapped by Bragg in Chattanooga. Besides Sherman's army from Mississippi, two corps from General Meade in Virginia were ordered to join the relieving force, though they would journey 1,157 miles across Ohio, Indiana, and Tennessee before reaching Chattanooga.

Longstreet's corps detraining at Ringgold, Georgia, preparing to move to Chickamauga

Burnside was ordered to hold what he already occupied and to draw upon the friendly citizens of East Tennessee for food and fodder. He could expect no replacements of ammunition, animals, or medical supplies, as his long supply line through the Cumberland Mountains was incapable of supporting a large army.

Burnside did send some scouting patrols southward. When these were detected by the Confederates, General Forrest was ordered to prevent them from cooperating with the Union army bottled up in Chattanooga. Proceeding up the valley from Chattanooga toward Knoxville by way of Cleveland, Forrest arrived at Charleston on September 26 and saw Union troops just across the Hiwassee River at Calhoun. Included in Forrest's cavalry were former soldiers of General John Hunt Morgan, who was now confined in jail in Columbus, Ohio, and they were spoiling for a fight.

"Remember, boys, your commanding officer is now in a felon's cell," cried Forrest. "Let Morgan be your watchword and give the Yankees hell!" [17]

Under cover of an artillery barrage, Forrest led his men across the Hiwassee River and drove the Union detachment northward. At Philadelphia, his advance units swooped down on Union cavalry under Colonel Wolford, defeated them, and captured 500 prisoners, 7 pieces of artillery, 82 wagons, and 600 stand of arms.

While operating in the vicinity of Athens on September 30, Forrest received an order from General Bragg to turn over his entire cavalry to General Joe Wheeler.[18] Already disgruntled with the ineptness of Bragg, Forrest was now incensed by what he considered a personal affront, and he stormed back to Bragg's headquarters in a towering rage. He took no further action in the Chattanooga campaign and about a month later, at his own request, was transferred to operations in West Tennessee and Mississippi.

*Brigadier General Bushrod Johnson, Confederate hero
at Chickamauga and Knoxville*

NOTES

1. Longstreet, p. 427. See H. S. Fink, "The East Tennessee Campaign and the Battle of Knoxville in 1863," East Tennessee Historical Society's *Publications,* No. 29 (1957), p. 84.

2. Humes, p. 220. Halleck had told Sherman that Burnside was instructed to move down the Tennessee River and cooperate with Rosecrans, should the Knoxville vicinity be free of Confederate forces. The instructions were repeated fifteen times, but Burnside failed to carry out the orders. W. T. Sherman, *Memoirs of General William T. Sherman,* I, 354.

3. *Battles and Leaders,* III, 680-81.

4. G. Moxley Sorrel, *Recollections of a Confederate Staff Officer,* p. 189.

5. Horn, p. 256.

6. *Battles and Leaders,* III, 664.

7. General Thomas Jordan and J. P. Pryor, *The Campaigns of Lieut.-Gen. N. B. Forrest, and of Forrest's Cavalry* (New Orleans: 1868), p. 338.

8. LaBree, p. 202.

9. John Fiske, *The Mississippi Valley in the Civil War,* p. 277. Lincoln told his secretary that "Rosecrans seemed stunned like a duck hit on the head."

10. O. R., Ser. I, XXXI, Part I, 192. Dana was on a mission for General Halleck to report on Rosecrans' movements. Halleck had complained that Rosecrans sent messages to Washington only if favorable.

11. Horn, p. 266.

12. Pollard, *Southern History of the War,* III, 126.

13. LaBree, p. 203.

14. O. R., Ser. I, XXX, Part I, 142.

15. Roy Basler (ed.), *The Collected Works of Abraham Lincoln,* VI, 480-81. Lincoln had a change of heart, and though the message was written, he never ordered it sent to the sensitive Burnside.

16. Sherman, I, 346.

17. *Confederate Veteran,* XXXVI (October 1928), 374.

18. Forrest refused to serve under Wheeler. Although the two men were personal friends, Forrest blamed Wheeler for an unsuccessful assault on Fort Donelson.

To Separate the Quarreling Generals

GENERAL Bragg's faintheartedness converted the Confederate triumph at Chickamauga into the "fruitless victory" that Longstreet had dreaded, and the latter's strategic plan for crushing the Federal armies in the West bogged down. The Union army was now safe in Chattanooga, impregnable to direct assault, and awaiting reinforcements from Mississippi and Virginia. Braxton Bragg stationed his troops on Missionary Ridge overlooking Chattanooga with the intention of starving the Federals into surrendering before help arrived.

Generals Longstreet and Polk, alarmed at Bragg's inertia, met secretly and decided to beseech the authorities at Richmond to act. Longstreet wrote Secretary of War Seddon that "Our chief has done but one thing that he ought to have done since I joined his army—that was to order the attack upon the 20th. All other things that he has done he ought not to have done. I am convinced that nothing but the hand of God can save us or help us as long as we have our present commander." He suggested replacing Bragg with General Lee.[1]

On October 4, the majority of the superior officers drew up a document addressed to President Davis outlining their indignation at Bragg's conduct, expressing their fears for the future defensive attitude of the army, and recommending Bragg's removal from command. This "round robin" petition willingly signed by the senior officers could hardly be ignored by Davis, who immediately left Richmond for Tennessee.[2]

Arriving at Bragg's headquarters on October 9, the President found the Army of Tennessee in a mood for open revolt. Davis called the generals

to a meeting at Bragg's headquarters. With Bragg himself present, each general was required in turn to give his opinion of Bragg's ability to command the army. Longstreet was called upon first. The general who had served with Lee minced no words in declaring that, although Bragg's intentions were good, he was incompetent to command an army in battle. Generals Buckner, Hill, and Cheatham sustained Longstreet's opinions.[3]

The President listened carefully to the generals, but for some incredible reason chose to ignore their advice. Instead, he circulated a letter chiding the commanders for their lack of con-

Brigadier General Mahlon D. Manson, U. S. A., commanding the 23rd Corps in the East Tennessee campaign

fidence. He then allowed Bragg to dismiss all of his dissenting generals except Longstreet, who was considered "untouchable" because of the strong personal loyalty of the troops of the First Corps, his obvious ability, and the fact that he was Lee's man on loan to the Army of Tennessee. When Davis departed, the army was more divided than ever and still without a plan for the fall campaign.[4]

At Knoxville, General Burnside was pleased with the Union military reorganization after the Battle of Chickamauga, for he could now deal directly with General Grant, a soldier in the field, rather than with the Washington authorities. Burnside had not been as idle as the War Department had implied in their frantic telegrams urging him to push forward to unite with Rosecrans. He was in effect trapped in upper East Tennessee, as his supply route through the Cumberlands was inadequate, and General Wheeler had sent large cavalry units to the outskirts of Knoxville to prevent Burnside from moving south.

By September 30, the whole Ninth Corps arrived in Knoxville, numbering 6,000 men, and immediately joined the 23rd Corps in mopping up operations in the upper regions of East Tennessee. Here, for the first time in the war, the Irishmen of the 79th New York Highlanders Regiment gazed at women chewing tobacco, using snuff, and smoking pipes. The 79th pitched camp a quarter of a mile east of First Creek, then "went recruiting" between Knoxville and Loudon, quite certain that the loyal people would flock to their banners. As it happened, the natives wouldn't join the foreigners—as one said, "Yer gwine too fur from home for we'uns to jine yer regiment." Not a man enlisted.[5]

Rollin Byrd, of the 44th Ohio Volunteer Infantry, wrote home that

We will stay here all winter as we have had orders to fix our quarters as comfortable as possible. Most of the boys are cutting down trees and building log huts which will make very good quarters. We have a very nice camping ground. It is situated in a grove called Pine Grove, and it ex-

Brigadier General Orlando B. Wilcox, a division commander under Burnside, later commander of the Ninth Corps

tends along the side of the river bank so that we have plenty of water. Knoxville has been a gay little town one day, but it being in possession of the Rebs until here of late, there is little or no hurrying going on in it at all. Rebel deserters still continue to flock inside of our lines and according to their report they are about whipped.[6]

But not all the men were cutting down trees in Knoxville. Brigadier General Julius White of Illinois was dispatched with the Second Division of the 23rd Corps to Loudon. Major General Samuel Carter held Bulls Gap, which was then the most advanced position of the United States troops up the valley, and Colonel Milo Hascall was supporting him at Morristown. Most of the Ninth Corps was sent northward under General Robert B. Potter toward Blue Springs, near Greeneville.

On October 2, General Burnside reported to Grant that he had 9,300 infantry, 4,500 cavalry, and supporting artillery units from the 9th and 23rd Corps for the defense of Knoxville, along with 8,950 other troops scattered in upper East Tennessee.[7] By the middle of October, Burnside had secured most of northern East Tennessee, and the Ninth Corps returned to Knoxville. A Confederate force under General Samuel Jones moved down from Kingsport and defeated the Federal garrison at Rogersville. Then nothing but cavalry fighting and foraging occurred around Knoxville until November 17.

The Second Division of the Ninth Corps, which included the 21st Massachusetts, the 48th Pennsylvania, and the 2nd Maryland Infantry regiments, was marched to Loudon. There the 21st Massachusetts ran a captured ammunition train off the south end of the trestle burned by General Buckner during his retirement in August. It plunged full speed into the Tennessee River in a cloud of steam.[8] On October 21, under the threats of possible Confederate cavalry attack, the Second Division moved to the north side of the Tennessee River and began removal of the pontoon bridge.

The bridge was made of a row of floating sections placed side by side to span the river with a ramp across them. The Federals needed the bridge at Knoxville. They pulled the floating sections, or pontoons, from the river and dragged them one-half mile to the railroad. Each pontoon was so heavy it took twelve mules to haul it.

While the bridge was being removed, a squadron of Confederate cavalry appeared on the opposite bank of the river. Captain Orlando M. Poe, who was the Chief Engineer of the Army of the Ohio and detailed to the task of transferring the bridge, expected the Rebels to open fire immediately, thus making it impossible to salvage the valuable equipment. To his surprise, Poe saw the Rebel leader waving and beckoning. Not knowing what to expect, Poe jumped into a canoe and paddled alone across the river. He was amazed to find that the Confederate just wanted to have a friendly talk. Seizing upon his good fortune, Captain Poe chatted amicably, reciting as many good war stories as he could recall until his men had removed the entire bridge.[9]

The pontoon bridge was successfully moved to Knoxville, where it was laid across the Tennessee River just east of Gay Street, and on November 1, General William Sanders' cavalry crossed over it to protect the southern approaches to the city.

Brigadier General Milo S. Hascall, commander of the Third Division, 23rd Corps, at Morristown and Knoxville

Sanders had first appeared in Knoxville as a colonel, leading a raid against the Rebels on June 20. On October 18 he had been brevetted brigadier general, and he now commanded the First Division of the Cavalry Corps of the Army of the Ohio.[10]

All of the available cavalry forces—the Sixth Indiana, the Eighth Tennessee, and six loyal Kentucky units—were dispersed on the south side of the river from Knoxville with instructions to guard it down to its junction with the Little Tennessee River opposite Lenoir City.

While Burnside was making preparations to defend himself, the War Department was urging Grant to "do something for Burnside's relief," because President Lincoln was deeply concerned. At the moment, Grant was not in a position to render aid; he himself was trapped in Chattanooga, where he had arrived on October 23, and was awaiting the arrival of Sherman's army from Memphis. However, Grant believed that if he stalled long enough, his adversary, Braxton Bragg, would make a mistake that would change the whole picture. And on November 4, 1863, General Bragg, prodded by Jefferson Davis, made the mistake.

While the Federals were concentrating their forces—Sherman was joining Grant and Thomas in Chattanooga—Bragg suddenly decided to divide his. From Atlanta on October 29, President Davis had suggested to Bragg that he "might advantageously assign General Longstreet with his two divisions to the task of expelling Burnside" from Knoxville.[11] Davis hoped by this move to separate his two quarreling generals. Furthermore, if Longstreet could move with the swiftness and decisiveness of a Stonewall Jackson, defeat Burnside, and return to Chattanooga before the arrival of Sherman, then the move would be a stroke of genius. On the dark side, should the move against Knoxville fail, there could not be a worse mistake.

Longstreet first heard that he was to be sent against Knoxville through camp rumors. When finally called to Bragg's headquarters to receive his orders, he suggested that instead of dividing the army, they withdraw it to a strong position behind Chickamauga Creek. From there, a

The 79th New York Highlander fatigue uniform and kilts

Brigadier General Julius White of Illinois, commanding the First Division, 23rd Corps, at Loudon and Knoxville

The 79th New York Highlander Regiment in parade uniform. The 79th, part of the
Ninth Corps, garrisoned Fort Sanders, Knoxville. *From Harper's Weekly, 1861*

larger force than two divisions could be sent against Burnside. Bragg refused to discuss this plan and ordered Longstreet to proceed against Knoxville with Hood's and McLaws' divisions, Alexander's artillery, and the four brigades of General Joseph Wheeler's cavalry. These 17,000 men would be sent against Burnside's 23,000 in East Tennessee, of which 14,297 were stationed at Knoxville.

Longstreet, who was a master defensive tactician, realized immediately that his force was inadequate for the offensive task assigned. He asked Bragg for more troops, was promised that as soon as possible General Buckner's corps would be sent forward, and was informed that four brigades of cavalry, commanded by Brigadier General Robert Ransom, were moving south from Virginia and would meet him at Knoxville. Bragg offered his departing general no military maps, engineers, or quartermasters, but generously tendered the services of a prominent Knoxville civilian, William G. Swan, the Confederate congressman, who would act as a guide and counselor.[12]

NOTES

1. O. R., Ser. I, XXX, Part IV, 705.

2. O. R., Ser. I, XXX, Part II, 65-66.

3. Charles M. Blackford, *Letters From Lee's Army,* pp. 221-22.

4. H. S. Fink, "The East Tennessee Campaign and the Battle of Knoxville in 1863," East Tennessee Historical Society's *Publications,* No. 29 (1957), p. 84.

5. William Todd, *The Seventy-Ninth Highlanders, New York Volunteers,* p. 349.

6. "Sydney Baker Papers, 44th Ohio Volunteer Infantry," Ohio Historical Society, Columbus.

7. O. R., Ser. I, XXXI, Part I, 756.

8. Charles F. Walcott, *History of the Twenty-First Regiment, Massachusetts Volunteers,* p. 279.

9. As told by Poe in a newspaper interview, Knoxville, date deleted, Ducloux Scrapbook, p. 225.

10. O. R., Ser. I, XXXI, Part I, 687.

11. O. R., Ser. I, LII, Part II, 554. Davis left the decision to send Longstreet to Knoxville or to retain him at Chattanooga to the best judgment of Bragg.

12. O. R., Ser. I, XXXI, Part III, 634-35.

17

More Like Romance Than War

ON THE night of November 4, Colonel Porter Alexander withdrew his twenty-three guns from Lookout Mountain. He was followed by Major A. Leyden with his battalion of twelve guns and the 5,000 cavalrymen of General Joe Wheeler's four brigades.[1] The next morning they marched to Tyner's Station, where they joined Longstreet's two divisions of infantry. Brigadier General Micah Jenkins now commanded Hood's Division, for the gallant Texan had lost a leg at Chickamauga. Major General Lafayette McLaws commanded the other division. The total Confederate expeditionary force numbered about 17,000 men.[2]

General Longstreet wrote a hasty note to Simon Buckner, who was the last Confederate commander at Knoxville and who was now in Chattanooga with Bragg.

Wednesday Nov. 5, 1863

My Dear General:

I start today for Tyner's Station and expect to get transportation tomorrow for Sweetwater. The weather is so bad, and I find myself so occupied that I shall not be able to see you to say goodbye.

When I heard the report around camp that I was to go into East Tennessee, I set to work at once to try and plan the means for making the move with security and the hope of great results. As every other move had been proposed to the general and rejected or put off until time had made them inconvenient, I came to the conclusion, as soon as the report reached me, that it was to be the fate of our army to wait until all good opportunities had passed, and then in desperation, seize upon the least favorable movement. . . .

Have you any maps you can give or lend me? I shall need everything of the kind. Do you know any reliable people, living near and east of Knoxville, from whom I might get information of the condition, strength, etc., of the enemy? I have

written in such a hurry and confusion of packing and striking camp (in the rain and on the head of an empty flour barrel) that I doubt if I have made myself understood. I remain,

Sincerely, your friend
J. Longstreet
Lieutenant General [3]

Buckner sent only a sketchy map of the roads and streams between Knoxville and Loudon. Bragg furnished a topographical outline of the country between the Hiwassee and Tennessee rivers to the rear of the proposed field of operations. No quartermaster or engineering officer was detailed to the expedition.

General Bragg's quartermaster was ordered to have the trains ready to transport the troops upon their arrival at Tyner's Station with the infantry troops receiving priority. The infantrymen were to ride in boxcars and the artillerymen on open flatcars.

At the station McLaws' troops boarded their cars as scheduled, but when Jenkins' infantry and Leyden's batteries arrived, their cars were not there, so they began walking. It was not until November 10 that Alexander's guns and men were loaded, and the horses and wagons were ordered forward on a dirt road. Longstreet's blitzkrieg was losing its "blitz" before it really got started.

Colonel Alexander later recalled that "it was a cold and windy night, and we suffered a great deal on the open cars. There was a very insufficient water and wood supply on the road, and the troops had to bail water and chop up fence rails for the engine. The journey of only sixty miles occupied the whole afternoon and night." [4]

"It was easy enough to travel during the day by sitting on the sides of the flatcars," wrote McKenzie Evans, an artilleryman from Richmond, Virginia, "but at night we had to crawl between the wheels of the guns and caissons to keep from being shaken off the train." [5]

John Coxe, of the Second South Carolina Regiment, recalled the trip in later years:

On November 9, we marched a few miles out to the crossing of the Western and Atlantic and East Tennessee and Georgia Railroads. We were on the way to capture Knoxville. As we got to the crossing, a cold, drizzling rain set in. We had been told we would find trains standing there to take us up to Loudon, but there were no trains, and we stayed there all night in the cold rain. About 10 A.M. the next day several trains backed down and the 2nd Regiment boarded one of them. . . . I recall that its name was the "Allegheny." We waited a long time, then it was given out that our engineer was missing and couldn't be found. Probably he was a United States loyalist and had "skipped." Soon another man who had been an engineer on that road, but was then a preacher, was found nearby, and he agreed to run us up to Loudon. As he mounted the cab we were much amused by his rather grotesque appearance in his long frock coat and silk plug hat. But he was all right and got up to Sweetwater, a little below Loudon, by midnight. [6]

Joe Wheeler's four cavalry brigades, two under General William T. Martin and two under General Frank C. Armstrong, later of Forrest's command, reached Sweetwater on the night of November 11. The next day the last of the brigades arrived.

Longstreet's men, who had started from Chattanooga on short rations, found no replenishments at Sweetwater. General Carter L. Stevenson, commanding the garrison there, told Longstreet, who expected to find supplies of food and clothing at Sweetwater, that General Bragg had given direct orders that all supplies would be shipped to the main army at Chattanooga.

At this juncture Bragg, suddenly awakening to the danger of an attack on his front, hastily recalled Stevenson to Chattanooga. The first train which carried Longstreet's troops to Loudon returned with those of Stevenson.

In his memoirs, General Longstreet recorded:

We had recently come from Virginia during the heated season, where we had left most of our clothes and blankets and all of our wagon transportation. Thus we found ourselves in a strange country, not as much as a day's rations on hand, with hardly enough land transportation for ordinary camp usage, the enemy in front to be captured, and our friends in the rear putting in their paper bullets. This sounds more like romance than war. [7]

The "paper bullets" were messages from Bragg urging a vigorous and rapid movement by Longstreet. But no movement could be vigorous without sufficient food and transportation. Foraging parties scoured the countryside, but seed corn was often the only ration. Due to the scarcity of horses, oxen were used to haul the caissons. Horseshoes and horseshoe nails were stripped

Brigadier General Frank C. Armstrong, Confederate cavalry brigade commander under General Joseph Wheeler

from dead horses and saved. In the artillery, shoes were taken from the drivers and given to the cannoneers, who had to march.

Loudon, the next point along the Confederate line of advance, is northeast of Sweetwater, on the south bank of the Tennessee River. In this area, the Tennessee flows generally westward. Upstream a short distance to the east, Lenoir City sits on the north bank, opposite the mouth of the Little Tennessee, and further east is Knoxville, also on the north bank. Downstream to the west is Kingston.

Longstreet planned to cross the Little Tennessee River—at that time he thought it was the French Broad—and, after capturing Maryville, to seize the heights on the south bank of the Tennessee River across from Knoxville. From these heights, he hoped his artillery, firing point-blank, would be able to drive the Union forces out of Knoxville into open ground, where

Brigadier General George G. Dibrell, commander of a Confederate cavalry brigade in the Knoxville campaigns, serving under Wheeler

the superior Confederate cavalry forces could be used to advantage.

To cross the Little Tennessee with the main force would require a pontoon bridge, but when the bridge arrived, there was not a sufficient wagon train to haul it to the river, and Longstreet had to change his plans. The change that was adopted hinged on the fact that at Loudon the railroad ran close to a bend in the Tennessee River which was some distance from the Union position on the north bank.

On November 13, Longstreet ordered General Joe Wheeler to leave enough horsemen to patrol the Tennessee River from Loudon to Kingston and with the rest of his cavalry, which could ford the Little Tennessee without a pontoon bridge, to attempt the task formerly set for the main force: to seize the heights south of Knoxville. The same day, Longstreet advanced his other forces to Loudon, with the intention of crossing the Tennessee River and thrusting directly at Knoxville. With Wheeler controlling Knoxville from the southern heights and Longstreet approaching from the west, the Union forces at Loudon would be trapped, and those at Knoxville would be easy prey.

The night of the 13th, the Confederate soldiers pushed their pontoons on flatcars into the Loudon railroad yards, preventing any noise that might alert Yankee pickets just across the river. They unloaded the pontoons west of the depot and took them to Hough's (Huff's) Ferry, west of town. There, downstream from the enemy and out of sight around a big bend to the north, the Rebels, almost unopposed, laid their pontoon bridge, and by the next day, November 14, they were moving across in force.

When General Burnside first learned of the Confederate's advance, he was not certain that he could hold Knoxville against them. He overestimated his enemy, believing Longstreet opposed him with 23,000 men. In private conversations with Dr. Humes and other civilian leaders, he expressed the fear that he might not be able to continue protecting them.

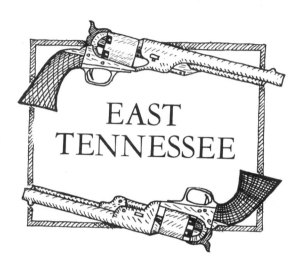

EAST
TENNESSEE

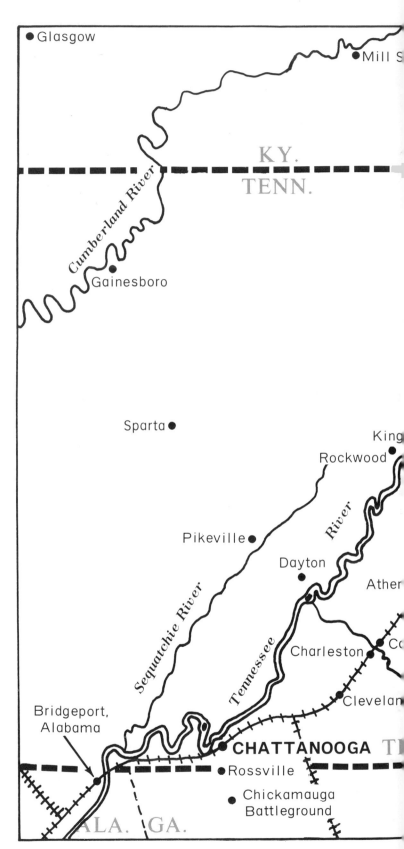

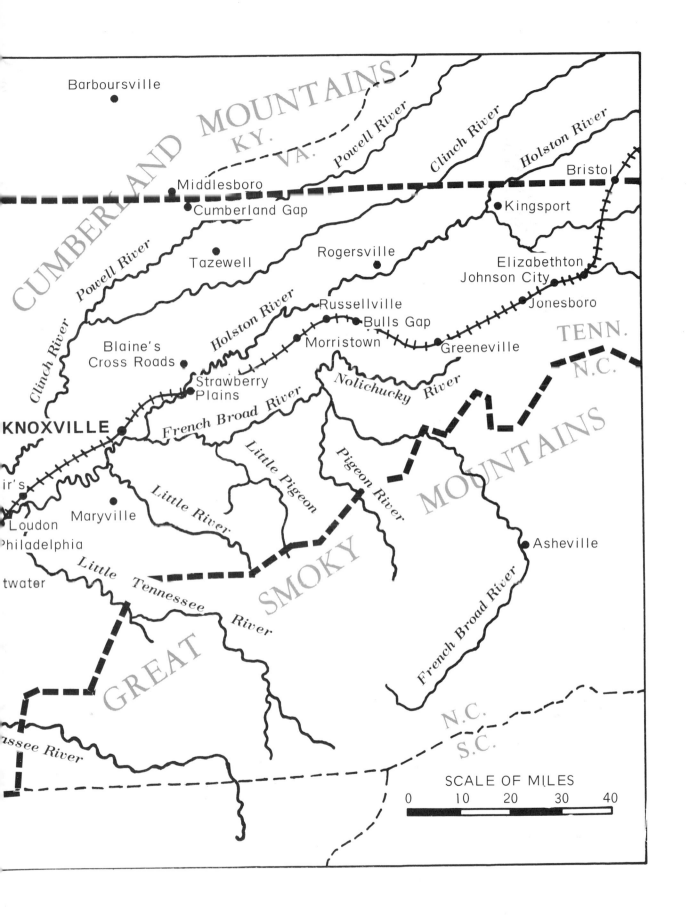

SCALE OF MILES

0   10   20   30   40

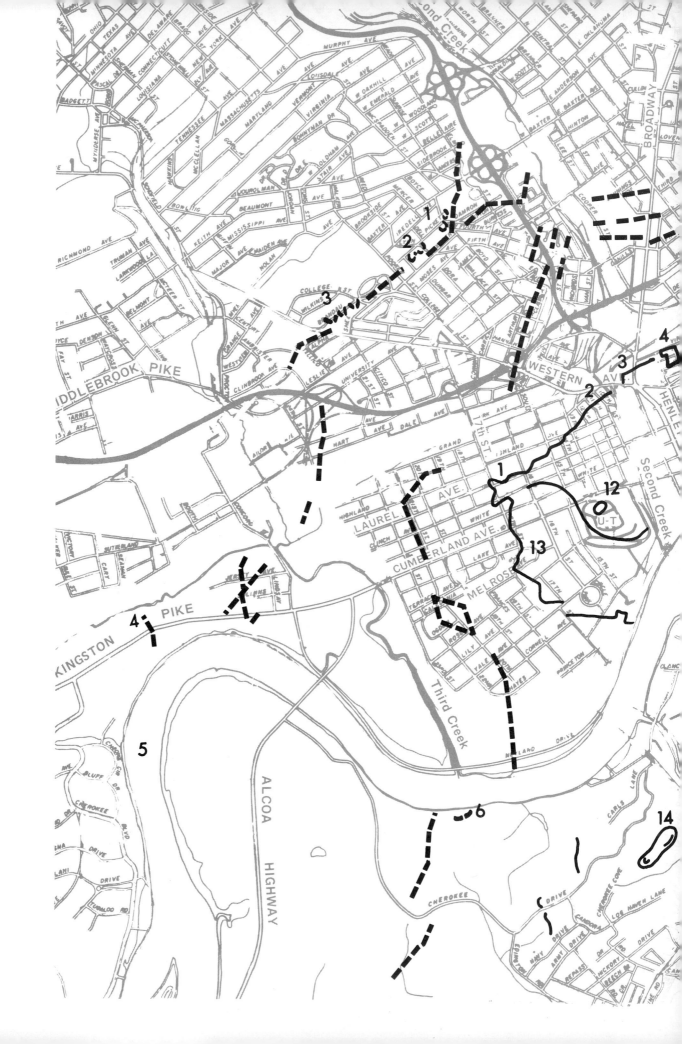

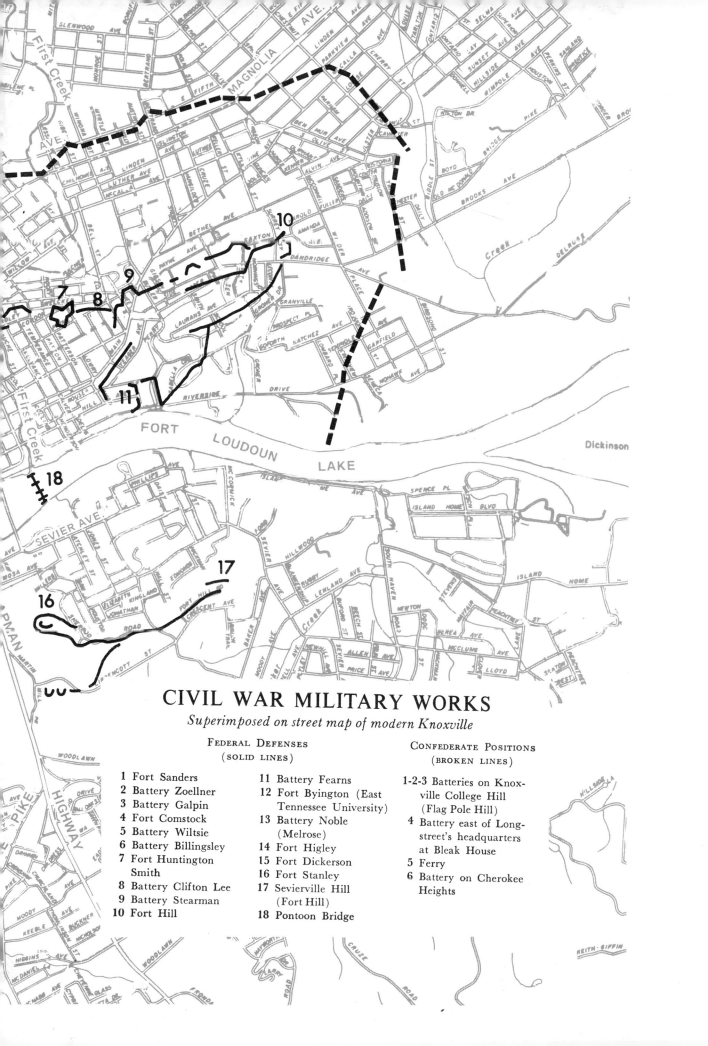

CIVIL WAR MILITARY WORKS
Superimposed on street map of modern Knoxville

FEDERAL DEFENSES
(SOLID LINES)

1 Fort Sanders
2 Battery Zoellner
3 Battery Galpin
4 Fort Comstock
5 Battery Wiltsie
6 Battery Billingsley
7 Fort Huntington Smith
8 Battery Clifton Lee
9 Battery Stearman
10 Fort Hill

11 Battery Fearns
12 Fort Byington (East Tennessee University)
13 Battery Noble (Melrose)
14 Fort Higley
15 Fort Dickerson
16 Fort Stanley
17 Sevierville Hill (Fort Hill)
18 Pontoon Bridge

CONFEDERATE POSITIONS
(BROKEN LINES)

1-2-3 Batteries on Knoxville College Hill (Flag Pole Hill)
4 Battery east of Longstreet's headquarters at Bleak House
5 Ferry
6 Battery on Cherokee Heights

Having been in East Tennessee now for ten weeks, Burnside had gained the unanimous respect of the Unionists, and even those hostile to his flag admired him for his fairness and good judgment. The General could not fully comprehend the bitterness and animosities which the war had produced among people who were former friends and neighbors in East Tennessee. He spoke of the deep division of the people with surprise and regret.

Although Burnside may have considered evacuating East Tennessee, President Lincoln and the War Department were strongly against abandoning the people or the railroad junction. In early November, daily telegrams were sent from Washington to Grant in Chattanooga, urging him to do something to relieve the army at Knoxville. Grant and Halleck corresponded with Burnside to determine the most important points to defend in East Tennessee. Colonel J. H. Wilson of Grant's staff and Charles A. Dana, Assistant Secretary of War, came to Knoxville from Chattanooga. They concurred with Burnside's conclusion that both Knoxville and Kingston should be held if possible, but certainly Knoxville.

As a result of the barrage of directives from his superiors, Grant on November 7 ordered General George Thomas, the "Rock of Chickamauga," to attack Bragg's right flank and perhaps panic Bragg into recalling Longstreet. Thomas replied that he could not execute the order because he had no horses or mules to move even one piece of artillery. Grant in turn notified Washington that he could do nothing until Sherman arrived and that Burnside would have to fend for himself.[8]

Grant believed that Bragg's position on Missionary Ridge was impregnable, and he had ordered Thomas to attack merely to placate the War Department. Burnside then wired Grant that he could hold Knoxville as long as his ammunition lasted and suggested that he would abandon all of the territory he held south and west of Knoxville, so as to draw Longstreet

farther away from his base and make it more difficult for Longstreet to get back to Chattanooga to help Bragg. Grant immediately saw the wisdom in Burnside's plan, and it was adopted.[9]

On November 14, Grant wired Burnside at Knoxville:

Sherman's advance has reached Bridgeport [Alabama]. His whole force will be ready to move from there by Tuesday at furthest. If you can hold Longstreet in check until he gets up, or, by skirmishing and falling back, can avoid serious loss to yourself, and gain time, I will be able to force the enemy back from here, and place a force between Longstreet and Bragg that must inevitably make

the former take to the mountain passes by every available road, to get to his supplies.[10]

On the same day as Grant's wire, Saturday, November 14, while Longstreet was crossing the Tennessee River just west of Loudon, General Burnside left Knoxville by train, accompanied by Mr. Dana of the War Department, Colonel Wilson of Grant's staff, and Congressman Horace Maynard. The train stopped at Lenoir City, but the General moved on to Loudon to assume personal command of the evacuation of his advance guard there.

As General Burnside made his presence known

Knoxville in April, 1864. This view looks directly north up Gay Street. At the far right is the military bridge erected by the U. S. Army Engineers. To the extreme left are the columns of the new jail. Just west of Gay Street, in the center background, is the dome of the courthouse. The Chisholm Tavern, now being restored, is the two-story white frame building on the river's edge to the right of Gay Street.

to the troops, when with his staff and battle flag he rode past, the cheers which rose from regiment after regiment testified to the confidence his men had in "Old Burnie." [11]

One soldier wrote home:

Notwithstanding the continued rain and the heavy roads, the presence of our commander produced a noticeable change in the spirit of the troops. An hour before, the men were deliberately covering themselves with mud, as if that were an appropriate mourning for their departed hopes, and their guns seemed naturally to seek a reverse position. But now they were all animation, and a slip here, and a fall there, was made the cause of laughing, notwithstanding the rain. I think the secret of it was that we reposed in our leader an almost perfect confidence resulting from long and tried association. Few corps commanders have ever won the affection of their men as Burnside did. [12]

Burnside made no serious attempt to hinder Longstreet's crossing of the Tennessee River.

"I shall withdraw my command to Knoxville," Burnside announced, after receiving a briefing from his staff. "Why so?" asked one of his aides. "You can easily beat the enemy as he is at present situated and drive him back across the river. If we start we are lost; he will bring his entire force against us and we shall be defeated and ruined."

Replied Burnside: "That may be true, but it will benefit Grant, if we can draw Longstreet away from his front, more than it will injure us. If General Grant can destroy Bragg, it is of no great consequence what becomes of ourselves. Order the troops to be ready to march in the morning." [13]

NOTES

1. O. R., Ser. I, XXXI, Part III, 631.
2. O. R., Ser. I, XXXI, Part I, 474.
3. Humes, pp. 380-81.
4. *Battles and Leaders,* III, 746.
5. *Confederate Veteran,* XXXI (November 1923), 424.
6. *Ibid.,* XXXII (September 1924), 340.
7. Longstreet, p. 486.
8. *Battles and Leaders,* III, 693.
9. *Ibid.,* p. 695.
10. *Ibid.*
11. Henry S. Burrage, *History of the Thirty-Sixth Regiment, Massachusetts Volunteers,* pp. 91-92.
12. Humes, p. 239.
13. Poore, p. 218.

Fighting Joe Wheeler — No Ordinary Man

GENERAL Longstreet had given diminutive "Fighting Joe" Wheeler very fluid orders at Sweetwater on November 13. Wheeler's cavalry was to capture the Federal cavalry outpost at Maryville, then move up to the south side of the Tennessee River at Knoxville and seize the heights dominating the city; if this were not possible, he was to harass and hold the Union troops in their forts while Longstreet moved against the Federal forces north of the river. If the objectives were not obtained, Wheeler was to withdraw and rejoin the main column.[1]

This was a rather monumental order to be given a man only twenty-seven years old, but Joe Wheeler was no ordinary man. Only five feet, five inches tall and weighing 120 pounds, he was filled with restless energy, was agile as a cat, and had a photographic memory. He was described by a friend as "the gamest little banty I ever seen."[2] Born in Augusta, Georgia, in 1836, he had been educated in Connecticut and appointed to West Point from New York, graduating in 1859. Joining the Confederate mounted infantry in 1861, he had quickly risen in rank, and by October, 1862, Braxton Bragg had appointed him a brigadier general and chief of cavalry over John Hunt Morgan and Nathan Bedford Forrest.

Following the Battle of Chickamauga, just before starting toward Knoxville with Longstreet, Wheeler and his men had made a smashing raid on Rosecrans' communications.[3]

On the dark night of November 13, he left five of his Georgia regiments with Longstreet at Sweetwater and struck out for Maryville with Colonel Dibrell's Tennesseans and General John T. Morgan's troops from Texas and Arkansas.

On finding that Maryville was held by only one regiment, the 11th Kentucky, Wheeler attacked quickly and dispersed the enemy into small parties which, however, escaped except for 150 men taken by Dibrell.

On the dawn of the 14th, Wheeler moved from Maryville toward Stock Creek, where Colonel Frank Wolford had brought up the balance of his Kentucky forces in opposition. The Federals fell back behind Stock Creek, destroyed the bridge, entrenched themselves behind a hill, and called for reinforcements from Fort Dickerson.[4]

Fort Dickerson, named for Captain Jonathan C. Dickerson of the 112th Illinois Mounted Infantry who was killed in a skirmish near Cleveland, was the first and strongest of the four earthwork forts which the Federal engineers were ultimately to construct on the heights south of the Tennessee River across from Knoxville. It was nearly opposite the mouth of Second Creek, just west of the present Chapman Highway.

The red clay heights, or knobs, on which the forts were built form a range whose crest runs parallel to the river at an average distance from it of about half a mile, with a wide valley beyond which sweeps to the Appalachian Mountains.

Fort Stanley, named for Captain C. E. Stanley of the 45th Ohio, who fell in battle at Philadelphia, Tennessee, was built on the highest hill, several weeks after Dickerson was constructed. This hill, just east of Dickerson, rises steeply 360 feet above the river directly opposite the south end of Gay Street and has been known for generations as "Gobbler's Knob."

A small fortification, unofficially known as

Fort Hill, was eastward from Fort Stanley across the Sevierville (Davenport) Road, on the adjacent height known as Sevierville Hill.

The western anchor of the chain of forts was Fort Higley, to the west of Fort Dickerson and the present railroad bridge. Fort Higley was lightly manned, and west of it a line of pickets extended farther downstream toward Cherokee Heights.

There were some entrenchments between the forts, but the defense line was not continuous except between Fort Stanley and Fort Hill. Communications were maintained with the city by means of the pontoon bridge set down near the mouth of First Creek.[5]

Forts Dickerson and Stanley were practically invulnerable to direct assault. On two sides, the contour of the land sheered from the military crest and dropped 200 feet straight down. The river prevented encirclement from the north. Any attack must be made from the south, from the open ground in the valley below.

The strategy of Grant and Burnside—to bring the Union forces from Loudon back inside the fortifications of Knoxville and hold out until

General James Shackelford of Kentucky, commander of the 23rd Corps cavalry opposing Wheeler at Knoxville

the arrival of reinforcements—depended upon the ability of the Federal soldiers to hold Forts Dickerson and Stanley and the pontoon bridge.

The pontoon bridge served to maintain communications with the fanatically loyal Unionists of the French Broad country, who could furnish food to the Knoxville garrison. The Federal army could not survive on the meager supplies that trickled down from Cumberland Gap.

If Forts Dickerson and Stanley, dominating the southern skyline of Knoxville, were to fall into Confederate hands, it would be disastrous for the Federal army occupying the city. Assuming Joe Wheeler could seize these heights, his siege guns could destroy the entire Union defense line, smash the city, and force Burnside's army into the open country to the northeast. There the Union army would be caught between Longstreet in the west and other Confederate forces approaching from Virginia.

The job of holding the southern heights was given to a handful of inexperienced Union cavalrymen of the recently organized 23rd Corps. Dismounted cavalrymen—1,700 men of the 25th Michigan, 118th Ohio, 16th Indiana, and 16th Kentucky—manned the supporting entrenchments. George Renwick's Elgin (Illinois) Battery had six three-inch rifled fieldpieces pointed to the steep southern ascent which Wheeler would be forced to assault if he hoped to take the heights. On these men depended the fates of the Army of the Ohio near Knoxville and the Army of the Cumberland entrapped in Chattanooga, the latter army still fearful of Longstreet's sudden return.[6]

Ironically, the commanders of the opposing cavalry forces, Confederate Wheeler and Union Sanders, were both Southerners.

When Wolford retreated toward Fort Dickerson, Wheeler, who had dismounted half of his command, crossed Stock Creek under cover of his artillery fire and sent the 8th and 11th Texas and 3rd Arkansas regiments after the fleeing Federals. A detail of men then spent the day repairing the bridge over Stock Creek which the

General Joseph Wheeler, Confederate cavalry chieftain who captured Maryville and attacked Fort Dickerson

Fort Stanley. See the map on pages 108-109 for the location of this and other fortifications in Knoxville.

Federals had destroyed, so that General Frank Armstrong and the remaining troops and the artillery could cross for the attack.[7]

The news of the Confederate cavalry advance toward Knoxville from the south side of the river burst upon the city in the form of fearful speculation. Rumors spread that Colonel Frank Wolford and an entire Federal regiment had been captured and that Knoxville was about to fall into Rebel hands once more. There were varied reactions in this town, deeply embittered, divided in sentiment, with more hatred between civilian factions than between the opposing armies.

Kentucky-born Federal Brigadier General James M. Shackelford and his staff rode down Gay Street across the pontoon bridge toward the threatened sector. To one Knoxville observer, Shackelford, astride his gentle, well-conditioned pacer and smoking the short-stemmed pipe of the common soldier, seemed "cool and calm to the point of indifference."[8] With Shackelford was his most aggressive subordinate, Brevet Brigadier General William Sanders, commander

Fort Dickerson. In this wartime photograph the entrenchments of Fort Stanley are seen in the foreground, the Tennessee River in the distance. Present-day Chapman Highway runs between the two forts. Fort Dickerson is in a remarkable state of preservation today.

of the First Cavalry Division of the Army of the Ohio, the leader of the brief Federal raid on Knoxville the previous June 20. Both Shackelford and Sanders were wise to the guerrilla tactics of Rebel raiders and were not going to take any chances on being caught unprepared.

General Samuel P. Carter, the Provost Marshal of Knoxville, expecting a combined Rebel assault from the south and west, did not believe the Union forces could hold the town and advised the most prominent Union citizens to escape with an escort he would provide. Several citizens, including Parson Brownlow, Samuel Rodgers, Thomas A. R. Nelson, O. P. Temple, John Fleming, M. M. Miller, and John Baxter, accepted General Carter's advice and fled.[9]

Many of the refugees, like Parson Brownlow, had only recently returned to Knoxville from exile in the North. Baxter, who had acted courageously in the courtroom defense of both the bridge burners and the locomotive stealers, could not trust his luck with the Confederate authorities many more times.

Quickly leaving their homes and families, the

East Tennessee University as seen from Fort Dickerson.
During the siege of Knoxville, College Hill was the site
of Fort Byington. Fort Sanders is behind and to the left
of the University. The small white house on the river
side of the University was the home of its president.
The stone piers in the river, right center, were built for
the Knoxville and Charleston Railroad. In the foreground are tents of Fort Dickerson's Union troops.

The University and terrain west of Knoxville. In this wartime view from Fort Dickerson, the square of tents enclosing the small evergreen trees indicates the approximate present location of Circle Park. The white house barely visible, top center of picture, is Thomas Powell's home, Melrose, location of Battery Noble; the mouth of Second Creek is in mid-foreground; and the University is at far right.

Unionists went with their military escort, led by Captain A. J. Ricks, to the picket lines eight miles northeast of town. From there the fleeing party departed after dark in a heavy downpour of rain along a road recently turned into a mire by the passage of 6,000 hogs brought in to supply the army. As the group reached Anderson County, they were met by an old woman coming out of her house with a torch in her hand.

"What in the name of goodness does all this mean, and where are you men going?" she asked. "Is Burnside retreating? Or who are you anyway?"

Someone in the crowd answered that Burnside was not able to retreat and that, further-

more, he and his whole army had probably been made captive.

"And you are running without firing a gun?" she cried. "I expect the next thing I'll hear will be that old Bill Brownlow is running, too!"

At this point, the Parson, unrecognizable in the darkness, spoke in a subdued voice unsuited to his fiery temperament. "Gentlemen, this is no place to make a stand. I think I'd rather encounter Longstreet's army or Vaughn's cavalry than that woman." [10]

At daybreak on November 15, General Sanders' entire First Division and an artillery battery moved out of the safety of their entrenchments at Fort Dickerson and made their way southward

The University and west Knoxville from the slopes of Fort Dickerson.
The University is at far left on the horizon. Beyond the University, to
the immediate right, the works of Fort Sanders can be seen on the
horizon. The home of James Cowan, which was General Kirby Smith's
headquarters during his command in Knoxville, is surrounded by trees,
below and slightly to the right of the Fort. The Knoxville Gas Works
is on the riverbank to the right of center. The prominent house on the
horizon, to the right of the Gas Works, was the home of Judge Mc-
Kinney, and the next house to the right was the home of Perez Dickinson. The Knoxville jail is at far right.

*Earthworks of Fort Dickerson, preserved by the city of
Knoxville, as they appear today*

down the slippery hillside to the valley below. In
the dark, foggy haze of this cold November
morning, Sanders was conspicuous on his snow-
white horse as the blue-clad Midwestern cavalrymen rode past. Accustomed to no more
excitement than chasing small parties of raiding
guerrillas or smashing behind enemy lines at
lightly held depots, the Union troops braced
themselves for their first real taste of warfare.

A fully loaded Union cavalry horse normally
carried 270 pounds of man and equipment, but
today the saddlebags and pommel bags were
left behind. Each horse was burdened with only
a trooper, his saber, revolver, single-loading carbine, cartridge box, forty rounds of carbine ammunition, and twenty rounds of pistol
ammunition.[11]

From his vantage point on the heights, General Sanders had spotted the long gray column
winding up the valley from Maryville. Their

gray pennants rippling defiantly in the breeze,
Joe Wheeler's ragged horsemen rode forward
to the attack. Although the Federals had better
weapons and uniforms, the Confederates had
superior numbers and experience. But numbers
could be effective only if the forces could be concentrated, and the rolling hills gave distinct advantage to a defending force.

Suddenly the advance troops of the two
columns ran head-on into each other some five
miles south of Knoxville. The alarm was
sounded and shots rang out. The buglers sounded
the call for attack, and the cry rang out: "Form
fours! Draw sabers! Charge!"

The Confederate force pushed its horses forward at a gallop and dispersed the Federal
advance guard. The Union cavalrymen disappeared behind the crest of a small hill, dismounted, and began firing as infantrymen.
Avoiding a direct assault on the blue line,

Inside Fort Dickerson today. The central magazine is enclosed by the mounds and small trees in the middle background. Contrast the present growth of trees with the appearance of the fort in the photograph on page 117.

Close-up of ammunition center. The author's children stand in the depression in the center of Fort Dickerson believed to have been the fort's central magazine.

With Terry's Texas Rangers. Private Achille Ferris, Company H, Eighth Texas Cavalry, C.S.A., helped drive the Federals back into Fort Dickerson.

Wheeler sent his men on one flanking maneuver after another trying to breach the Federal position. As each Union line was outflanked, their bugler sounded "Boots and Saddles," the order "to horse, to horse" was given, and the men beat a hasty retreat to a new position behind another hill.

The opposing masses of horsemen appeared to undulate over the rolling hills as they wheeled and turned, each seeking weaknesses in the other's lines. For seven hours the Confederates, always the aggressors, tried in vain to work behind Sanders' mobile forces.

Finally, Terry's Texas Rangers, supported by the 3rd and 11th Arkansas brigades, broke the center of Union resistance. Wheeler said the "entire mass of the enemy swept on toward Knoxville in the wildest confusion. The charge was continued successfully for three miles to within less than half a mile of the river opposite the city. The bulk of the enemy dashed over their pontoon in their flight into the city, creating the greatest consternation. Great numbers scattered over the country and many plunged into the river, some of whom were drowned." The Confederates took 140 prisoners, and the dead and wounded of both commands were strewn out over the countryside.[12]

The Federals who had not galloped across the river or hidden in the hills scrambled and clawed their way back up the steep trail, breathing sighs of relief as Renwick's rifled guns in Fort Dickerson came into the fray, stopping the pursuing Confederates.

The Texans had outrun their main force, which was still some four miles to the rear. The Confederates exchanged a few rifle shots with the entrenched soldiers, but it was obvious to Wheeler that a direct assault on Fort Dickerson at that time would be suicide. The Rebel cavalrymen then reconnoitered all the fortifications on the south bank and found them too formidable for direct assault. As darkness was approaching he led his command back to Stock Creek, the only area suitable for foraging.[13]

Wheeler returned with his full command the next morning, but he found the Federals had reinforced the garrison at Fort Dickerson during the night. He withdrew his men from effective cannon range to plot his next move. After he had retired from any further attack upon Fort Dickerson, General Wheeler received a message from Longstreet: "Unless you are doing better service by moving along the enemy's flank than you could do here, I would rather you should join us and cooperate. I presume that you could unite with us by crossing the Holston [Tennessee]."[14]

Wheeler moved west fifteen miles down the river to Louisville, Tennessee, before he could find a ford to cross and did not rejoin Longstreet until November 17. Meanwhile, through no fault of his own, he had been at the wrong place at the wrong time.

NOTES

1. O. R., Ser. I, XXXI, Part I, 456.
2. H. D. Milhollen, J. R. Johnson, A. H. Bill, *Horsemen Blue and Gray*, p. 39.
3. Horn, p. 282.
4. O. R., Ser. I, XXXI, Part I, 540-44.
5. *Ibid.*, p. 312.
6. *Battles and Leaders*, III, 751-52.
7. O. R., Ser. I, XXXI, Part I, 540-44.
8. Humes, p. 244.
9. *Ibid.*, pp. 245-46.
10. *Ibid.*, pp. 381-82. Of course, it was not Vaughn's cavalry but Wheeler's that Brownlow was eluding.
11. Francis A. Lord, *They Fought For the Union*, p. 75.
12. O. R., Ser. I, XXXI, Part I, 540-44.
13. *Ibid.*
14. *Ibid.*, p. 544.

19

Like Moves Upon a Chessboard

AT FOUR o'clock in the morning, November 15, Burnside began evacuating his men from their position east of the Tennessee River, across from Loudon. On the same morning, one mile to the west of Loudon, but five miles downstream via the northward loop of the river, the last of the main body of Longstreet's troops crossed to the north side of the Tennessee over the pontoon bridge laid down at Hough's Ferry. Burnside's troops, the Ninth Corps and the Second Division of the 23rd Corps, numbered about 5,000. Against these, Longstreet had about 12,000 infantry and artillery immediately at hand, besides Wheeler's 5,000 cavalry south of Knoxville.

While Burnside retreated eastward toward Lenoir City, Longstreet advanced along a parallel route just to the north, the Hotchkiss Valley Road. Burnside's forces spent the night of November 15 at Lenoir City. The air was bitterly cold, but only one fire was allowed to each company to avoid observation by the enemy.[1] Longstreet's men bivouacked two miles to the north, at the east end of the Hotchkiss Valley Road, a mile and a half south of a place called Eaton Crossroad. Eaton Crossroad was on the old Kingston Road, which is parallel to and a little south of the modern Kingston Pike. The old Kingston Road ran eastward from Eaton Crossroad to Campbell's Station (one-half mile west of modern Farragut) and on to Knoxville.

The East Tennessee and Georgia Railroad ran from Lenoir City through Concord to Knoxville, but Burnside dared not try to follow this route all the way. To his right was the Tennessee River, to his left the old Kingston Road. These converged with the railroad just west of Knoxville. If Burnside tried to follow the railroad all the way to Knoxville while Longstreet rushed along the old Kingston Road, he might be gradually squeezed into a trap between Longstreet and the river. Burnside's only salvation was somehow to get on the old Kingston Road ahead of Longstreet. The key to the problem was Campbell's Station on the old Kingston Road, in the line of march of both armies.

From Longstreet's position two miles north of Lenoir City, Campbell's Station via Eaton Crossroad was nine and three-fourths miles east, and from Campbell's Station to Knoxville it was fifteen miles further. From Lenoir City, Burnside had to go about eleven miles to Campbell's Station via Concord and Turkey Creek Gap. The possession of Campbell's Station was therefore of great moment to Burnside; should the Rebels get there before him his retreat would surely be cut off. This is exactly what Longstreet intended.

About 2:00 A.M. on November 16, Burnside ordered the Ninth Corps, commanded by General Robert B. Potter, to break camp at Lenoir City and withdraw to Knoxville.[2] On the same morning Longstreet advanced in two columns. On the left, along the old Kingston Road, marched the forces of Major General Lafayette McLaws, Longstreet's forty-two-year-old division commander, a West Point graduate from Augusta, Georgia. On the right, Longstreet himself accompanied Hood's Division, commanded by General Micah Jenkins, as it followed Burnside eastward from Lenoir City. If all went well for the Confederates, Jenkins would drive Burnside's

At Campbell's Station and Knoxville. Brigadier General Robert B. Potter of New York commanded the Ninth Corps, Army of the Ohio.

Colonel John F. Hartranft of Pennsylvania, who commanded the Second Division, Ninth Corps

army into McLaws' guns at Campbell's Station.

Both armies, Federal and Confederate, sent advance parties to try to hold Campbell's Station. Just before daylight, Colonel John F. Hartranft of Pennsylvania, commanding the Second Division of Burnside's Ninth Corps, and Colonel James Biddle, leading the Sixth Indiana Cavalry, were ordered to push ahead as rapidly as possible along the Concord Road. Longstreet detached Hampton's Legion and Captain William Parker's Artillery Battery to rush forward ahead of the main column on the old Kingston Road. With each side aware of the importance of seizing the junction of these two roads, the race for Campbell's Station was on.[3]

Meanwhile, the progress of the main columns —Union retreat and Confederate advance—was made extremely difficult by a heavy rain, which

fell for several hours and was followed by a cold north wind. The condition of the roads for the movement of wagons and artillery was almost impossible. Where the wheels did not sink in the mud they were blocked by rough rocks. The horses had been overworked for the past twenty-four hours and were by now so balky as to be almost useless for hauling.[4]

The Federal column moved along out of Lenoir City at a snail's pace. The first three miles took eight hours. At last, their patience exhausted, the men broke ranks and caught hold of the muddy rims of wheels or parts of gun carriages, wherever a hand could seize them, and pushed and shoved to assist the poor animals. Fences along the road were burned to light the way.

The 79th New York Highlanders were detailed to escort the wagons. Although they had to leave many wagons intact, some one hundred wagons, whose mules were needed to draw the artillery, were destroyed, along with bacon, coffee, sugar, and other supplies the soldiers could not carry but did not wish to fall into

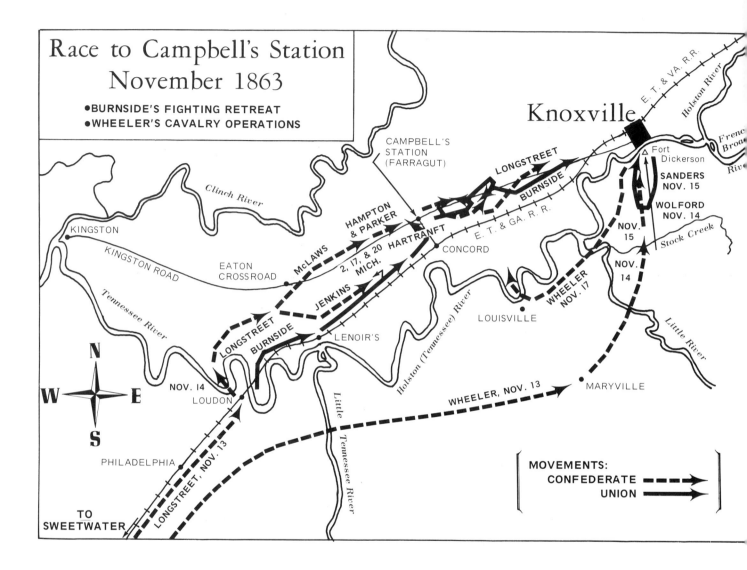

Race to Campbell's Station November 1863

- BURNSIDE'S FIGHTING RETREAT
- WHEELER'S CAVALRY OPERATIONS

Rebel hands. Officers' baggage, books, and some ammunition were burned.

The pursuing Confederates, feeling their way through the weird gray of the morning, came upon a long line of what appeared to be sharpshooters, but were instead merely stumps in the road. They pushed on and in a moment came upon a sight heaven-sent to the Confederate soldier: before them was a scene of an encampment deserted in ignominious haste. They found eighty well-stocked wagons containing food,

camp equipment, spades, picks, axes, and ammunition. The wagons had apparently been left behind so that their horses could be used by the artillery, because it sometimes took sixteen to twenty of the beasts to pull one Federal gun through the mud.[5]

In the Union retreat, the 35th Massachusetts Regiment was detailed to help in the withdrawal of Lieutenant Samuel Benjamin's battery. Toward daylight, Lieutenant Benjamin, discerning that unless the command made greater speed his

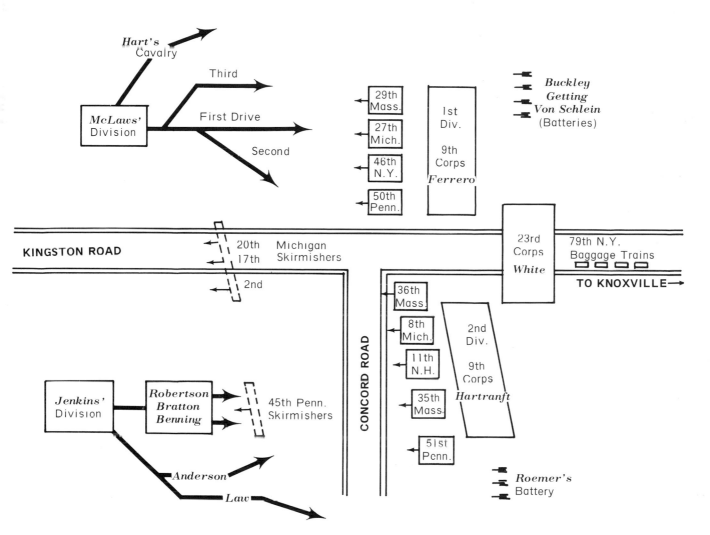

The Battle of Campbell's Station. On November 16, 1863, at present-day Farragut Community, Burnside's troops held off Longstreet while Union forces retreated into Knoxville. The delaying action allowed Federal forces extra time to strengthen the city's defenses.

guns would fall into Rebel hands, ordered a part
of the ammunition and the lagging rear caisson
destroyed, but found that he did not even have
an axe.[6] Benjamin, a cool veteran of many a
hard fight in Virginia and a man who had
learned the art of patience in the protracted
siege at Vicksburg, talked calmly to his men as
if all were progressing favorably. Ropes with
hooks and toggles were brought out and attached, and the guns were slowly dragged
through the mire by hand.

In the confusion of the retreat, Company B
of the 111th Ohio Infantry, which was on picket
duty, was overlooked in the orders issued by a
staff officer and was captured by the advancing
Confederates.[7]

General Jenkins' Confederates, ordered to advance at double time, moved along quite well,
but were constantly hampered by the rear guard
action of the 2nd, 17th, and 20th Michigan
troops of Colonel William Humphrey. Meanwhile, McLaws' men trudged along the old
Kingston Road in normal cadence. Disturbed by
the slow pace of his infantry and artillery, Longstreet sent orders for Colonel John R. Hart's
cavalry brigade to come up and try to get to
Campbell's Station ahead of the Federals.[8] Hart
was on patrol between Loudon and Kingston, a
few miles to the rear of the advance, where he
had been left by Wheeler when the latter departed to attack Maryville. Longstreet, traveling
with Jenkins, apparently forgot that he had a
large force of cavalry jogging along the old
Kingston Road with McLaws' infantry.

J. W. Minnich of Morgan City, Louisiana,
a cavalryman of the Sixth Georgia, wrote
years after the war that he was riding with
Colonel C. C. Crews and five regiments of
Georgia cavalry when they passed right by about
8,000 Union troops off to the right. (The enemy
always looms larger than life—Burnside had only
5,000.) "We were some 200 yards northeast on
the Kingston-Knoxville road," he remembered,
"and though that mass of infantry passed within
easy range we did not molest them nor did they

Drawing artillery through the mountains of East Tennessee. This drawing from *Harper's Weekly*, November 21, 1863, graphically illustrates the difficulties of Burnside's retreat into Knoxville, as well as his advance the previous August 16 (see page 83).

molest us. . . . Our policy was to let them go by quietly since they appeared to be decent." [9]

Much to Longstreet's disgust, Hartranft's mounted troops reached Campbell's Station ahead of any Confederates, and the main body of Burnside's command arrived around noon of November 16, a good fifteen minutes before McLaws' Confederate men.[10] If "Fighting Joe" Wheeler's cavalry had been riding with Longstreet's columns on this day, they might easily have beaten the Federals to Campbell's Station.

When McLaws' men reached the west side of Campbell's Station, they found their way to the junction with the Concord Road blocked by a battle line of Federal troops deployed across the Kingston Road. Behind this battle line, approaching on Concord Road from the right, other Federal troops, wagons, and artillery were streaming through the junction, turning onto the Kingston Road ahead of McLaws, and moving on toward Knoxville.

The head of the advancing gray column quickly engaged the blue battle line in an effort to force its way through and prevent the passage of the Union wagon trains; but the Rebels were still strung out and therefore could not yet attack in force, and the blue line held. Soon Burnside had his forces through the junction and deployed for a holding action during his retreat to Knoxville. He intended to hold off Longstreet as long as possible to gain time while Captain Orlando Poe, of the Corps of Engineers, strengthened the defenses within the city.

Burnside ordered General Potter to direct the movements of the 5,000 Union troops and six guns which opposed the 12,000 attacking Confederates. Potter placed the Second Division of General Julius White's 23rd Corps directly across Kingston Road to the rear of the junction with Concord Road. Facing west, the left of the line on the bordering hill was anchored by the 51st Pennsylvania. The 35th Massachusetts, the 11th New Hampshire, the 8th Michigan, and the 36th Massachusetts were deployed in a north-south line, the north end of the 36th's line just reaching the south side of the old Kingston Road. The 45th Pennsylvania was placed further forward as skirmishers. Captain Jacob Roemer's 34th New York Artillery Battery was placed to the rear in support.[11]

To the right of Kingston Road, Potter deployed the First Division of General Edward Ferrero of the Ninth Corps. From the north side of the road, the 50th Pennsylvania, the 46th New York, the 27th Michigan, and the 29th Massachusetts stretched across an open field to the wooded hills on the right. The Second Artillery Battery of Lieutenant Samuel Benjamin, Captain William Buckley's First Rhode Island, and the batteries of Lieutenants Getting and Von Schlein were placed on these hills for support.[12]

The battle was not going as Longstreet had planned, but it was still possible for him to win by outflanking the Union position. The Federal forces were stretched across a valley between two ranges of low, heavily wooded hills about a mile apart. Longstreet rode forward, examined the enemy's deployment, and ordered McLaws to send Colonel Hart's cavalry on a wide swing to his left beyond the hills, a move intended as a diversion to the Union right wing. McLaws' main force would push forward along the old Kingston Road. Jenkins was ordered to have General E. McIver Law take his own brigade and that of General G. T. Anderson, swing far to the Confederate right, then advance along a well-concealed route beyond the Federal left flank, wheel to the left, and fall on the rear of the Federals.

Leaving General Law to command the flanking movement, Jenkins rode to the brigades of General Jerome Robertson, General Henry Benning, and Colonel John Bratton to direct the main assault.[13]

Longstreet, leaving his staff behind to avoid drawing the enemy's fire, rode to the center front. Upon his appearance, the eager veterans sprang forth to charge the enemy, but Longstreet called them back to await the development of the flanking movement on the right.[14]

Captain Orlando M. Poe of Ohio, Burnside's chief of engineers. Poe directed the fortification of Knoxville and completed the construction of Fort Sanders.

Suddenly it was evident that Law had changed his direction so that his entire flanking force was in front of the Union lines instead of to the rear. Jenkins reported that "to my surprise, I received a message from General Law that in advancing his brigades he had obliqued so much to the left as to have gotten out of its line of attack. This careless and inexcusable movement lost us the few moments in which success from this point could be attained." [15]

A staff officer reporting to Longstreet on the error indicated that Law, jealous of Jenkins for command of Hood's division, had deliberately delayed the attack. He told his commander that "at the time it was currently reported that Gen-

Defended Fort Sanders. Brigadier General Edward Ferrero of New York commanded the First Division, Ninth Corps.

General J. B. Robertson of Texas, a Confederate brigade commander in Jenkins' Division

eral Law said he might have made the attack successfully, but that Jenkins would have reaped the credit for it, and hence he delayed until the enemy got out of the way." [16]

Watching the attack on their lines from a position in an orchard on a plateau about two-thirds of a mile to the rear, Burnside and Potter could clearly see the plan of investment that Longstreet was developing. Burnside had the troops ordered back to the position he and Potter now occupied as observers. As the Union lines fell back, General Lafayette McLaws promptly attacked them, but was delayed by artillery fire and the approach of darkness.

The Federal men of the 35th Massachusetts also observed the action from a vantage point. About noon of that day, exhausted, they were finally relieved of pulling Lieutenant Benjamin's guns through the mud and were sent scurrying

USA

Lieutenant Colonel Ralph Ely, who commanded the Eighth Michigan Regiment, First Brigade, First Division, Ninth Corps

Colonel Joshua Siegfried of Pennsylvania, commander of the First Brigade, Second Division, Ninth Corps

CSA

Colonel John Bratton of South Carolina, commander of a brigade in Jenkins' Division at Campbell's Station

Colonel Henry Benning, a brigade commander in Jenkins' Division

up into the wooded hills south of Kingston Road. From this position they could see both armies, and their historian recorded that

it was a grand sight. The Confederates came out in line with colors flying, fully expecting, apparently, that as soon as they got close to us we would retreat as before; but they were mistaken, for no sooner were they in sight than our batteries poured shells and shrapnel into their ranks with terrible effect; we could see the shells burst upon them, and they would break and run for the woods. . . . About noon, we could see their batteries take posi-

tion in a field near the road we had passed over and send shells in our direction, which burst in too close proximity to be pleasant; but their guns were soon silenced by our batteries. We could also see their infantry marching across from the Kingston road in the woods upon our left. Their attack commenced upon the right of the line, Ferrero's Division, and, being repulsed, worked towards our front, avoiding a direct assault upon the centre, White's Division. . . . They kept on, however, working around in the woods on the left, and to prevent being flanked it became necessary to withdraw the whole line of battle, between three and four o'clock, to a new position in the rear, upon the top of the hill we were occupying.[17]

The 29th Massachusetts, which occupied the hill and woods anchoring the Union right position, a mile away from their Bay State compatriots, had no sooner formed their line than they were likewise attacked. Colonel Ebenezer Peirce, commanding the 29th, had just placed his men in position and covered his front and flank with skirmishers when the blue uniforms of his rear guard were seen, then the skirmishers, the latter crossing the fields, "creeping along the fences, and coming to the road, guns in hand, occasionally pausing to load and fire. Now and then a soldier in gray showed himself on the edge of the woods, but he would soon dart back out of sight." [18]

Companies A and I had been detailed to the flanks and had proceeded but a short distance into the woods when they came upon the Rebels, who were approaching stealthily from tree to tree,

evidently attempting what Colonel Benjamin Christ had feared: namely, to flank the Brigade.

State historical marker on Kingston Pike, across Concord Road from Farragut High School

A brisk fire began at once, but our men kept their line intact and maintained perfect coolness. After the lapse of about an hour, the officers of the skirmish line discovered that the enemy were gradually overlapping the right of the Brigade and promptly informed Colonel Christ of the fact. The skirmishers were ordered to come in at once, and the Brigade changed front and began to fall back. This movement was not made a moment too soon, for a dense mass of the enemy's infantry immediately poured out of the woods in the rear of the retreating Brigade; while the flanking party, which had not yet lapped over our old position, also at the same moment, emerged from the woods, and, with loud yells, joined in the pursuit, firing an occasional shot and with terrible oaths, shouting to our men to surrender and lay down their arms.

Our men loading as they marched, halted by files, turned about and fired. . . . At last the regiment, which was in the rear, reached a sunken road, and leaped into it . . . meanwhile over the heads of the men played the cannon of our reserve batteries. The slaughter wrought upon the pursuing enemy is described as terrible; and as the Twenty-ninth came up the hill, gaining the plateau on the Knoxville side, Generals Burnside and Ferrero, standing on either side of the road, clapped their hands as it filed proudly between them." [19]

Before Longstreet could mount another offensive thrust, the darkness closed in, and his artillerymen could no longer spot the retiring Federals. Colonel Alexander eagerly looked forward to the next day's fighting, as he found opposite him once again Benjamin's battery of twenty-pound Parrotts which he recalled had been his "vis-à-vis at Fredericksburg," where it had pounded him from Marye's Heights.[20]

From Lenoir City on the night of November 15, Burnside had sent orders recalling General Sanders and his cavalry division back north to the Tennessee River. Now, to cover his retreat from Campbell's Station on the night of the 16th, Burnside ordered Sanders to perform delaying actions along the old Kingston Road, which in the vicinity of Knoxville followed the same course as modern Kingston Pike. With one brigade of 700 men, Sanders rode swiftly forward until he contacted the Confederate forward point. Then, by skirmishing slowly, he fell back upon a hill just north of the road (the site of the present Second Presbyterian Church), a mile west of the main Union defensive position in Knoxville, and about eight hundred yards west of where Kingston Pike crosses Third Creek. Two regiments of mounted infantry, commanded by Colonel C. D. Pennebaker, made a stand where the Clinton Road (modern College Street, which runs in front of Knoxville College) crossed the mountain ridge about a mile northwest.[21]

The retreating Federal army had had about sixteen miles of forced night marching before they could retire to prepared defensive positions in Knoxville. This was to most of the men the third night without sleep, and their condition was pitiable. Moreover, since the previous morning, they had marched twenty-four miles and fought a battle, "the evolutions of which were like the moves upon a chessboard and were executed with a precision seldom displayed in active field service in thickly wooded country."[22] Ferrero's division began moving out at 6:00 P.M., followed by Hartranft and White. Many of the men recalled that they almost slept while marching; the officers dozed in the saddle, and men who dropped were spurred on with warnings that to rest was a sure preliminary to Libby Prison.

At midnight the 79th New York Highlanders reached the outskirts of Knoxville, and Captain William Montgomery positioned them in the earthworks that the Confederates had called Fort Loudon. Companies B, H, and K manned the northwest bastion. It was 4:00 A.M., November 17, before the rear of White's marching columns finally got to Knoxville, and the men threw themselves on the ground for a quick two-hour nap before the dawn and the inevitable Confederate onslaught.

Dr. James Park, Presbyterian minister and the one-time superintendent of the Tennessee School for the Deaf—which had been converted into a hospital, first for the Confederates and then for the Union army—sat on the porch of his home in Cedar Springs and watched the passage of both armies. The weary, dragging Federal officers stopped for a drink and told him they were expecting a quick defeat. Later, as the Confederates trudged by, General Longstreet came into the house, seeking information about the local roads. He also ventured to ask the good minister what strategy he should pursue. "You need only to march straight against the city," replied Dr. Park, who had seen the condition of both armies, "and send in a flag of truce with a summons . . . to receive an immediate surrender."[23]

NOTES

1. O. R., Ser. I, XXXI, Part I, 481.
2. *Ibid.*, p. 350.
3. William H. Osborne, *The History of the Twenty-Ninth Regiment of Massachusetts Volunteer Infantry in the Late War of the Rebellion*, p. 263.
4. Sumner Carruth, *History of the Thirty-Fifth Regiment, Massachusetts Volunteers*, p. 180.
5. Longstreet, p. 491.
6. Carruth, p. 180.
7. O. R., Ser. I, XXXI, Part I, 350.
8. Longstreet, p. 492.
9. *Confederate Veteran*, XXXII (January 1924), 10.
10. Osborne, p. 263.
11. Burrage, p. 95.
12. Osborne, p. 263.
13. Longstreet, p. 493.

14. *Ibid.*, p. 495.
15. O. R., Ser. I, XXXI, Part III, 756.
16. O. R., Ser. I, XXXI, Part I, 526.
17. Carruth, pp. 182-83.
18. Osborne, p. 263.
19. *Ibid.*
20. *Battles and Leaders*, III, 747.
21. *Ibid.*, p. 737.
22. Carruth, p. 183.
23. As quoted by H. W. Field, a friend of Dr. Park, in the New York *Evangelist*, February 7, 1889. In 1867 Dr. Park was chosen as pastor of the First Presbyterian Church in Knoxville. He retired in 1905, but continued as Pastor Emeritus until his death in 1912, two months before his ninetieth birthday. His first task in the church was the restoration of the building which had been used and pillaged by the Union army.

20

Prettiest Shot of the War

GENERAL Burnside reached his Knoxville headquarters at Crozier House in the early dawn hours of November 17. But before he could enjoy a brief, welcome sleep, he was handed a message which Grant had sent from Chattanooga on the 15th.

"I do not know how to impress on you the necessity of holding on to East Tennessee in strong enough terms. It would seem that you should, if pressed to do it, hold on to Knoxville. . . . Should Longstreet move his whole force across the Little Tennessee, an effort should be made to cut his pontoons on that stream, even if it sacrificed half the cavalry of the Ohio army." [1] Apparently, Grant believed that Longstreet would move eastward south of the Tennessee River and attack Knoxville from that side, since the Little Tennessee flows into the south side of the Tennessee about twenty-five miles to the west, at Lenoir City.

Burnside telegraphed Grant informing him of his delaying tactics from Loudon to Knoxville, to which Grant immediately replied: "Your dispatch received. You are doing exactly what appears to me to be right. I want the enemy's progress retarded at every point, all it can be, only giving up each place when it becomes evident that it cannot longer be held without endangering your force to capture." [2]

Grant immediately wired to Halleck in Washington that "Burnside speaks hopefully," and issued battle orders for the Federal armies in Chattanooga, where General Sherman, up from Memphis, had recently joined General Thomas. [3]

General Longstreet's troops followed the Union army very cautiously to the outskirts of Knox-ville on the 17th. The Rebel commander did not choose to follow Dr. Park's advice to show his strength and demand immediate surrender.

Always the master of defense against superior attacking forces thrown against him in Virginia, Longstreet knew full well the hazards of an ill-timed and ill-prepared assault such as Burnside had made against him at Fredericksburg. Furthermore, after Chickamauga the brilliant dash which had always distinguished Longstreet was gone. The exasperating delays and inefficiencies of his logistical support in the Knoxville campaign had sapped his initiative.

The Confederate forces spent the entire day of November 17 establishing their lines in an arc around Knoxville, leaving open the country south of the river. In the early hours Colonel Hart's cavalry brigade moved toward the Clinton Road. As Jenkins' infantrymen came up toward Hart, the latter moved east to the Tazewell Road to prevent Burnside's "escape," should such an idea occur to the Union commander. [4] McLaws' Division remained about one thousand yards west of the first Union defense line beyond Third Creek. Longstreet kept the bulk of the infantry massed to the west from Middlebrook Pike to the river, while the cavalry moved north and as far east as Boyd's Ferry. Longstreet thus simplified his supply problem. He also wanted to trick Burnside into trying to escape to the east where the latter would be at the mercy of the Confederate cavalry in open country. [5]

On the hill north of Kingston Pike about eight hundred yards west of Third Creek (at the site of the present Second Presbyterian Church), General Sanders had dismounted the 700 men

Confederate Memorial Hall, originally known as Bleak House. Confederate Generals Longstreet and McLaws used this house at 3148 Kingston Pike, Knoxville, for their headquarters during the siege of Knoxville. Its tower is obscured by the trees at left.

of the 11th and 12th Kentucky, 8th Michigan, and 45th Ohio cavalries and posted them squarely in front of the Rebel advance. With the 112th Illinois Infantry in front as skirmishers, Sanders occupied the ground from the railroad to the river.[6] For many of the men of the Twenty-third Corps, who had remained in Knoxville while the Ninth Corps was retreating from Loudon, an attack would mean their first fight.

Burnside had no intention of sacrificing his inexperienced troops. Colonel C. D. Pennebaker of the 27th Kentucky Mounted brought his troops from the area of the Clinton Road and anchored the extreme left flank of the Union line from the river's edge to Kingston Pike. The Eighth Michigan entrenched themselves, behind rail pilings, from the road to the top of the hill on the farmland of Jacob L. Thomas. At the top of the hill was a solitary cedar tree which marked the center of the defense line, which continued north down a steep declivity to the railroad tracks. Sanders established his command post seventy-five yards behind the cedar tree in a depression under cover, but he frequently walked up to the tree, where he could direct

The tower of Bleak House. Sharpshooters in this tower fired upon General Sanders' defense line.

the fire of the Eighth Michigan. This regiment was armed with the breechloading Spencer rifle,[7] a seven-shot repeating rifle that could be fired effectively fifteen times per minute.[8] The average Confederate soldier, armed with a muzzle-loading weapon, could at best fire only two accurate shots per minute.

About noon of November 17, Brigadier General Joseph B. Kershaw, forty-two-year-old former state senator of South Carolina, massed his brigade of McLaws' Division for an assault upon Sanders' position. But for the rest of the day, Kershaw's veterans were held in check by Sanders' green troops who were well protected behind barricades made of the fence rails. Colonel Porter Alexander's Rebel batteries were used sparingly against the rails, as powder and shot were too scarce to waste on isolated pockets of resistance. By nightfall, the Confederate troops abandoned the attempt to drive Sanders from his hill and camped west of the city, near Middlebrook Pike.[9]

At 11 P.M., General Burnside sent for Captain Poe to report to headquarters at the Crozier House. General Sanders was present. The three discussed the urgent need to hold Longstreet in check for another day in order to complete the defense works of the city, particularly the various forts. Poe said he could finish the job by noon the next day. Sanders said he could hold his line until that time or longer, if necessary. Sanders accompanied Poe to his quarters, where the two talked until midnight.[10]

Just before daylight of the following morning, November 18, alerted by a guard, Sanders mounted his white charger and rushed out to the rail piles in time to see several Confederate infantry regiments attempting a frontal assault. When a few of the Federal troops began to break from their positions behind the rails, Sanders, according to Poe, would walk up there and "stand erect with fully half his height exposed to a terrific fire at short range until every retreating man, as if ashamed of himself, would return to his proper place."[11]

Inspired by Sanders' presence and his iron-like perseverance, the defenders beat off the assault and held their ground, to the amazement of the rest of the Federal army watching the fight from the positions nearer the town. But the defenders were continually harassed by eight or ten sharpshooters who had positioned themselves in the tower of the brick house belonging to the family of Robert H. Armstrong on the south side of Kingston Pike 750 yards southwest of Sanders' position.[12]

Distinguished from the ordinary sharpshooting riflemen, these were men from the selected twenty in Longstreet's Corps armed with the thirteen-pound English "Whitworth Rifle." This fine English piece, costing $1,200 each, was a muzzle-loader firing a one-inch projectile propelled by a three-inch powder charge. It was equipped with a fourteen-and-a-half-inch telescopic sight. The men entrusted with this weapon were excused from the ordinary soldierly duties of guard mounts, drills, and inspections. Each

man acted as his own free agent, subject only to orders from the division commanders or Longstreet himself.[13]

Annoyed by the accurate fire from these sharpshooters, General Sanders sent a request to Lieutenant Samuel Benjamin in Fort Loudon (later named Fort Sanders by the Federals), located where Laurel Avenue and 17th Street intersect today, to see if his artillery could scare the sharpshooters from their advantageous post. Captain Poe, who was in the fort at the time, watched with some skepticism evident on his face as Benjamin, cigar in mouth, lined up a twenty-pound Parrott, the largest field rifle in use. When set to an elevation of twelve degrees, the maximum the carriage would allow, this piece would fire 3,000 to 3,500 yards. Estimating the distance from the fort to the Armstrong House to be 2,500 yards, Lieutenant Benjamin took careful aim. He and Poe stepped back a few paces to get away from the powder blast that would obscure their vision. Benjamin's gunner then sent the first shot directly through the compartment of the tower, and Rebels were seen scurrying from their loft.

Poe declared it to be "the prettiest single shot of the entire war" and, beside himself with wonderment, called for another shot. But Benjamin had established his reputation, and, concealing his obvious satisfaction, he walked away.[14]

About noontime, Longstreet realized that Sanders was not going to be dislodged by infantry firing alone, and he ordered Colonel Alexander to destroy the fence rails with fire from his brass howitzers. For two hours the howitzers pounded the rails, scattering them in every direction, but the Federals held on by steadily replacing them.

His patience exhausted, Longstreet once more ordered the hill carried by assault. Colonel James D. Nance was detailed to lead the Third South Carolina Infantry in a direct charge, while Colonel John Kennedy led the Second Carolina on a flanking movement to the right.[15]

Nance pointed out two lone cedar trees on the

Killed in the tower of Bleak House. Portrayed by an anonymous artist on an inside wall of the tower are these three unknown Confederate sharpshooters killed there. The author of the script caption, done before the United Daughters of the Confederacy began restoration of the mansion, also is unknown. The sketches are remarkably well preserved.

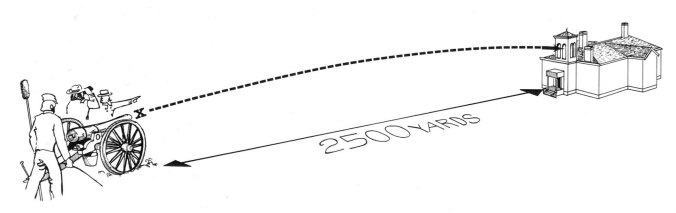

Prettiest shot of the war. Using a twenty-pound Parrott field gun at Fort Loudon (later named Fort Sanders), Lieutenant Samuel Benjamin sent a cannonball directly through the tower of Bleak House, on a hill 2,500 yards distant. This "prettiest shot of the war" dislodged sharpshooters who had harassed the lines of General Sanders west of Knoxville.

Fires the prettiest shot. Lieutenant (Brevet Major) Samuel N. Benjamin, Second U. S. Artillery, commanded the defenses of Fort Sanders.

hill some thirty yards in front of the enemy's lines, smaller than the lone tree in the Federal center, and told his men to advance upon them, to carry the rails, but to go no further. To soften the resistance, Alexander ordered Captain Osmond Taylor to open fire with two of his twelve-pound Napoleon guns and Captain G. V. Moody's Louisiana battery to hurl shrapnel into the rear of the rails with twenty-four-pound howitzers.[16]

Shortly after the cannonade began, Sanders' men started deserting the rails and striking out for shelter behind the hill. Colonel Nance, his long gray overcoat buttoned to the neck, raised his sword high in the air and in his great bass voice thundered, "Forward, guide left, march!" Then men sprang up and swept along in grand style to the base of the hill. Then Nance bellowed out again. "Double-quick, march!" The Second closed in from the right, and the Third dashed up the hill.[17]

The Federal officers rallied their men gallantly and brought most of them back into line, pouring a heavy fire into the Carolinians. The Third advanced rapidly without returning the fire until they reached the two cedar trees thirty yards in front of the Federal line. Here they mistakenly halted, dropped to the ground, and opened fire. They had misunderstood their orders and had stopped at the cedar trees instead of the Federal line beyond.[18]

At the first sign of the fire fight, General Sanders, his aide Major R. E. Lawder of Mexico, Missouri, and Colonel Wolford left their shelter to the rear and began walking up the hill to the cedar trees. Sanders, sending Wolford to the right, walked with Lawder over to the center of the line. Lawder said that "the Union line had begun to break, when from the left, which was held by the 8th Michigan, armed with Spencer carbines, there was opened, as from the furnace of death, an enfilading fire . . . it was more than human bravery could endure and the [attackers] turned and ran." [19]

Sanders and Lawder thought that the repulse was complete, and they deliberately turned away

Wounded in the Assault on Fort Sanders. Colonel John Kennedy commanded the Second South Carolina Regiment which overran Sanders' defense position near the present Second Presbyterian Church on Kingston Pike.

Colonel Frank Wolford, who succeeded Sanders in command of the Union cavalry

from the fire fight and began walking slowly to the rear. However, they had not gone far when they turned around and were standing near the solitary cedar tree at the center of the line, the balls from myriad rifles whizzing through the air close to their heads. But they seemed not to notice the danger, as their eyes remained transfixed on a lone horseman.[20]

For at this moment occurred one of those dashing feats of individual gallantry in wartime that defy all the rules of self-preservation. Captain Stephen Winthrop, an Englishman, formerly Captain of Her Britannic Majesty's 24th Infantry, who had joined the Confederate ranks and was on duty with Alexander's artillery battery stationed several hundred yards to the rear, saw the infantry charge toward the rail piles.[21] Seeing the charging men fall short of the mark, then wince from the galling fire of Sanders' troops, Winthrop jumped on his horse and dashed across the road, the only horseman in the melee. He rode right through his own troops firing from the ground, up to the very works of the enemy. A hundred rifles were aimed at him, but he moved on. With a dozen muskets blazing at him from close range, he fell forward on his horse's neck, a Minié ball through his collarbone, his scabbard broken and the point of his sword sheared off. Carried from the field, the plucky Britisher survived.[22]

Winthrop's gallant charge rallied the wavering Confederate line. Nance's troops no longer were confused and no longer seemed to care that the right flank of the Second hadn't moved up the hill. Inspired by Winthrop's dash, the entire Third Brigade sprang to their feet and charged up to the summit of the hill.[23] As the surging mass of Lee's veteran troops, screaming their defiant roars, swarmed up the crest, a few of the rookies in the Federal lines yelled out, "We surrender!"[24]

Seeing the apparent surrender, Colonel Nance joyfully ordered the Confederates to cease fire. But the main body of Federal troops opened fire again. The stunned Nance ordered his men forward once more, and in two minutes the South Carolinians gained the hill. Leaping over the rail piles, they found thirty dead Federal soldiers, from whom they took the clothes and the filled haversacks.

The tired but relieved Colonel Nance ordered his men to occupy the hill and to take a deserved rest. "It is but truth to state," he said, "that this was the most desperate encounter in which my command was ever engaged, and as it was perhaps one of the most brilliant charges of the war, I cannot speak too highly of the conduct of my comrades."[25]

NOTES

1. Burrage, p. 102.
2. *Ibid.*, p. 103.
3. *Ibid.*
4. O. R., Ser. I, XXXI, Part I, 471.
5. Personal communication from Dr. H. S. Fink, January, 1963.
6. *Battles and Leaders,* III, 737.
7. Knoxville *Tribune,* October 26, 1882.
8. Lord, p. 164.
9. *Battles and Leaders,* III, 747.
10. *Ibid.,* p. 737.
11. *Ibid.*
12. *Ibid.,* p. 738. The Armstrong home, Bleak House, is now called Confederate Memorial Hall.
13. *Confederate Veteran, XXX* (July 1922), 247.
14. *Battles and Leaders,* III, 738. Poe visited Knoxville in 1899. In an interview with the Knoxville *Journal and Tribune* he gave the details of this incident. A copy of this interview, date deleted, is in the Ducloux Scrapbook, Lawson McGhee Library.

15. O. R., Ser. I, XXXI, Part I, 509-12.
16. *Battles and Leaders,* III, 747.
17. *Confederate Veteran,* XXX (September 1922), 340.
18. *Battles and Leaders,* III, 747.
19. R. E. Lawder, interview in the Knoxville *Journal and Tribune,* 1899, date deleted, in the Ducloux Scrapbook.
20. *Ibid.*
21. *Battles and Leaders,* III, 747.
22. E. A. Pollard, *Southern History of the War* (Blue and Gray Edition), III, 142-43.
23. *Battles and Leaders,* III, 747.
24. O. R., Ser. I, XXXI, Part I, 509-12.
25. *Ibid.* Colonel Nance and Kershaw's Brigade had borne the brunt of the Southern fighting the second day of the Battle of Gettysburg. The hard fighting outside Knoxville was a tribute to the gallantry and determination of the men of General Sanders' command. After the skirmish General Kershaw made his headquarters in the

home built by Drury P. Armstrong in 1823, known as "Crescent Bend." The house, at 2728 Kingston Pike, is still used as a residence today.

Captain B. F. Thompson of the 112th Illinois said that "Colonel Nance rode up to within 30 yards of our lines and demanded we surrender. Major Dow of the 8th Michigan politely told him to go to hell, and ordered Corporal Williams of Company A to shoot him, but others fired at him and he fell dead in our front." Thompson remembered the details after twenty years and was confused. It was Captain Winthrop who was shot and appeared dead. Colonel Nance was unharmed. Some of the confusion regarding the apparent surrender and resumption of fighting was due to the nature of the troops. Lt. Colonel Alfred O'Brien of Louisiana, a Rebel officer whose sister was married to William G. Brownlow of Knoxville, said that he thought the Union soldiers were "new troops and didn't know enough to run," and that all his men had to do was to go up and "take them in." When the Yankees refused to be "hollered" out of their position and repulsed the Rebel charges on several occasions, Captain Thompson of the 112th Illinois said that the Rebels then made it a point of honor to break the line. The Eighth Michigan, whose left flank was on the river and whose right flank hugged Kingston Pike, held firm. The 112th Illinois held steady in the center of the line from the Pike to the crest of the hill. The 45th Ohio holding the right salient broke quickly, exposing the rest of the Union troops to deadly enfilade fire. The 112th Illinois lost one-third of the regiment trying to escape the trap.

Alone in His Glory

GENERAL Sanders and his aide, Major R. E. Lawder, had watched as the gray line swarmed up the hill against the Federal position on Kingston Pike. Suddenly, they saw Captain Winthrop, the lone Confederate horseman, charging, like some heroic figure from the Middle Ages, directly into a murderous fire of rifles. Fascinated, they watched until he slumped forward on his horse.

"It was," said Lawder, "a charge unequalled in the war." They turned and began to retreat for cover behind the hill. Bullets whistled over their heads, fired by the attacking Confederate brigade. Sanders exclaimed, "What a gallant fellow he was." Just as Sanders finished speaking, Major Lawder heard the sickening and unmistakable thud of lead ripping into flesh.

"I'm hit!" cried Sanders, reeling. "I'm no further use, go, leave me here." [1]

Lawder caught the general in his arms and quickly collected a few men, who carried their bleeding commander to the Anderson House, 400 yards to the rear. There they found an old ladder and used it as a stretcher to move Sanders to a room at the Lamar House, on the southwest corner of Gay Street and Cumberland Avenue, where he was examined by Dr. J. C. Hatchitt. The doctor, a Kentuckian and an old friend of the twenty-eight-year-old cavalryman, found that a Minié ball had entered the left side and torn the spleen. As was the custom in those days, Sanders was told that the wound was mortal. [2]

All through the night of November 18, General Sanders lay quietly in his bed at Lamar House, surrounded by devoted comrades-in-arms, surgeons, and ministers summoned to the deathwatch. In full possession of his mind, the young hero calmed the uneasiness of those about him:

"Soldiers, I am not afraid to die. I have done my duty and served my country as well as I could." [3]

Following the din of battle by day, the night seemed quiet by contrast. Only the crackling of innumerable campfires, the whinnying of starving mules, the muted strains of a distant band, and the infrequent sharp cracks from pickets' rifles disturbed the bedside vigil.

On the following morning, November 19, Dr. Hatchitt informed Sanders that he had but a few hours to live. At 10:00 A.M., the dying man was baptized by the Reverend J. A. Hyden of the Methodist Episcopal Church, and the end came shortly afterwards. [4]

"It was the saddest death I ever witnessed," the doctor remembered. "In his delirium before dying he continually thanked God that he was not shot in the back." [5] Burnside, clasping Sanders' hand, wept unashamedly as "suddenly the strength of the dying soldier failed, and like a child he gently fell asleep." [6]

There was a sudden awkward silence, finally interrupted by an unidentified soldier who lifted up an Episcopal Book of Common Prayer and, in a hushed voice, intoned, "Let us pray." Major Lawder said the soldier, with head bowed, and "with trembling tearful tones, lifted up his voice to the God of battles in the beautiful prayer which begins: 'Oh Father of mercies and God of all comfort, our only help in time of need, we fly to Thee for succor.' Then pent up sorrow burst its gates, the fountains of their hearts were broken up and those battle-scarred men wept like children." [7]

Viewing the body, General Burnside ex-

147

Brigadier General William Pitt Sanders, the only Southern-born Union general officer killed in the Civil War. Fort Loudon was renamed Fort Sanders in his honor. Today a hospital, a school, a church, a street, an apartment building, and many business establishments in Knoxville bear this name.

claimed, "I told Sanders not to expose himself, but he would do it." [8]

General Sanders' personal effects were entrusted to his West Point classmate, Captain Poe. Dr. Thomas Humes was asked to conduct the funeral service.[9]

It was decided that, for sake of the morale among the soldiers, General Sanders' death would be concealed for the time being. Dr. Hatchitt said that "Such was the confidence the army had in him that General Burnside requested that his death should not be made known, and the surgeons were accordingly urged to keep up the impression that Sanders was living some time after he was dead." [10]

The funeral, with graveside service, would be

held at night, as silently as possible—no music, no death march, no rifle salute over his grave. He was buried in the graveyard next to the Second Presbyterian Church, which at that time was on the west side of Market Street between Clinch and Union avenues.

Burnside and Dr. Humes led the funeral procession from Lamar House to the grave. Dr. Jackson, medical director for the army, carried a lantern to light the way. No sound of drum or carriage disturbed the night.

"I am reminded of the lines on 'The Burial of Sir John Moore,' " said Dr. Humes.

General Burnside, striking his leg for emphasis, quickly responded, "I have thought of them twenty times today."

As the body was lowered into the grave, the learned warrior could silently recall the lines of "The Burial of Sir John Moore."

Not a drum was heard nor a funeral note
   As his corse to the ramparts we hurried,
Not a soldier discharged his farewell shot
   O'er the grave where our hero we buried.

We buried him darkly at dead of night,
   The sod with our bayonets turning,
By the struggling moonbeams' misty light,
   And the lantern dimly burning.

Few and short were the prayers we said
   And we spoke not a word of sorrow,
But we steadfastly gazed on the face of the dead
   And we bitterly thought of the morrow.

.   .   .   .

Slowly and sadly we laid him down
   From the field of his fame, fresh and gory,
We carved not a line, we raised not a stone
   But we left him alone in his glory.[11]

But the eerie quiet and stillness, interrupted sporadically by the deep booming of a distant cannon, was overpowering to Captain Poe. With a nod to the others that they quickly understood, Poe directed the officers, who drew their pistols, raised them in the air, and fired a parting salute to General William P. Sanders, a cousin of Jefferson Davis and the only general of Southern birth killed while serving in the Union army.[12]

Strangely enough, in view of the secrecy of the burial, the first sergeant of Company K of the 35th Massachusetts Regiment recorded in his diary on November 19: "I was awakened from sleep by the playing of Webster's March at the funeral of General Sanders; the effect in the stillness of night was solemn and impressive." [13]

Burnside realized that he could not keep up his well-meaning deceit for long, and in a field order five days later he announced the death of his young friend and subordinate.

HEADQUARTERS ARMY OF THE OHIO
IN THE FIELD, November 24, 1863
GENERAL FIELD ORDER NUMBER 31

The Commanding General has the sad duty of announcing to his army the death of one of the bravest of their number, Brigadier General W. P. Sanders.

A life rendered illustrious by a long record of gallantry and devotion to his country has closed while in the heroic and unflinching performance of duty.

Distinguished always for his self possession and daring in the field, and in his private life eminent for his genial and unselfish nature and the sterling qualities of his character, he has left, both as a man and as a soldier, an untarnished name.

In memory of the honored dead, the fort, in front of which he received his fatal wound will be known hereafter as Fort Sanders.

By command of Major General Burnside
LEWIS RICHMOND, Assistant Adj.-Gen.[14]

NOTES

1. The details of the death of General Sanders have been shrouded in mystery and controversy. Major R. E. Lawder, Sanders' aide, was a brother-in-law of Captain W. P. Chamberlain of Knoxville. Lawder visited Knoxville in 1882 and again in 1899, and the local papers interviewed him on each occasion (see the Knoxville *Sentinel*, December 25, 1899). The Knoxville *Tribune*, on October 26, 1882, also quoted extensively from an interview Lawder gave to the *National Tribune* in April of that year. In one

account Lawder was quoted as saying Sanders was wounded just as he had finished observing Captain Winthrop's magnificent charge. In another interview he describes the location of Sanders' shelter; the actual fire fight; and the difficulties he encountered carrying the 200-pound wounded general to the rear for treatment. In all accounts Lawder specifically stated that he and Sanders were walking back toward their rear shelter, while bullets were whizzing all about them, when Sanders was wounded.

This evidence contradicts many legends, old and current, regarding the manner of the general's death. William Rule in *Standard History of Knoxville, Tennessee,* p. 166, states that Sanders was shot from his white horse by a sharpshooter concealed in the tower of the Armstrong House. According to Mr. Robert Cunningham of the Knoxville *News-Sentinel,* several men have claimed to have known who fired the fatal shot. One version told Mr. Cunningham was that Jake Warren, who became Sheriff of Monroe County, shot the general off his horse. Recently it was claimed that Hiram M. Vineyard, whose son Fred is still living, deliberately selected a man on a white horse, presumably the general, aimed, and fired. He believed he had wounded him.

Since the 2nd and 3rd South Carolina regiments were charging up the hill, backed by the fire of the 8th and 15th South Carolina infantries on the slope near the river's edge, it is possible that any number of men could have thought they wounded the general. In the engagement in which Sanders was wounded, 119 Federal soldiers were killed or wounded and 75 were captured. The Southerners had 140 casualties including Colonel Gist, commanding the 15th South Carolina.

2. Knoxville *Tribune,* October 26, 1882.
3. *Ibid.*
4. Humes, pp. 254-55.
5. Knoxville *Tribune,* October 26, 1882.
6. Humes, p. 255.
7. Ducloux Scrapbook, p. 46.
8. Humes, p. 256.
9. *Ibid.,* pp. 255-56.
10. Knoxville *Tribune,* October 26, 1882.
11. Humes, pp. 257-58.
12. Ducloux Scrapbook, p. 46.
13. Carruth, p. 187.
14. Captain Poe, who was General Sanders' only West Point classmate present at the siege of Knoxville, said that it was at his suggestion that the fort was renamed Fort Sanders. O.R., Ser. I, XXXI, Part III, 241.

Earthworks Grow Like Magic

LONGSTREET'S mission was to destroy Burnside quickly at Knoxville and return to the assistance of Bragg, who, for the moment, had Grant trapped in Chattanooga. Burnside, on the other hand, had to delay Longstreet in order to increase Grant's chances of defeating Bragg and breaking out of the trap.

Burnside had lured Longstreet as far from Chattanooga as he could. Now, he himself was enclosed, but Knoxville's hilly terrain might lend him the defensive strength to withstand a prolonged siege.

At that time, the city of Knoxville covered little more than the tableland, nearly a mile square, on the north bank of the Tennessee River, about 150 feet above river level but with many higher points. The tableland was cut then as it is today by three small streams running from north to south and emptying into the Tennessee River. These streams were and are called, quite naturally, First, Second, and Third creeks, in that order from east to west. The main portion of town was between First and Second creeks. The larger section of the tableland, between Second and Third creeks, was sparsely populated.

The valley bounding the northwest side of the tableland, averaging about fifty feet above river level, contains the tracks of the present-day Southern Railway, then known to the east as the East Tennessee and Virginia and to the west as the East Tennessee and Georgia.

Just east of First Creek is Temperance Hill, overlooking the railroad tracks from a height of 225 feet. Further east, beyond a depression, is Mabry's Hill, 230 feet high, the highest point north of the river within cannon range of the

town. Flint Hill, to the southwest of Temperance, rising 162 feet, overlooks the river and the mouth of First Creek. Just west of Second Creek, near the river, is a 160-foot elevation then known as College Hill, site of East Tennessee University, now the main campus of the University of Tennessee. Northwest of College Hill is the 198-foot elevation where stood the old Confederate earthworks bastion which the Federals renamed Fort Sanders.[1]

From Campbell's Station on November 16, General Burnside had sent instructions to Captain Orlando Poe, chief engineer of the Army of the Ohio, at Knoxville to prepare lines of defense for the town, employing the engineering battalion of the 23rd Corps and such civilians as he could impress into service.

Beginning with simple rifle entrenchments, Poe directed the development of a continuous defense line, backed in places by second and third lines, the whole system of which formed a rough rectangle, elongated to the east and west, with the Tennessee River as the southern side.

Starting a quarter of a mile west of the mouth of Second Creek, the line extended from the river at an angle of about 82 degrees, running northwestward for 900 yards to the front of Thomas Powell's home, Melrose (site of the new University of Tennessee men's dormitory on Melrose Place), where it was reinforced by a section of Buckley's battery. This point was called Battery Noble, in honor of Lieutenant William Noble of the Second Michigan Infantry.

Then bending abruptly 50 degrees northward, the defense line continued across the old Kingston Road (Cumberland Avenue at Melrose Place)

View from East Tennessee University. In this wartime photograph of Knoxville, Second Creek runs from left to right in the ravine in the foreground. Hill Avenue, at the left, climbs toward downtown Knoxville, and above it on the horizon Flint Hill appears at the bend of the river. Note the Union cannon in the right foreground.

and up the hill to Fort Sanders. The west front of this fort was in the vicinity of 17th Street between Clinch and Laurel avenues, with the northwest bastion near the present site of Fort Sanders Manor, an apartment building at the intersection of 17th and Laurel.

At the northwest bastion of Fort Sanders, the defense line changed direction 65 degrees eastward and went parallel with the river some 1,600 yards to Battery Wiltsie, south of the Southern Railway Depot. This battery was named in honor of Captain William Wiltsie of the 20th Michigan.

Included in this part of the defense line were earthen forts designed to give extensive artillery cross fire over the valley to the north, each one named for a Federal officer killed in recent fighting. Battery Zoellner, named for Lieutenant Frank Zoellner of the Second Michigan, was located between Fort Sanders and Second Creek, at modern Forest Avenue between 11th and 13th streets. Battery Galpin, named for Lieutenant Galpin of the Second Michigan, was just east of Second Creek, at present-day Vine Avenue between Broadway and Locust Street. Fort Comstock, named for Lieutenant Colonel C. Comstock of the 17th Michigan, originally built by the Confederates, and Battery Wiltsie, at modern Vine Avenue between Locust and Gay streets, anchored this portion of the defense line.

From Wiltsie, the entrenchments continued along the crest of the bluff over Temperance Hill to Mabry's Hill, a distance of 2,400 yards. Battery Billingsley, named for Lieutenant J. Billingsley of the 17th Michigan, was placed just west of First Creek, on present Commerce Avenue between Gay and Central streets. Fort Huntington Smith, for Lieutenant Colonel W. H. Smith of the 20th Michigan, occupied Temperance Hill at present Payne Avenue. Battery Clifton Lee, for Captain Lee of the 112th Illinois, was set in the depression between Temperance Hill and Mabry's Hill, and Battery Stearman, for Lieutenant William H. Stearman of the 113th Kentucky, was just to the east. Fort Hill, for

Union encampment. The encampment in the center foreground is just west of the inner defense trenches. Fort Higley, beyond the river on the left, was occupied by Federal forces, and Cherokee Heights, out of the photograph at the right, was a Confederate emplacement.

Captain Hill of the 12th Kentucky, anchored the extreme easterly point of Mabry's Hill. From this point, the defense line curved sharply to the southwest for 1,300 yards to a ravine 1,000 yards east of the mouth of First Creek.

Dams were built across First and Second creeks, flooding extensive parts of the line and forming obstructive wet ditches, and various entanglements were placed in front of the trenches at several points.

Continuous infantry lines connected all the forward positions. A second line ran from the present intersection of Clinch Avenue and 16th Street at the rear of Fort Sanders southeastward to the mouth of Second Creek. It included Fort Byington, named for Major Cornelius Byington of the Second Michigan, on top of College Hill, where the University's main building, Ayres Hall,

now stands. A third line extended from Temperance Hill to Flint Hill, terminating at the river at Battery Fearns, named for Lieutenant Charles Fearns of the 45th Ohio.[2]

The pontoon bridge across the Tennessee River just east of Gay Street connected these fortifications with the positions on the south side of the river which "Fighting Joe" Wheeler had assaulted but failed to capture.

The siege of Knoxville effectively began November 17, 1863, when the Confederates surrounded Knoxville except where it was bounded on the south by the Tennessee River. The Union troops, ordered by Burnside to retreat no farther, to stand or die in Knoxville, now began to number the days of the siege.

The third day, November 19, was memorable, for in the early hours of the morning, the 79th

Melrose from the University. From Fort Byington (the University), the road on the right, leading straight up the hill, is Rose Avenue. The large white house to the right of the road is Melrose, Thomas Powell's home, the location of Battery Noble. Union rifle pits can be seen curving across the immediate foreground. Confederate artillery occupied Cherokee Heights, on the far left horizon.

New York Highlanders inside the earthwork fort erected their flagstaff, and for the first time the Stars and Stripes flew over the red clay ramparts. All along the entrenched line, the flag was greeted with cheers. Colonel Alexander saluted it with a furious burst of artillery fire but did not hit its fluttering folds.[2]

Longstreet brought his men closer to town, searching for a soft spot at which to push his main assault. Out from the woods east of First Creek, Captain William Parker of Richmond, Virginia, led his battery of guns, the cannoneers mounted on their white and gray horses that the men of the 79th had respectfully dubbed "Scots Greys." They fired three shots into the tents of the men of Company K of the 35th Massachusetts, the last one flying near the head of

General Burnside, who was behind a parapet looking through his binoculars. Burnside showed his white teeth, and "sighting one of the guns, quickly sent the white horses flying." [4]

Companies A, B, D, and G of the 36th Massachusetts, on picket duty near the river at Third Creek, were driven back. Their place in the line was taken by the 45th Pennsylvania. The relieved companies retired to College Hill to support Roemer's 34th New York Battery, but they spent most of the day scrubbing the buildings so recently used as a Confederate hospital.

Companies C, E, F, H, I, and K moved into the freshly dug rifle pits in front of Thomas Powell's house, Melrose, south of Kingston Pike. This elegant brick residence, built by slave labor in 1858 by John Craig, had walls more than one foot thick and ceilings thirteen feet high. Down-stairs was a great reception hall with a curving stairway of sweet gum, flanked by two large drawing rooms entered through massive door-ways.

General Burnside ordered loopholes made in the southwestern and northwestern fronts of the house and instructed two companies of the 36th to guard the house. Mr. Powell, a staunch Union-ist, agreed. "All right. Lay this house level with the ground if it is necessary." He invited Colonel David Morrison, commander of General Fer-rero's First Brigade, and Major William Draper of the 36th to make the house their headquarters. They assigned one room to the wounded.[5]

It was on this day, the 19th, that the men of the 36th Massachusetts erected Battery Noble, a small earthwork a few feet from the south-western front of Melrose, for part of Buckley's artillery battery. All the while the men were digging and knocking holes in the walls, fresco painters were at work ornamenting the parlors and halls of the great house.[6]

Friday, November 20, was a foggy day with extremely limited visibility. The Confederate gun which yesterday had shelled the town from the Tazewell Road remained quiet. The Rebels could not waste ammunition in indiscriminate firing, especially with half the Knoxville citizens on their side.

Inside Fort Sanders, Negro gangs were kept busy building up the parapets with cotton bales to protect the men. The cotton bales were cov-ered with rawhide to keep them from igniting from musket fire.[7]

All day bullets bit into the red clay embank-ments or went whistling over the heads of the defenders. Every man from General Ferrero to the drummer boy ducked and dodged as he went about his duties. "Long Andy," the cook for the 79th New Yorkers, ventured out during the day to deliver bread to the picket line in front of the fort. Rebel snipers kicked up the dirt around his heels, until in exasperation he clenched his fist and bellowed, "You bastards, do you want a

Melrose, home of Thomas Powell. This house was used as a hospital and observation post by the 36th Massachusetts Regiment, as well as being the site of Battery Noble.

bite?" The firing ceased, for every Southerner on the line felt sure the bread would be his when. Longstreet gave the word to attack.[8]

For the previous three days, the Confederate force had ringed the town but had not made a serious demonstration at any single point. It was not easy to find a weak spot, especially as the be-siegers were unfamiliar with the locality and did not even have maps of the city. But on November 20, offensive lines began to appear as Longstreet ordered the construction of entrenchments, start-ing from near the Armstrong House, running across Kingston Pike, and following the ridge near the present site of Knoxville College (north of the railroad—not to be confused with College Hill) on a line nearly parallel to the Union forti-fications.

"The earth-works on each side seemed to grow like magic, but we were apparently digging more than they," said Poe.[9]

To strengthen their "diggings," the Union troops reinforced their lines with every material on hand until the defensive position resembled the pattern of a World War I battlefield. Imme-diately in front of the rifle pits were constructed chevaux-de-frise — pointed stakes, thickly and firmly set in the ground and inclining outward at an angle of 45 degrees. The stakes, nearly five feet in height, were bound with wire so that they could not be easily torn apart by an assaulting party. In front of Fort Comstock on the north side of town, the chevaux-de-frise were constructed with the 2,000 pikes captured at Cumberland Gap. In front of these formidable barriers, abatis were arranged of felled trees firmly set in the ground with the branches facing the enemy.[10]

The Ninth Corps, under Brigadier General Robert Potter, defended the line from the Tennessee River north to Fort Sanders, then east to First Creek. General Edward Ferrero's First Division occupied that portion of the works from the river to Second Creek. Colonel David Morrison's brigade was entrenched from the river's

Major William Draper, 36th Massachusetts, who used Melrose as his headquarters

edge to the fort, with Colonel Benjamin Christ's and Colonel William Humphrey's brigades extending from the fort eastward to Second Creek. Colonel John Hartranft's Second Division was dug in between Second and First creeks.

The 23rd Corps of Brigadier General Mahlon D. Manson was assigned the defense of the eastern and southern approaches to the city. Colonel Marshall Chapin's brigade was posted from the Bell House on the north side of Mabry's Hill across to Temperance Hill, and Colonel James Reilly's First Brigade continued across to Flint Hill and the river. Colonel Daniel Cameron's infantry brigade and General James Shackelford's dismounted brigade held the forts south of the city on the bluffs.

Supporting the riflemen, Burnside had fifty-one guns in position, including eight on the south side of the river. Captain Joseph Sims, 24th Indiana, and Captain Edward Henshaw of Illinois had four of the small six-pound howitzers and six James rifles atop Temperance Hill. The James rifles were old smoothbores rebored to fire rifled projectiles of doubled weight, or up to eighty-four pounds.[11]

Captain Joseph Shields, 19th Ohio, and part of Captain Wilder's Ohio Reserves occupied Mabry's Hill with one section of three-inch rifle guns and six of the twelve-pound Napoleons. The Napoleon gun, being smoothbore, was not effective beyond 2,000 yards, but at short range its twelve-pound charge could be fired about 300 yards in a fairly even pattern, with a spread of about twenty yards.

The Unionist Tennessee Eighth Battery, with a section of twelve-pound howitzers, guarded Flint Hill. Captain Jacob Roemer's 34th New York Battery of four three-inch rifles dug in on the campus of the East Tennessee University, and Captain Joseph Sims' 24th Indiana guarded the southern approach at Fort Dickerson.[12]

Fort Sanders was the most heavily fortified emplacement. Lieutenant Samuel Benjamin commanded his own battery of four twenty-pound Parrotts and the six twelve-pound Napoleons and

Looking toward Fort Sanders. In this rooftop view from the University, Fort Sanders appears directly above and behind the small pond, on the first ridge. At the far right on this ridge is Battery Zoellner. To the left of Fort Sanders, and more in the foreground, are the tents of Colonel David Morrison's First Brigade, Ninth Corps. Cumberland Avenue angles from the far right, foreground, to the left center of picture. Union rifle pits, meandering through the foreground, are interrupted at one place by Cumberland.

two three-inch rifles of Buckley's First Rhode, Island. The Parrott gun, easily recognized by the heavy wrought-iron jacket reinforcing the breech, was the most effective siege gun used in the war. But neither the Parrott nor the smoothbore could destroy earthworks.[13]

Burnside's gunners had four types of projectiles for their smoothbore artillery. For long-range targets, they fired the solid shot, the explosive shell, or the spherical case. The solid shot was used more frequently than the others, but to be effective it had to slam into a target head-on. The explosive shell, containing a black powder bursting charge, more often than not failed to shatter into more than two fragments. The spherical case was the most effective long-range projectile, when the fuse worked properly; the exploding fragments burst into a fairly dense pattern. "Canister," which was a tin can of small iron or lead balls, was used for close work against assaulting parties.

All of the Federal guns were protected by earthworks and guarded by infantrymen. Since most of the pieces were accurate only to 1,200 yards, their crews were particularly vulnerable to Longstreet's roving snipers armed with the Whitworth rifle with its fourteen-and-one-half-inch telescope and effective range of 1,800 yards.

Opposing Burnside's fifty-one guns, Colonel Alexander had only thirty-four, in three batteries from Georgia, five from Virginia, and one from Louisiana. By the afternoon of the 20th, Longstreet and Alexander had reconnoitered most of the Federal positions and had determined that there was but one point at which an assault could be made with any hope of success—the works the Confederates had called Fort Loudon which, on November 24th, the Federals would officially rename Fort Sanders.[14]

Both sides knew that, although this fort was constructed according to classical engineering principles, with a profile of moat, embankment, and parapet, its northwest bastion, a prominent salient in the main Union line of defense, had been built upon a hill which fell off sharply to

Batteries Zoellner and Galpin. Looking from the University, the encampment barely visible on the first ridge at far left is Battery Zoellner. On the same ridge, in the center of the picture, is Battery Galpin. The white house prominent in the foreground was the home of **Hugh Lawson White, a** Knoxvillian who was Van Buren's opponent for the Presidency of the United States in 1836. In the distance at far right, the four neat rows of tents indicate the location of Fort Comstock. The valley of Second Creek cuts between Comstock and Battery Galpin on the left.

View of Knoxville from Fort Dickerson. Union defensive positions arrayed from left to right on the hills immediately beyond Knoxville were Battery Galpin, Fort Comstock, Battery Wiltsie, and Battery Billingsley. At the extreme left, the large white house was James Cowan's home. In the center of the picture, Sharp's Gap is distinctly visible on the horizon. At the right, the photograph looks directly up Prince Street, present-day Market Street. At the base of Prince Street, on the riverbank and partly obscured by trees, is the city's boat dock. In the block to the right of Prince is the old courthouse; the next street to the right, much broader, is Gay Street, and at the far right, in the middle distance, the large white building is the First Presbyterian Church.

the northwest. Beneath the brow of this hill a large attacking force could approach within 100 yards without being exposed to view or to fire either from the fort or from the adjacent rifle pits.[15]

Longstreet returned to his headquarters and wrote to Bragg that the Union position at Knoxville was stronger than that at Chattanooga and asked that he "hurry the Virginia troops up to help me to shut up the place." [16]

The general who had been sent on a mission demanding speed, a quick assault, and a return to the main force of the army wrote as if he were intending to starve the enemy out, a process requiring more time and more troops. The slow process of starvation would succeed only if the town were completely encircled. Up to this point, Longstreet had made no move to blockade the south side of the river or to destroy the pontoon bridge across the river. Moreover, he was confused as to the course the river followed above and below the town.

His map indicated that the French Broad River joined the Tennessee below Knoxville at Lenoir City, whereas in reality the French Broad and the Holston converge four miles upstream, east of Knoxville, to form the Tennessee River, and it is the mouth of the Little Tennessee which is opposite Lenoir City.

When Longstreet called a group of Knoxvillians of Confederate sympathies to a conference on a hill near the McDonald farm and asked them how he might starve the Union army, they pointed out to him the location of the mouth of the French Broad and said he couldn't starve them out.

The French Broad, south of the Holston, was not patrolled by Confederate troops. Barges could be floated unchecked down this river to its junction with the Holston, just east of Knoxville, and unobserved at night on the Tennessee for the remaining short distance to the city.

John M. Brooks, the mayor of Knoxville in 1909, reported that his father, General Joseph Brooks, Captain James S. Boyd, Mr. Robert H. McNutt, and Dr. J. G. M. Ramsey each protested in vain after Longstreet "hooted at them and told them that they did not know what they were talking about or else were unfriendly to him and his cause, as he knew and they knew that the mouth of the French Broad was some miles below Knoxville opposite the little village of Lenoir's." [17]

Longstreet, because of caprice or ignorance, thus failed to heed the advice of those seeking to aid his cause. As a result, Captain George W. Doughty, of the Unionist 17th Tennessee Cavalry, was able to safely obtain food from the rich counties of Sevier and Jefferson. Doughty's agents and friendly partisans brought the supplies by wagon to his headquarters at Bowman's Ferry, (modern Riverdale Ferry), ten miles up the French Broad, and from there they were floated down the river under cover of darkness and fog into Knoxville.[18]

Colonel Alexander, more aggressive than his commander, made preparations for assault, not siege. He arranged all of his thirty-four guns in such positions that they could fire upon Fort Sanders and enfilade the adjacent lines. He put most of his guns on the hill on which Knoxville College now stands and a few in front of the Armstrong House. He rigged four howitzers as mortars to drop shells behind the Federal parapets. Finally, patching up an old flatboat, he made it into a ferry, drawn back and forth across the river with telegraph wire, on which he carried Captain Parker's rifle guns to the south side of the river to establish a battery on Cherokee Heights. From here he could enfilade Fort Sanders some 2,600 yards away. Law's and Robertson's brigades moved across the river to protect Parker's battery.[19]

Thus, by the night of November 20, the physical divisions of offensive and defensive lines were clearly drawn. But where was the sharp line that divided friend from foe? Both armies destroyed homes and property indiscriminately. One little Knoxville girl remembered that "all the houses facing west were used by Federal

Colonel James C. Luttrell, mayor and post-master of Knoxville

soldiers as the Confederates were coming that way." Finally, they burned the house in which she lived because it obstructed the fire of their guns. But the next day, as she was going to the spring near Dr. William Morrow's house to draw water, a Union soldier said to her, "Here, give me your bucket. I'll get your water even if you are a little Rebel." [20]

A little boy who had the run of both lines when there was no firing asked a Federal soldier, "Why don't you shoot the Rebels?" Pointing westward, the soldier replied, "Hell, them guys are our friends. They gives us our tobacco!" [21]

What were the thoughts that night of James C. Luttrell, the mayor and postmaster of Knoxville? His son, Samuel B. Luttrell, who had been a corporal in the Union army, was now his clerk. His namesake, James Churchwell Luttrell III, was a lieutenant in Wheeler's cavalry besieging the city.

In the besieged city, divided in loyalties, the ring of blue uniforms was reinforced by regiments of recently recruited Unionist Tennesseans in homespun uniforms. A Massachusetts soldier wrote: "It was a strange sight to see citizens clothed in gray or butternut, with long rifle in hand, come down and take places by our side in the trenches for the defense of their homes. We had been so long accustomed to look upon that color as hostile, its appearance in our ranks was very cheering to the men." [22]

NOTES

1. *Battles and Leaders,* III, 734-36.
2. *Ibid.*
3. Todd, p. 369.
4. Carruth, pp. 186-87. The 79th New Yorkers were of Scottish descent and nicknamed the enemy detachment for the famous Second Dragoons Scottish Regiment, the "Royal Scots Greys."
5. Burrage, p. 104.
6. "Melrose Art Center Publication," Knoxville, 1930.
7. Carruth, p. 187.
8. Todd, p. 374.
9. *Battles and Leaders,* III, 738-39.
10. Burrage, p. 105.
11. Humes, pp. 251-52.
12. *Ibid.*
13. *Battles and Leaders,* III, 742-43.
14. *Ibid.,* pp. 747-48.
15. E. Porter Alexander, *Military Memoirs of a Confederate,* p. 483.
16. O. R., Ser. I, XXXI, Part III, 739.

17. John M. Brooks, in an address recorded by the Knoxville *Journal and Tribune,* November 29, 1902; O. P. Temple, *East Tennessee and the Civil War,* pp. 505-10.
18. Samuel W. Scott and Samuel P. Angel, *History of the Thirteenth Regiment, Tennessee Volunteer Cavalry U.S.A.,* pp. 124, 128. Temple refers to the man as "James A. Daughty." A Knoxville newspaper (date deleted, Ducloux Scrapbook, p. 232) refers to the man as Captain J. A. Daughty, a resident of Knoxville who lived at 3rd and Laurel Avenue around 1900, and who at the time of the Civil War was a captain in the First Tennessee Infantry. This newspaper states that it was General Burnside who incorrectly identified the man as "Doughty." However, in a letter to H. S. Fink, January 24, 1957, Richard H. Doughty says that Temple was incorrect in his reference. Nonetheless, Doughty or

Daughty, according to the Chattanooga *Times,* October 7, 1890, brought into Knoxville by his "cracker train" some 10,000 bushels of corn, 6,000 bushels of wheat, 1,000 cattle, 1,500 hogs, and a quantity of butter and eggs. Operating first at night, the agents soon became bold enough to float supplies during the day right by the noses of the Confederate pickets. On November 30 Longstreet finally sent General W. T. Martin and two brigades of cavalry to stop the flow of supplies from Sevier County. Dr. Humes says that after this date the food scarcity was critical (Humes, p. 290).

"When the supply of forage began to run low, and there were more mules to feed than forage to feed them, heroic treatment was resorted to for the purpose of reducing the number. Scores and hundreds of poor mules were taken to the river along the south side of the city, driven into the water and shot, their carcasses floating away down the stream. These animals were so starved that it was no unusual thing to get up in the morning and find the tongues of wagons with the whiffle-trees devoured by the mules in a single night." Captain Chamberlain in the Knoxville *Journal,* May 7, 1893.

Colonel Alexander of the Confederate artillery said his men watched for the dead mules floating down the stream. The men would wade in after the carcasses, pull them ashore, and strip the animals of their precious shoes and nails. *Battles and Leaders,* III, 750.

19. *Battles and Leaders,* III, 748.

20. Mrs. A. D. Plant in *Confederate Veteran,* XXXVI (April 1928), 129.

21. As told by Colonel James O. Andes of Knoxville.

22. Carruth, p. 185.

"One of My Children Isn't Dead"

ON SATURDAY, November 21, the fifth day of the siege of Knoxville, rain poured down on both armies, and there was no significant change in the positions of the lines. Around 3:00 P.M., the First Creek dam gave way, and Federal men were immediately set to work repairing it.[1]

The garrison troops in Fort Sanders were cut to quarter-rations of black bread. No more coffee was issued except to the hospitals. The 79th Highlanders sent a man to town to buy the "Jeff Davis Substitute" for seventy-five cents a pound, but derided the mixture as a fraud of wheat and chicory.[2] A stray cow wandered into the lines of the 35th Massachusetts and was milked for four precious quarts.[3]

Longstreet communicated once more with Bragg, informing his commander that "I am close in under the enemy's works, but cannot bring him to battle, as he has the other side of the river for foraging. I think that my course is hardly strong enough to warrant my taking his works by assault." Later in the day, he implored Bragg to send him one more division.[4]

Longstreet's philosophy of attack was the same that he would have preferred at Gettysburg, that is, to move into enemy territory, select a defensive position, and entice the enemy into attacking from a disadvantageous angle. But Burnside, whose mission was defensive, had no intention of leaving his fortifications and attacking in open ground. He was well entrenched in a position similar to Longstreet's against Burnside at Fredericksburg.

Sunday, the 22nd, was clear and pleasant, and although there was less firing than usual, several Union men were hit by Rebel snipers as the guard was changed in daylight hours at Fort Sanders. The besieged regiments were ordered to police their campsites for Sunday inspection.[5]

By nightfall, General McLaws reported to Longstreet that his pickets had advanced near enough to Fort Sanders to warrant an assault, and he was ordered to attack immediately. Jenkins was ordered to support the attacking columns, and Wheeler's cavalry was instructed to demonstrate against the entire northeast lines to divert attention from the assault upon Fort Sanders. However, during the discussion preceding the issuance of orders, the officers of General McLaws' division unanimously agreed that they preferred a daylight attack. Longstreet concurred, since night attacks were seldom successful.[6]

Just before dark, a bottle with a piece of paper corked inside was seen floating down the river past Knoxville. The bottle was retrieved by Union soldiers and carried to the Officer of the Day. It contained a message from a woman living near Boyd's Ferry, on the Holston River north of Knoxville, informing General Burnside that near her house the Confederates had commenced constructing a raft.[7] She had heard that they hoped to float the raft downstream and smash it into the pontoon bridge, cutting Union communications with the forts south of the river.

To thwart the Rebel plan, Captain Poe gathered all of the iron bars he could find and by 9:00 A.M. next day had constructed across the river a continuous iron cable boom about 1,000 feet long, supported by wooden floats. Two days later a boom of logs, fastened end to end with

North Knoxville from the University. The cluster of tents at left, on the bank above Second Creek, is the camp of the Engineer Batteries. The spire of old Second Presbyterian Church, where General Sanders was buried, appears prominently at center; just to the right of it on the horizon is Fort Huntington Smith on Temperance Hill. On the far right, Main Avenue can be seen climbing toward downtown Knoxville.

chains, was stretched across the river farther upstream.[8]

On the 23rd, Longstreet received word from Bragg that a large force was advancing from Kingston against the Confederates at Knoxville. Longstreet immediately withdrew most of Wheeler's cavalry from the line and sent them toward Kingston to block the progress of the unknown force pressing from the rear.[9]

Bragg, sensing an attack upon his own position at Missionary Ridge, decided to recall Longstreet from Knoxville. He dispatched Brigadier General Danville Leadbetter, his chief engineering officer, to Longstreet to personally urge either an immediate Confederate assault or a hasty withdrawal.[10]

The night of the 23rd the Union picket lines between First and Second creeks were driven in,

Braggs' engineering chief Brigadier General Danville Leadbetter, who selected Fort Sanders as the assailable point in the Union lines

crackled with an unearthly sound, casting a broad belt of dazzling light over the fields and into the forests. In the roundhouse of the railroad, there was stored a large amount of condemned ammunition, and when the flames reached that, there was an explosion that shook the earth, and startled the anxious residents of the city." [11]

As the flames crackled through the night, Longstreet read a message from Bragg that should have caused him to abandon the siege immediately and return to Chattanooga. The Union army had moved out of Chattanooga and attacked Bragg. Grant and Sherman were on the move.

Tuesday, November 24, it rained again most of the day, and there was very little picket firing. The Second Michigan attempted to regain an advance parallel Confederate line in front of Fort Sanders. Sixty-seven of the Michigan men fell in the futile assault, including Major Cornelius Byington, the commander, who was left on the field mortally wounded. [12] A flag of truce carried out by the Federals seeking to collect their dead was fired upon by the Confederates.

and it appeared that a general engagement would result. Burnside ordered his troops to set fire to the long line of buildings north of the railroad between the two armies. They burned homes, the railroad machine shops, and the former Confederate arsenal, lest they become shelters for Rebel sharpshooters. The flames lighted up the wintry sky, and the whole town was illuminated by the blazing buildings "which roared and

Fort Huntington Smith from the east. Rutledge Pike crosses the shoulder of Temperance Hill between the fort and the Tennessee River, which is at far left. Knoxville itself is hidden behind the hill.

Inside the fort, a former deserter from the 79th Highlanders, who had recently been returned, tried, and sentenced to execution, but was placed back on duty because of the shortage of troops, was sitting in his tent calmly smoking a pipe. A stray Minié ball fired from a distant trench struck him in the back of the neck, and he fell forward, apparently dead. Suddenly he got up, blew smoke out of his mouth, spit the Minié ball into his hand, and sat down to await the arrival of the litter which would bear him to the hospital. His commanding officer, realizing that the man was now granted a reprieve from his sentence of death, declared, "That's what you might call shooting a man to save his life!" [13]

Most of the day, the Confederates were occupied in establishing their rifle guns on Cherokee Heights south of the river, from which they could enfilade the western side of Fort Sanders. The attack was ordered to commence at sunrise of the 25th. The mortars would open the barrage to get the range, and then the direct-fire guns would bombard the front of the fort. Rebel sharpshooters were to capture the outlying Union rifle pits, enabling the assaulting force to gather behind the steep slope 100 yards from the northwest bastion, the salient to be attacked. [14]

Before the orders could be issued to the subordinate officers, Longstreet learned that the brigades of Generals Bushrod Johnson and

*Union soldiers encamped on the grounds of the Deaf
and Dumb Asylum (now City Hall)*

Knoxville from Fort Stanley. Around east Knoxville were the defenses of Fort Huntington Smith, Battery Clifton Lee, Battery Stearman, and Fort Hill. At left, on the opposite bank of the river, are the buildings of the Knoxville Pork Works. The military bridge seen in the photograph on pages 110-111 crosses the Tennessee River at far left.

Archibald Gracie, about 2,600 men, were on their way to reinforce him and would arrive the night of the 25th from Loudon. The attack was postponed once again.[15]

Wednesday, November 25, was clear and pleasant again, and the troops of both armies washed their clothes, cleaned their weapons, and in general seemed inclined not to molest one another. An order was issued to the troops in Fort Sanders forbidding the use of matches to light pipes, because the Confederate pickets were attracted by such inviting targets. Union and Confederate bands played throughout the day.[16]

General Leadbetter arrived at Longstreet's headquarters after dark with orders from Bragg to attack and crush Burnside quickly. Longstreet suggested that, with 2,600 reinforcements expected that very evening and more in the next few days, the town could be so completely invested that the Union troops could be starved into surrender without the needless expense of Confederate lives in an assault that, after all, might not be successful. He added that if an assault must be made it should be directed against the northwest bastion of Fort Sanders.

Leadbetter, the oldest military engineer in the Confederate service, an 1836 graduate of West Point and Bragg's chief engineer, had been at Knoxville during the Confederate occupation and was listened to with respect by Longstreet's staff. Leadbetter agreed that Fort Sanders, which he himself had originally laid out as Fort Loudon, was the most opportune target for assault, but requested that the final decision be delayed until he could make a thorough reconnaissance.[17]

Thursday, November 26, was fair. General Leadbetter, accompanied by Longstreet, Jenkins, and Alexander, scouted the entire Federal line. Leadbetter decided that it would be better to direct the attack against the troops at Mabry's Hill. Alexander then spent all night moving his guns from Cherokee Heights to points opposite Mabry's.[18]

The 26th was Thanksgiving Day for the

Forts Stanley and Dickerson. Here the viewer looks from the roof of the University past Union caissons, lower left, rifle pits in the foreground, and the mouth of Second Creek, at right, toward Fort Stanley, left, and Fort Dickerson.

Union soldiers. Burnside issued General Field Order Number 32, in which he expressed the hope that the day would be observed by all, as far as military operations would allow. His soldiers got a full ration of bullets but only a half-ration of bread.[19]

Burnside had more to be thankful for than he realized. In the Battle of Chattanooga on the preceding day, General Grant's besieged army had broken out of its trap and driven Braxton Bragg from Missionary Ridge. The Confederate army was in full retreat toward Dalton, Georgia. Since neither Longstreet nor Burnside had complete communications with his superior in Chattanooga, neither officially knew that the battle had been fought.[20]

Grant hardly had time to report the full particulars of his success to Washington before President Lincoln sent his congratulations by wire, adding "Remember Burnside." [21]

Grant was far ahead of his superiors in remembering Burnside at Knoxville. Even before he began the Battle of Chattanooga, he had made preparations for the corps of General Gordon Granger to move up to the south bank of the Tennessee River, accompanied by a steamboat loaded with rations and ammunition.

After the battle, Grant sent General William Sherman and the Army of the Tennessee on a forced march toward Maryville and Knoxville. In his instructions to Sherman, Grant stated that he had lost all faith in Granger's "energy or capability to manage an expedition of the importance of this one" and reminded Sherman that the "last advices from Burnside himself indicated his ability to hold out with rations only to about the 3rd of December." [22]

On the morning of the 27th, Generals Leadbetter and Longstreet made another reconnaissance of the Federal lines. This time they concluded that an attack upon Mabry's Hill was impossible, because the hill was strongly fortified, the approaches were inundated, and there was no cover within a mile for the formation and advance of an assaulting column. Leadbetter admitted that the best policy would be to wait and starve the Union army, but since he was under orders to force an attack, he had to advise Longstreet to proceed. [23]

On the way back from observing Mabry's Hill, the reconnoitering party stopped about four hundred yards from Fort Sanders and, while observing it with glasses, saw a man cross the ditch in front of the northwest salient. They took this to mean that the ditch was not more than five feet deep and would prove no obstacle. Apparently, it did not occur to them that the man might be walking across a plank bridging a ditch much deeper than their estimate. [24]

In the afternoon, Colonel H. L. Giltner arrived with five battalions of cavalry from Virginia, and the six battalions of Brigadier General William E. Jones were only a day's march away.

Along the Federal lines, November 27 was quiet until evening, when cheers and strains of music were heard coming from the Rebel camps. Was it possible, they wondered, that Grant had been defeated? Or had the Confederates received reinforcements?

While on picket duty, the men of the 36th Massachusetts could hear the Rebels "chopping on the knob that they had so recently occupied on the opposite bank of the river. They were clearing away the trees in front of the earthwork which they had constructed the day before. Would they attack at daybreak? So we thought, connecting the fact with the cheers and music of the earlier part of the night." [25]

In Washington, also, there were fears of an attack of disastrous consequences. Lincoln's private secretary rushed to the White House with the news that Burnside had been calling for help lest he be forced to surrender. The secretary was astonished and taken aback when Lincoln replied that he was "glad of it."

Said Lincoln: "Why, you see, it reminds me of Mrs. Sallie Ward, a neighbor of mine in Illinois, who had a very large family. Occasionally, one of her numerous progeny would be heard crying in some out-of-the-way place, upon which Mrs. Sallie would exclaim, 'There's one of my children that isn't dead yet.' " [26]

NOTES

1. Carruth, p. 187.
2. Todd, p. 373.
3. Carruth, p. 187.
4. O. R., Ser. I, XXXI, Part III, 739.
5. Carruth, p. 187.
6. O. R., Ser. I, XXXI, Part I, 484.
7. *Battles and Leaders*, III, 739.
8. *Ibid*. A portion of this iron cable boom and one anchor fashioned from railroad rail were dredged from the Tennessee

River near the mouth of First Creek in December, 1962. These ninety-nine-year-old relics were presented to the United Daughters of the Confederacy, Chapter 89, and are in the Confederate Memorial Hall yard.

9. O. R., Ser. I, XXXI, Part III, 733-34.

10. *Ibid.*, p. 736.

11. Osborne, p. 267.

12. Major Byington's leg was amputated by Confederate surgeons. Two days later he was returned to the Union lines, but died from sepsis.

13. Todd, pp. 377-78.

14. *Battles and Leaders,* III, 748.

15. *Ibid.*

16. Todd, p. 739; Carruth, p. 187.

17. *Battles and Leaders,* III, 748.

18. *Ibid.*

19. O.R., Ser. I, XXXI, Part III, 248.

20. *Ibid.,* p. 310.

21. *Battles and Leaders,* III, 704.

22. Sherman, I, 336.

23. *Battles and Leaders,* III, 748.

24. Burrage, p. 116.

25. *Ibid.,* pp. 109-10.

26. Poore, p. 223.

24

Rush To It Without Hallooing

ON SATURDAY, November 28, the siege of Knoxville went into its twelfth day, and it might have lasted many days longer except that General Leadbetter delivered General Bragg's order to attack immediately. On the other hand, this high-ranking message bearer had delayed the assault himself by his faulty reconnaissance.

Now, Longstreet ordered General McLaws to strike at Fort Sanders as soon as it became visible in the morning sun of the 28th, but there was no sunlight that day. It was extremely cold and foggy. Once more Longstreet cancelled the attack order, since his artillery could not see the fort to find the range.

As the siege dragged on, opposing pickets in the front lines sometimes made truces while they came together and exchanged coffee, tobacco, and "war stories." Usually such comradeship occurred at night, when the officers were sleeping; besides, at daylight the sight of a head or rifle on one side was an invitation to a sniper's bullet from the other.

Inside the fort, to relieve the monotony of the constant daylight vigil, the Union men would hold their hats up on the ends of their guns to test the accuracy of the Confederate sharpshooters. Sergeant Campbell, of the 79th Highlanders, had been playing this old game for several days. One evening, just as he began waving his hat, he cried out, "Damn it, I'm hit!" A wise sniper had aimed two feet below the cap, and that ended the "hat game." [1]

By the 28th, the Confederate pickets had advanced close enough to Fort Sanders to shout at the men inside and exchange jibes.

"How are you, Vicksburg," the Rebels taunted the besieged men.

"You hain't got us yet," came the defiant answer. "A bird in the hand is worth two in the bush." Fortunately for the defenders, they had more protection than a bush. [2]

Although faulty in plan, Fort Sanders was well constructed in detail. A slightly lopsided quadrilateral, it stood on the crest of an east-west ridge. Its western side was about 95 yards long, following approximately the course of modern 17th Street between Clinch and Laurel avenues, as previously noted. The northern and southern sides, approximating the courses respectively of Laurel and Clinch avenues eastward from 17th, were each 125 yards long. The east end, or rear, of the fort, near 16th Street, was about 85 yards across. [3]

On the sides of the fort facing the Confederates—the northern, the western and part of the southern—the embanked earthen walls were thirteen feet high and were surrounded by a ditch averaging twelve feet in width and six to eight feet in depth—but at some points eleven feet deep. The parapet atop the walls was raised in places with cotton bales to protect the riflemen. There was a sheer slope down the embankment, at an angle of 45 degrees and a distance of about thirteen feet, from the outer base of the parapet to the top of the ditch. The scarps, or excavated slopes, between the bottom of the ditch and the parapet proper were cut nearly vertical, at depths of six to eight feet. Captain Poe had eliminated a possible toe hold for an assaulting party by removing the "berme," a one-foot-wide ledge around the outside base of

The point of attack. The northwest bastion and ditch of Fort Sanders are viewed from the north. The fort was located between 17th and 16th streets and Laurel and Clinch avenues.

the fort between the edge of the ditch and the parapet.[4]

The western side of the fort, facing Longstreet's greatest concentration of troops, was more fully completed than the other sides. Bastions, or V-shaped salients, projected outward diagonally from the northwest and southwest corners of the fort. Through embrasures in the walls of these two bastions protruded the muzzles of twelve-pound Napoleons, which could set up a deadly cross fire into the ditch in front of the west wall. Sandbags and barrels were arranged to cover the embrasures. The banquette tread, or rifleman's ramp, behind the parapet on top of the west wall would hold forty men who could fire in the direction of the ditch.

Three embrasures were cut in the north wall of the fort for twelve-pound Napoleons. The distant Batteries Zoellner and Noble could each fire effectively into the ditch surrounding Fort Sanders.[5]

From the northeast corner of the fort, on a line with the northern wall, infantry entrenchments extended eastward to Battery Zoellner and beyond. From a point about midway along the southern side of the fort, the main western infantry entrenchments ran southward past Battery Noble to the Tennessee River. The secondary western defense line ran southeast from the rear of the fort past Fort Byington to the river near Second Creek. The east end of the fort was left open, providing access to the three lines of entrenchment.

Rifle pits were constructed thirty and eighty yards in front of the fort. Between these pits and the fort was an entanglement feature left there by the Confederate engineer Leadbetter, who had laid out the fort when his side occupied Knoxville. Leadbetter had had trees felled in front of the walls, leaving stumps five inches in diameter and eighteen inches high. The Federals were now using these stumps to their own end. Mr. Hoxie, superintendent of the East Tennessee and Virginia Railroad at Knoxville, volunteered several miles of rusted telegraph wire

Close-up of defense ditch on the perimeter of Fort Sanders, with the University in the background

which Poe strung from stump to stump in front of the northwest bastion. An abatis was also placed there. [6]

The most novel, perhaps unique, feature of the external barriers was peculiarly deceptive. The whole open space in front of the western wall was plowed with furrows which converged to a point in the ditch in the direct line of fire from the cannons in the fort. The furrows were wide and well defined. Since it is natural for veteran troops, when passing over open ground, to avoid ridges and to follow smooth places and hollows, the Union engineers hoped that the converging furrows would funnel the instinct-driven Confederates to the point of maximum Union fire power.[7]

The intensive efforts to strengthen the defense of the fort against an attack from the northwest stemmed from weaknesses of the fort in that direction which were known to both the Federals and the Confederates.

The defilade or steep drop-off of the ridge north of the fort provided protection from the guns of the fort for as many as 4,000 troops scarcely more than one hundred yards from the northwest bastion.

No massed infantry fire could be directed against an assaulting force coming from the northwest. To fire against such a force, defending troops to the east of the fort would have to fire a considerable distance almost down the line of their own entrenchment. Infantrymen in the entrenchments south of the fort could not fire toward the approach to the northwest bastion, because of the intervening southwest bastion and the crest of the ridge on the west side of the fort. Defensive riflemen behind the parapet on the walls would be hampered by Confederate sharpshooters.

Because no embrasure could be built in the northwest bastion from which a gun could fire to the northwest, there was a blind sector facing straight ahead. Narrow along its northwest axis, the bastion would allow only one gun at a time to fire in that direction, and that one

Lieutenant Colonel George Hawkes, commander of the 21st Massachusetts Regiment

must fire over the parapet, "en barbette," where the gunners would be exposed to infantry fire.

Finally, the northwest bastion was oriented with its narrow northwest axis, its weakest direction of fire, pointing toward the drop-off of terrain about one hundred yards away, giving the Confederates an almost unopposed avenue for an assault from the northwest.[8]

First Lieutenant Samuel N. Benjamin, of the Second United States Regular Artillery, was in command of Fort Sanders and the 105 artillerymen who manned the twelve cannons. His guns and troops were supported by 335 riflemen from the 79th New York Highlander Regiment, the 29th Massachusetts, and the 2nd and 20th Michigan infantries.[9]

Forty men from the Second Michigan under Captain Charles Hodskin occupied a banquette behind the counterscarp or outside slope of the ditch in front of the west wall. If their position became untenable, they were to pick up the planks over which the Federal pickets crossed the ditch, run through the ditch southward, and enter the fort at the eastern front.[10]

Lieutenant Benjamin had certain misgivings concerning his ability to utilize either his maximum firepower or the support of his infantry troops. His riflemen were of questionable value, since for the past few days any time that a Yankee gun or head protruded from the fort, a hail of lead forced it down quickly; Rebel sharpshooters had an easy time with silhouetted targets.

If an attacking force brought scaling ladders and crossed the ditch and the parapet, the battle for the fort would end quickly. Benjamin's small garrison would be no match for Longstreet's overwhelming numbers — veterans of Lee's campaigns—who could then sweep straight through to the heart of town, the Union defenses being primarily constructed to stop an initial assault. But if the defenders could stop the attackers in the ditch, the assault might be halted in time for reinforcements to reach the fort from other points in Knoxville.

Benjamin realized that his cannons were capable of firing only two solid shot or three canister rounds per minute under ideal field conditions. The gun barrels had to be swabbed out after each firing with a wet sponge, or otherwise lingering sparks might set off the new charge as the gunmen rammed it home. Since an attacking force could assemble so close that with one quick rush it could be in the ditch within fifteen to twenty seconds, Benjamin also realized that his cannons would each be capable of firing only one effective round. After that, as the gunners attempted to swab the barrel, they would be picked off by riflemen in the ditch.

Recalling some of the clever strategy employed by the Confederates whom he had helped besiege in Vicksburg, Lieutenant Benjamin gathered about fifty of his spherical shells which were to be ignited by time fuses. Wooden and paper fuses were used interchangeably. They were notched to indicate time intervals in seconds and could be cut to the desired length with a knife. The metal or Borman fuse consisted of an outer surface of lead with notches around the periphery ranging from one to five seconds. These could also be cut with a knife and, when fired from a cannon, were ignited by the flame of the powder which expelled the projectile.[11]

From the Vicksburg defenders, Benjamin had learned that the fuses could also be lit by a torch and the shells hurled as hand grenades. On the night of November 28, he carefully cut the fuses of fifty shells to the three-second interval and laid them out on the banquette tread for instant use. By using these shells as grenades, he hoped to stop the assault in the ditch, but his men were apprehensive of their presence, wishing "the damned things were somewhere else." [12]

The Union commanders were quite certain that the Confederate assault would be aimed at the northwest sector of Fort Sanders, because it was obviously the weakest point in the entire defense perimeter in spite of the artillery firepower it possessed. Nevertheless, they conceived a unique plan to warn all sections of the defense of the point where the attack would begin. In addition to telegraphic communication between General Burnside's headquarters and all of the main earthen forts, Roman candles were issued to each of the artillery batteries and would be fired into the air to indicate the direction of the assault.[13]

On Cherokee Heights, across the river from Fort Sanders, Sergeant J. P. Polley of the Confederate Texas brigade gazed down upon the campfires of his comrades and of the enemy. Later, when time would permit, he would write to his fiancée.

Charming Nellie,
So much has happened since my last letter from

Colonel James P. Simms. Commanding the 53rd Georgia of Bryan's Brigade, he was wounded in the assault on Fort Sanders.

Cleveland. . . . Since encountering the Western men who fight under the Star-Spangled banner, Longstreet's Corps has somewhat modified its estimate of what Bragg "might have done in the way of whipping them." The Yankees who fled before us at Chickamauga had as little grit and staying power apparently as any we were in the habit of meeting in Virginia, but Burnside had troops at Knoxville that not only stood well, but shot well. The hardest and most stubbornly contested skirmish fighting I ever witnessed took place there, and our lines needed to be frequently reinforced. . . . On the evening of November 28th Company F was detailed for picket duty. Three inches of snow lay on the ground and an icy wind, from whose severity we could find little protection, chilled us to the marrow. I went on duty about 9:00 P.M., my post being at the edge of a high bluff overlooking Knoxville and the valley opposite me, and one-half mile away I could see lights moving back and forth in the enemy's fort on College Hill.

I was growing numb and sleepy with the intense cold, when the flash and report of a rifle, followed by a scattering and then a continuous roar of small arms, awoke and informed me that an attempt was being made by the Confederates to capture the fort. . . .[14]

Sergeant Polley had witnessed an attack by the Rebel picket line on both sides of Fort Sanders. After some two hours of sharp fighting, fifty Union prisoners were taken, the Union picket trenches were occupied, and no Union sentries remained farther than twenty yards from the fort. Colonel Alexander was furious because Longstreet and McLaws had changed the plan of attack that he had devised and they had earlier accepted. Alexander regretfully admitted later that he "was then too young and modest to say a word of objection." [15]

Alexander's original plan called for the assault to begin with a massive artillery bombardment upon the fort by all of the thirty-four guns and mortars. A large number of sharpshooters would capture the Union rifle pits within 120 yards of the fort, completely enveloping the north and west fronts of the fort and keeping down the fire from the embrasures or parapets. Then would come the storming of the northwest bastion by two brigades of 4,000 men with fixed bayonets, accompanied by pioneer troops with spades and axes to cut steps in the steep slope of the embankment. The attack would occur in daylight and would proceed suddenly and

Colonel William L. Brandon, commander of the 21st Mississippi. His unit, as part of Humphreys' Brigade, was assigned to the storming of Fort Sanders.

continuously so that there would be an element of surprise.

About 9:00 P.M. of the 28th, Longstreet had changed Alexander's plan after consultation with Leadbetter and McLaws. The attack was ordered to begin in the darkness just before sunrise, preceded by only a few rounds of artillery fire to encourage the infantry, and the assault would be made by the infantry alone. The sharpshooters were ordered to advance their lines during the evening to be in a position to hold down the return fire from the fort during the dawn assault. But as the Rebel sharpshooters advanced into position about eleven o'clock that evening, Burnside's entire command was alerted to the point of attack.[16]

From within Fort Sanders, a few Roman candles were fired into the air. Sergeant J. H. Granberry of Waverly Hill, Georgia, a member of the 20th Georgia Infantry, was lying in a ditch about two hundred yards to the west of the fort. As the sharpshooters advanced beyond his position, he noticed something that disturbed him considerably. He recalled that "there was a peculiarity about the shells fired from the fort that night such as I never observed

Rushed to aid the Rebels. Bushrod Johnson's Brigade, including Colonel Young M. Moody (above) and his 43rd Alabama, was rushed to Knoxville to reinforce the Confederate attack.

elsewhere; there were three separate and distinct explosions from each shell. They exploded like skyrockets!"[17]

In his comfortable headquarters in the downstairs rooms of the Robert Armstrong House on Kingston Pike, General Longstreet reviewed the assault plans in their final form with Generals Leadbetter, McLaws, and Jenkins. The assault was to be made upon the fort after a token artillery fire, as soon as the weather cleared the view. The assaulting thrust was to be made by three McLaws' brigades, those of Wofford, Humphreys, and Bryan. His fourth brigade under Kershaw was to advance on the right and carry the trenches in its front as soon as the fort was taken.

Three brigades of Hood's Division, commanded by Jenkins, were to follow in echelon on the left of McLaws' column at 200 yards distance. G. T. Anderson would follow McLaws on the left and assault the entrenchments in

Brigadier General Archibald Gracie of Alabama, brigade commander under Bushrod Johnson

Teen-age officer. This portrait of Lieutenant Henry H. Cook, Company F, 44th Tennessee Regiment in Johnson's Brigade, was made in 1861 when he was seventeen years old.

his front. But in case of delay in McLaws' assault, Anderson was to wheel to the right and take the fort through its eastern end, which was open. Bushrod Johnson was to follow Mc-Laws with Buckner's Division and also with Archibald Gracie's brigade, which had recently arrived from Chickamauga.

General McLaws passed along specific instrucstructions to his subordinates as to the nature of their assignments.

First. Wofford's Georgia and Humphreys' Mississippi brigades to make the assault, the first on the left, the second on the right, this latter followed closely by three regiments of Bryan's brigade; the Sixteenth Georgia Regiment to lead the first and the Thirteenth Mississippi the second assaulting column.
Second. The brigades to be formed for the attack in columns of regiments.
Third. The assault to be made with fixed bayonets, and without firing a gun.
Fourth. Should be made against the northwest angle of Fort Loudon or Sanders.
Fifth. The men should be urged to the work with a determination to succeed, and should rush to it without hallooing.
Sixth. The sharpshooters to keep up a continuous fire into the embrasures of the enemy's works and along the fort, so as to prevent the use of the cannon, and district, if not prevent, the fire of all arms.[18]

The third section of the order, calling for a strict bayonet charge without gunfire, was given for a good reason. If all went well, the men would be assembled under cover about one hundred yards from the fort. With one quick rush, the fort would be reached before small arms fire would be necessary.

The experienced Civil War infantryman could fire three rounds per minute at most. In the excitement of battle, no more than 25 per cent of the troops fired a muzzle-loading rifle correctly, many failing to remove the ramrod, some inserting five or six charges of powder or bullets into the chamber. Eleven separate steps were required to fire the rifle from the time the soldier tore open the powder charge with his teeth and emptied the powder into the barrel until the gun was aimed and fired. A man on the run usually missed his target completely.[19]

The Confederate officers ordered their men to charge without firing a shot so that the moment they crossed the ditch and entered the fort, each rifle would be ready for one quick, well-aimed shot at the defending soldiers. After the initial volley, the assault could degenerate into hand-to-hand combat, with the biting, clubbing, kicking, knifing, and even rock-throwing which characterized the climax of Civil War assaults, in which the Confederates would have an overwhelming ten-to-one superiority.

The attacking force was ordered to rush without "hallooing," as the commanders hoped they would be making a surprise attack. However, it was foolish of the officers to presume that the men could withstand the temptation to burst forth with the "Rebel Yell" which was second nature to them by now—their high-pitched, canine yelps adopted from the Texas Rangers. Also, some of the Confederate officers had told the attacking force that the fort was manned, not by veteran soldiers, but by newly-recruited Unionist East Tennessee troops.[20] And from their experiences at Bull Run, the men of Longstreet's Corps knew that nothing frightened a Union greenhorn in battle more than the shrill Rebel Yell.

General McLaws' order specifically mentioned that the men "should be urged to the work with a determination to succeed." But there were clear indications that McLaws himself and General Jenkins had serious doubts of the wisdom of their assignments. Possibly to protect his own military reputation, McLaws set forth his objections in writing to Longstreet, to become a part of the official records, even though the two generals were quartered in the same household.

HEADQUARTERS DIVISION,
November 28, 1863
GENERAL,
It seems to be a conceded fact that there has been a serious engagement between General Bragg's forces and those of the enemy, with what

result is not known so far as I have heard. General Bragg may have maintained his position, may have repulsed the enemy, or may have been driven back. If the enemy has been beaten at Chattanooga, do we not gain by delay at this point? If we have been defeated at Chattanooga, do we not risk our entire force by an assault here? If we have been defeated at Chattanooga, our communications must be made with Virginia. We cannot combine again with General Bragg, even if we should be successful in our assault on Knoxville. If we should be defeated or unsuccessful here, and at the same time General Bragg should have been forced to retire, would we be in condition to force our way to the army in Virginia? I present these considerations, and with the force they have in my mind I beg leave to say that I think we had better delay the assault until we hear the result from Chattanooga. The enemy may have cut out communication to prevent this army reinforcing General Bragg, as well as for the opposite reason—viz., to prevent General Bragg from reinforcing us, and the attack at Chattanooga favors the first proposition.

Very respectfully,
L. McLAWS
Major-General.[21]

After conferring with General Archibald Gracie, who had been in Knoxville earlier in the year with General Buckner, General Jenkins learned that the ditch in front of the fort was deeper than Longstreet had thought and that the assaulting party would need either to place scaling ladders against the embankments or to fill the ditch with fascines (bundles of sticks) to walk across. He mentioned this to McLaws, but with a sweep of his hand, the latter showed Jenkins that there was not a tree in sight with which to make ladders or fascines. Alarmed, Jenkins then sent Longstreet a letter indicating his fear of the ditch and its great depth.

But General Longstreet, who up to this moment had found many excuses for delaying the assault, suddenly became firm and fixed in his determination to attack the following dawn. He immediately replied to Jenkins: "General, Your letter is received. The work of the enemy is not enclosed. The ditch is probably at some points no more than three feet deep, and five

or six feet wide. At least, we so judged it yesterday in looking at a man walk down the parapet and over the ditch. I thought that you saw the man, as you had been with us. I have no apprehension of the result of the attack, if we go at it with a determination to accomplish it. . . ." [22]

Longstreet also promptly replied to McLaws: "I am not at all confident that General Bragg has had a serious battle at Chattanooga. . . . It is a great mistake to suppose that there is any safety for us in going to Virginia, if General Bragg has been defeated, for we leave him at the mercy of his victors; and with his army destroyed, our own had better be also, for we must not only be destroyed, but disgraced. There is neither safety nor honor in any other course than the one I have already chosen and ordered. . . ." [23]

There were to be no more delays. Longstreet had listened to all manner of advice. The decision to attack Fort Sanders at dawn was clearly his own. His mind was now at ease.

The night was wretched with freezing temperature and falling mist. The attacking troops lay upon their arms without fires and suffered greatly. At about 3:30 A.M., the regiments assembled in assault formations. The atmosphere was still damp and penetratingly cold. The men were thinly clad and numbers of them were barefoot; their suffering was incalculable as they stood clasping with numbed hands the cold barrels of their muskets. But despite the cold, hunger, nakedness, and approaching peril, the brave soldiers were full of spirit, and a stout heart beat hopefully beneath each ragged gray jacket. General Gracie, riding through his brigade on the day before, had pointed significantly toward Knoxville and remarked, "There are shoes over there, boys," and visions of comfortable brogans were floating through the minds of those barefoot Confederates.[24]

There was little noise save the low hum of subdued voices, the rumble of moving artillery,

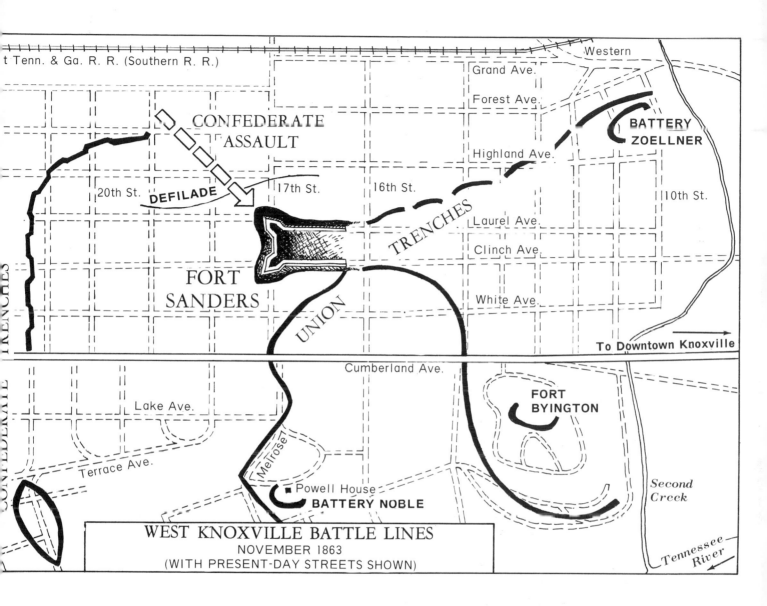

t Tenn. & Ga. R. R. (Southern R. R.)

CONFEDERATE ASSAULT

DEFILADE

20th St. 17th St. 16th St.

Grand Ave.

Forest Ave.

Highland Ave.

Western

BATTERY ZOELLNER

TRENCHES

10th St.

FORT SANDERS

UNION

TRENCHES

Laurel Ave.

Clinch Ave.

White Ave.

To Downtown Knoxville

CONFEDERATE TRENCHES

Cumberland Ave.

Lake Ave.

Melrose

Terrace Ave.

Powell House
BATTERY NOBLE

FORT BYINGTON

Second Creek

Tennessee River

WEST KNOXVILLE BATTLE LINES
NOVEMBER 1863
(WITH PRESENT-DAY STREETS SHOWN)

the steady tramp of different bodies of troops advancing to their allotted positions. The night was dark. But the Federals, anticipating the movement, filled the heavens with streams of artificial light, which threw shadows of the columns far to the rear and was reflected by many an unsheathed sword and burnished barrel.

J. B. Boothe, of the 21st Mississippi, would for the rest of his life remember the bitter cold and the frozen ground. "At the dawn of the day," he said, "the lines already had been formed, and they were almost as silent as a funeral procession. Nothing could be heard except the suppressed commands of 'Attention, battalion! Order arms! Fix bayonets!' Then there was the rattle of steel against steel as the bayonets were adjusted, and then again the modulated command of 'Shoulder arms! Forward: Guide Center! March!' " [25]

NOTES

1. Todd, p. 381.

2. *Ibid.*, pp. 381-82.

3. *Battles and Leaders,* III, 736, 742.

4. *Ibid.*, p. 749.

5. *Ibid.*, p. 742.

6. Burrage, pp. 105-108; *Battles and Leaders,* III, 741. William Hamilton, *op. cit.*, p. 65, says that this was the first time that wire had been used to stop an infantry assault on the American continent.

7. Osborne, p. 267.

8. *Battles and Leaders,* III, 747-48. It has often been written that the northwest bastion was the strong point of the fort. However, Alexander in this book states that the large declivity in front of the fort, to which the salient angle of the bastion had been injudiciously turned by the original Confederate engineers, was an outstanding weakness known to both armies. Poe, the Union engineer, said, "Its existence caused us great anxiety." The capital of the bastion had a completely blind sector of fire, the only such fault in the entire Union line at Knoxville. While on a visit to Knoxville after the war, Poe said that if he had been a deserter from the Union army, he would have told Longstreet to attack the northwest bastion, using ladders, as at no other point would an assault likely succeed. Ducloux Scrapbook.

9. *Battles and Leaders,* III, 742.

10. *Ibid.*, 743.

11. Bell Irwin Wiley and Hirst D. Milhollen, *They Who Fought Here,* p. 135.

12. Todd, p. 383; Carruth, p. 192.

13. Miller, VIII, 332-36.

14. *Confederate Veteran,* V (April 1897), 153. Polley wrote that during the entire campaign he had played "hide and seek with the enemy" while barefooted.

15. E. P. Alexander in a letter to Will H. Brearley, October 18, 1870. Colonel Alexander was by choice an artilleryman. He and General Hunt of the Union army were considered "the master gunners" of the Civil War. Beyond this, Alexander was a man of extremely varied and gifted talents. He helped develop a method of signal communication before the war and used this system to relay information which helped turn the tide of the Battle of Manassas. His system was not substantially changed until the advent of the "walkie-talkie" in World War II. Alexander was used by his superiors for reconnaissance and for staff officer duties. Jackson wanted him for an infantry general. J. E. Johnston wanted him to command the artillery of the Western Army. He was made brigadier general in February, 1864. After the war he was a very successful businessman in the field of transportation. President Cleveland named him as commissioner to adjust a border dispute between Costa Rica and Nicaragua. See Miller, VIII, 308-20; E. P. Alexander, *Military Memoirs of a Confederate,* ed. by T. Harry Williams (Bloomington, Indiana: 1962).

16. The exposed salient of the fort was so obviously an inviting target that the Federals were still alert to the possibility that Longstreet would try a surprise attack at another sector of the line.

17. *Confederate Veteran,* XVIII (January 1910), 24; XXXI (October 1923), 372.

18. O. R., Ser. I, XXXI, Part I, 460-61; *Ibid.*, pp. 86-87.

19. For a full description of the steps necessary to fire the Civil War rifle, consult Francis A. Lord, *They Fought For the Union,* pp. 154-55.

20. Todd, p. 399.

21. O. R., Ser. I, XXXI, Part I, 491.

22. Burrage, p. 116.

23. O. R., Ser. I, XXXI, Part I, 494.

24. Shaver, *History of the Sixtieth Alabama Regiment,* pp. 24-27.

25. *Confederate Veteran,* XXII (June 1914), 266.

Twenty Minutes at Fort Sanders

DURING the cold night of November 28, the Union soldiers in Fort Sanders ate and slept fully armed, crouched behind the parapets in six inches of mud. One man in four was detailed to stay awake, to keep things quiet, and to observe any signs of a dawn attack. Forty men were assigned to duty in the counterscarp of the ditch in front of the northwest bastion, where an attack was expected. The 29th Massachusetts Regiment, which had been driven from its outpost picket lines at eleven in the evening, was on special duty in the rear of the fort, with Major Chipman commanding.[1] The ammunition boxes were opened, spare rifles loaded, cannon double and triple shotted with canister, and the fuses double shorted.[2]

Just before dawn on Sunday, November 29, the Confederate troops moved forward at the command "Guide Center! March!" In the darkness the leading echelon became confused and halted some 200 yards back of the intended attack line. Bushrod Johnson's brigades had formed about 1,000 yards back, almost too far for close support.[3]

At six o'clock a low signal lantern swinging indicated to Colonel Alexander that the brigades

Brigadier General William T. Wofford of Georgia. His brigade led one assaulting column against Fort Sanders.

Losses heavy at Fort Sanders. Brigadier General Benjamin Humphreys' Mississippi brigade lost heavily in the initial assault on the fort.

were in battle formation. Instantly, a signal gun was fired from near the Armstrong House, followed in quick succession by flashes from Parker's Battery on Cherokee Heights south of the river and from the battery on the ridge north of the East Tennessee and Georgia Railroad. There followed a terrific rattle of musketry as the sharpshooters opened fire on the parapet. For a few minutes a dozen cannon poured a hot stream of fire into the fort and the supporting entrenchments, the shells lighting up the dark skies like meteors. There was no response from the fort.[4]

Now Alexander was infuriated because Longstreet had not let him train all thirty-four of his guns on the fort, as even in the dim light he could see at least twenty shells find their mark. He aimed several guns at the Powell House in the rear of Battery Noble, striking the tower. Federal Captain Roemer, of the 34th New York, immed-iately responded to this challenge by firing his guns from College Hill toward the Confederate cannon.[5]

The Confederate storming column remained crouched in position in the defilade northwest of the fort. Realizing that they were too far back, the supporting troops in the rear moved up. The historian of the 60th Alabama Regiment of Gracie's Brigade recorded that

At length, the ominous silence was broken by the discharge of a single piece of artillery from the brow of a hill to our right. Artillery had been planted on each of the hill-tops in the vicinity—some being occupied by the enemy, and some by ourselves—and now, in a few moments after the discharge of this pioneer piece, a brisk fire was opened from them all. Thunder peals burst forth and answered each other in quick succession; and, like destroying angels, the huge missiles flew through the dense atmosphere with an unearthly shrieking. Under the exhilaration of this stirring martial serenade, and the animating words of the

Confederate artillery on Cherokee Heights—bluffs south of the river—firing the signal to assault Fort Sanders

colonel of the regiment (who seemed everywhere present), the line was put in motion, and, encountering a creek [Third Creek], plunged through regardless of the cold.[6]

At the first flash of the signal gun, the Federal pickets in the counterscarp put their heads down and hugged the ground, the ditch being as safe a place as any during the artillery bombardment. Some of the shells struck the tree stumps, splintering them to atoms, and the chips went flying over the heads of the pickets. The screeching sound of the shells was fearsome enough to make green troops shudder, but these veterans knew they were safe from infantry assault until the bombardment was over.[7]

Suddenly, the roar from the cannon stopped. Instantly from the northern defilade came the unmistakable high-pitched yells and jerky canine yelps, which at a distance seemed shrill like boys' voices, but were terrifying in their savagery as they came nearer. With all the "hallooing" they could muster, the "recumbent ranks of gray sprang to their feet and formed for a charge, not so famous in history as Pickett's charge at Gettysburg, and not so inspiring a sight to see, for only the flashes of guns were visible in the dim light, but a charge that illustrated as well as Pickett's or any other ever made those splendid qualities of Longstreet's Infantry which made them at once an admiration and a delight to their comrades in the artillery."[8]

A few Federal sentries out about twenty yards in front of the ditch sprang to their feet and ran for their lives. One Irishman hollered to his fleeing comrades, "Deil tak the hinmost, but look out for the wires!" The forty men in the ditch hastily grabbed up the planks used for crossing, ran around to the southwest corner, then struck out for the open sector at the east as fast as they could go.[9] At the same instant Major Chipman hastily dispatched a courier toward the river to recall four companies of his regiment which had been pushed out of their rifle pits the evening before.[10]

With a rush and a yell the surging gray column advanced up the hill toward Fort Sanders. As they neared the fort the leading lines crashed through the brush barriers and bowled them aside like tenpins, but in the darkness the men tripped and stumbled over the telegraph wires stretched between the stumps.[11] As the lead troops began tearing and kicking at the wires, they were knocked over by the sheer weight of numbers of the rest of the onrushing troops. At this moment of delay and confusion, one cannon "en barbette" in the fort fired two quick rounds of canister into the storming party, but quickly closing their ranks the Confederates reached the ditch and chased away the gunners exposed on the platform.[12]

The rapid advance in almost complete darkness over terrain filled with obstacles and converging furrows brought the attacking force together into a packed mass whose officers could no longer distinguish their own men. Hesitating only momentarily, the men swarmed into the ditch which they had been told was no more than four feet deep. They expected to get a toe hold on the berme and scale the parapet with one leap. But as they surged into the ditch they discovered to their horror that in places it was more than eleven feet deep, the embankment was slippery and icy, the berme had been cut away, and the parapet had been built up very high with cotton bales. Many of the men, not knowing what else to do, fired into the embrasures at any of the Federals foolish enough to show their heads.[13]

Sergeant Isaac Garretson, of the 100th Pennsylvania Infantry, sensing the disorganization of the attackers, shouted to the men in the fort, "Pick the officers! Pick the officers!" As he turned to shout again, a Rebel bullet smacked into the back of his head, and he tumbled from the parapet into the fort.[14]

Private A. J. Cone of Raleigh, North Carolina, said that Colonel S. Z. Ruff, commanding Wofford's Brigade, seeing that the men could not pass the ditch, tried to get them to climb out and attack the breastworks leading off from the fort

Confederates outside the ditch at Fort Sanders being raked by enfilad-ing cannon fire

"which we could easily have done if it had been understood by our men." As Colonel Ruff climbed to the western edge of the ditch to make himself heard, he was cut down immediately by a bullet fired from the fort.[15]

Direct fire from the parapet had ceased except for an occasional musket raised overhead to the level of the interior crest and fired without aim. The cannon of the fort were useless against the Confederates in the blind sector of the ditch. Colonel Alexander said that "the fort was so nearly silenced that looking on from the guns we thought it had surrendered, though some fire continued to come from the left."[16]

The Confederates, with their battle flags of red with cross of blue floating defiantly above their heads, now lost the aspect of an assaulting column and became merely a mass of armed men who could not go forward but were determined not to fall back. Many of the officers, color-bearers, and men attempted to scale the parapet using bayonets and swords to hack out footholds in the slippery dirt.[17] In the darkness and confusion, what happened seemed different to different observers.

Colonel Alexander, who had fought with Lee's army in all the Virginia campaigns and with Bragg at Chickamauga, said that "Nowhere in the war was individual example more splendidly illustrated than on that fatal slope and in that bloody ditch."[18] Alexander said that Adjutant T. W. Cumming of the 16th Georgia scaled the parapet, entered the fort through an embrasure, and was captured inside, where he assured his captors "they would all be his prisoners within a few minutes."[19] After the war Private B. F. Red of Little Rock, Arkansas, wrote that "No one went over that fort except Adjutant Cumming of the 16th Georgia Regiment. An old Federal soldier here says that he saw Cumming knocked in the head with an axe." [20]

Lieutenant Bostick of Company C of the 20th Georgia clawed his way to the top of the parapet. He afterwards said that the Federal soldiers were lying down and that the fort could have been

Rebel troops in the ditch attempting to scale the parapet

taken easily if the ditch had not been so hard to cross.[21] Private Red substantiates Bostick, writing that "There is another old soldier living in Arkansas who says he was in that fort when we charged it. They all ran out, but when they found out that we could not get over it they came back and threw all the picks, shovels, and hand grenades they had over on us. They had poured water on the edge of the fort, and it ran down and froze. . . ."[22]

William Osborne, a fort defender with the 29th Massachusetts, graphically recorded:

The Confederates, led by fearless officers, crowded the ditch, and crossing it on each other's shoulders, began to ascend the bank; one of their standard-bearers came running up and planted his colors upon the parapet, in the very faces of Major Chipman's men; but he had hardly performed his deed of daring, when one of our soldiers shot him through the heart, and he fell forward into the works. Inspired by the example of their color-bearer, a large body of the Confederates, led by a gray-haired old officer (Colonel H. P. Thomas of the 16th Georgia), with wild shouts made a dash up the bank. All seemed lost; but at this moment Companies A, C, D, and K of the regiment came running into the fort, and ranging themselves along the parapet, opened a deadly fire upon the assaulting party. The gray old leader of the enemy, while waving his sword and shouting to his men to come on, was shot dead. Many of his brave followers suffered the same fate, and the handful of survivors fell hurriedly back into the ditch. At the same instant, like scenes were transpiring all along the works.[23]

The Federal defenders, now more encouraged than ever, were inspired by the individual heroics of the attackers and responded in kind. As one Rebel officer got to the top and shouted, "Come on, boys, the fort is ours!" he was seized by Lieutenant Munsford of Company A, 100th Pennsylvania, pulled into the fort, and clubbed to death.[24]

From a burning stick held by Captain Baird of the 79th New Yorkers, Lieutenant Benjamin now began lighting the time-fused shells he had prepared in advance and throwing them over the parapet as hand grenades. The explosions took a terrible toll among the Confederates crowded in the ditch and threw some of them into a mad scramble to get out and retreat. The elated Benjamin then lit one shell with his cigar, tossed it over, and hollered: "Look out, over there, some of you will get hurt!"[25] The Rebel troops cursed, thinking they were being shelled by their own artillery. Longstreet thought the same thing when he saw the flashes from the explosions, and he ordered Alexander, who had continued to hurl artillery at the enemy flanks, to cease fire.[26]

In spite of the panic, the Confederates bravely tried to keep up the assault. Lieutenant Munger of the Ninth Georgia pushed through an embrasure and found himself all alone with the Federal troops. Without a moment's hesitation, he emptied his revolver at the Union gunners and made his escape. Colonel Kennon McElroy of the 13th Mississippi fell in front of the ditch, and Lieutenant Colonel Fiser of the 17th Mississippi lost an arm on the parapet.[27]

The massed assault had degenerated into a frenzied trial of individual strength marked by beating, gouging, taunting, and swearing. One fearless Rebel officer climbed right into the front of the muzzle of a twelve-pound Napoleon gun that the defenders had been saving for emergency use and defiantly thundered: "Surrender, you damned Yankees!" "Yes, we'll surrender this to you," the artillerymen responded as they yanked the lanyard and blew the Rebel officer into a thousand pieces.[28] By now the flags of the 16th Georgia and the 13th and 17th Mississippi regiments had been planted on the parapet, and the defenders were trying to pull them down.[29]

Private Seaburn Shepherd of the Ninth Georgia crossed the ditch and reached the flagstaff which held the Stars and Stripes. He attempted to scale the pole, but was clubbed in the head and promptly retreated into the ditch. Private Robert Thompson of the Ninth Georgia seized one of Benjamin's shell grenades and hurled it back into the fort, where it exploded.[30] One Rebel soldier was seen trying to cover an unexploded shell with red clay before it discharged and blew him to bits.[31]

The darkness gave way to the gray light of early dawn. Federal infantry in the trenches to the east and the south of the fort began to fire effectively at Confederates outside of the ditch who had spread eastward and southward from the northwest bastion. The cannon in the southwest bastion and at Battery Noble, 500 yards south, enfiladed the attacking Confederates not yet in the ditch.[32] Sergeant Boothe of the 21st Mississippi, who had watched the entire fight from the sharpshooters' line, said that the Confederates "were determined and were capable of accomplishing anything within the range of possibility. . . . With scaling ladders the entry into the fort would have been comparatively easy, but without them the gallant stormers at its base were as impotent as the foolish king who stood upon the seashore and commanded the waters to cease their ebb and flow. . . ." Some of the men began to fall back, muttering that they needed ladders, but they were still determined to renew the assault, as they "preferred the hardship and peril of war and death to dishonor." [33]

As the original attackers began to fall back, the men of Anderson's Brigade of Jenkins' division, waiting to the left and rear of McLaws' column and ordered to attack only if the assaulting column was successful, were unwilling to see the attack falter and rushed forward into the ditch to try it themselves.[34]

Osborne of the 29th Massachusetts noted that about this time the assault slackened; but in a few moments another column of the enemy came rushing towards the fort, and with almost sublime courage faced the withering fire of our troops, and large numbers of them gained the bank. The first terrible scenes of the battle were re-enacted; three of the enemy's standards were planted simultaneously upon the parapet, but they were quickly torn away by our men. The resistance was as desperate as the assault; officers freely used their swords, the men clubbed their muskets, others used their bayonets, and others still axes and the rammers of the cannon. A struggle to severe as this could not be otherwise than of short duration. In a few moments the enemy's soldiers began to falter, and fall back into the ditch. Seeing this, General Ferrero, who was in command of the fort and closely watching the fight, ordered one company of the Second Michigan on the right, to go through the embrasures and charge the disorganized enemy. Sweeping down the ditch, these commands captured about two hundred of the enemy, and drove them into the fort, the little squad of the Twenty-Ninth following their captives and bearing triumphantly two battle-flags of the foe; the capturers of which were Sergeant Jeremiah Mahoney of Company A and Private Joseph Manning of Company K, both of whom afterwards received the medals of honor voted by the Congress of the United States.[35]

The bloody fight had lasted only twenty minutes. General Longstreet had approached the fort with the support brigades of Bushrod Johnson and got no closer than 500 yards from the ditch when the first wounded were borne back by their comrades. Major Goggin, who was McLaws' adjutant, rushed back to inform Longstreet that the fort was surrounded by a network of wire and that it was impossible for the men to get in without axes. Placing full confidence in this hasty report, Longstreet ordered the troops to withdraw, but his command came too late to stop Jenkins' second assault at the ditch. Bushrod Johnson pleaded with Longstreet to continue the attack, but was overruled. Instead, Longstreet ordered a diversionary attack on the south side of the fort, which if successful would allow his troops to sweep into the open end at the east.[36]

After the troops had been ordered back, it suddenly occurred to Longstreet that his decision had been too hasty. He had seen the men pass the wire entanglements and climb the parapet. Goggin had been in error, but Longstreet's confidence had been shaken, and he was too far back

The Rebel assault on Fort Sanders. On the following two pages appears a *Harper's Weekly* sketch of the bloody fight.

to know the true cause of the repulse—the deep ditch.[37]

Longstreet now witnessed the terrible scenes at the rear of a battle, the kind of scenes about which Union General William Sherman wrote: "I never saw the rear of an army engaged in battle but I feared that some calamity had happened at the front—the apparent confusion, broken wagons, crippled horses, men lying about dead and maimed, parties hastening to and fro in seeming disorder, and a general apprehension of something dreadful about to ensue; all these signs, however, lessened as I neared the front, and there the contrast was complete—perfect order, men and horses full of confidence, and it was not unusual for general hilarity, laughing and cheering. Although cannon might be firing, the musketry clattering, and the enemy's shot hitting close, there reigned a general feeling of strength and security that bore a marked contrast to the bloody signs that had drifted rapidly to the rear. . . ."[38]

The bloody signs that drifted to the rear where Longstreet rode with Johnson's and Gracie's brigades made a lasting impression on the historian of the 60th Alabama Regiment, who sadly recorded the events.

After ascending a hill, and advancing a few hundred yards in the open field beyond, the command was suddenly ordered to fall back, and accordingly faced about and moved in retreat to the brow of the hill just passed, where it occupied a line of rifle-pits located at that point. This retrograde movement, suggestive of ill, and at first inexplicable, was soon accounted for in a manner that filled every heart with sorrow, and shrouded every countenance in gloom. We had been in the rifle-pits but a short time when day began to dawn. The firing ceased for the most part; only a stray shell now and then ricocheted through our line, or burst above our heads. While thus waiting in the rifle-pits, expecting, with much solicitude, the denouement, a solitary litter was seen advancing toward us over the field in our front; then another and another, and anon a sad procession was silently threading its way to the rear. No words were required to convey the sad tidings. The blood dripping from the litters, and the occasional groans of their mangled occupants, who had led in the charge, as they passed through our line on their way to the rear, apprised us, more unmistakably than language could have done, of the woeful fact of the morning's disaster. The charge, though gallant, was unsuccessful, and five hundred noble Mississippians lay dead or dying in the moat that surrounded the fort upon which the attack had been made. . . .

Among the many inexpressibly sad days of our military career, no member of the regiment will, I am sure, fail to recognize this, the 29th day of November, 1863, as one of the most sad. All through that dismal day the words were ever recurring—"These are they who have passed through great tribulation." [39]

Federal Captain Poe, who had completed the construction of Fort Sanders, said that for the Confederates in the ditch "Advance and retreat were about equally difficult, and it needed but a very short exposure to convince them that if any were to leave the ditch alive it could only be by the promptest surrender. Those who were able to walk were brought through the ditch to the south-eastern angle and there entered our lines as prisoners. Such of the assaulting forces as had not entered the ditch fell back, at first sullenly and slowly, but flesh and blood could not stand the storm of shot and shell that was poured upon them, and they soon broke in confused retreat." [40]

Sergeant Granberry of the 20th Georgia, who had watched the whole fight from the sharpshooters' line, said that there were few casualties during the retreat. "The enemy appeared above the walls of the fort and fired one volley into the fleeing columns and there was one discharge of artillery. There was no other firing done by the enemy. If a head appeared above the walls of the fort it was at once fired on from the heavy picket line."[41]

Sergeant Boothe of the 21st Mississippi said that the enemy "did not dare follow as the Confederates were too wrought up."[42] The men felt that without ladders they were not given a fair chance, and they wanted another crack at the fort.[43] General Jenkins pleaded with Longstreet and finally obtained permission to renew the assault. But this time Alexander was to concentrate all of his guns on the fort, 1,000 sharpshooters would silence the infantry within the embrasures, and the storming column would come equipped with ladders, fascines, and axes to cut footholds in the escarp, the inner bank of the ditch.

While the plans were being made for the renewed assault, a courier suddenly arrived from Major General Robert Ransom at Rogersville with a telegram President Jefferson Davis had sent to Ransom on November 27 to relay to

Longstreet. The message informed Longstreet that General Grant had broken out of the Chattanooga encirclement and driven General Bragg's army from Missionary Ridge. Longstreet was ordered to abandon the siege of Knoxville and to move promptly to join Bragg near Ringgold or Dalton, Georgia. Orders were at once given to move the Confederate trains to the rear in preparation for a retreat southward that night.[44]

As soon as it became evident to General Burnside that the assault was over, he ordered General Potter to arrange a thirty-minute truce with Colonel Sorrel of Longstreet's staff in order to care for the wounded and bury the dead.[45]

NOTES

1. Osborne, p. 267.
2. Todd, pp. 382-83. Mr. E. J. Sanford, a Knoxville native, not in the army, joined the defenders in the fort. He told Judge O. P. Temple that Burnside had put 4,000 loaded rifles in the fort. Temple, p. 492.
3. Alexander, *Memoirs*, pp. 487-88.
4. *Confederate Veteran*, XVIII (January 1910), 24; *Battles and Leaders*, III, 743, 748-49.
5. *Battles and Leaders*, III, 749; Burrage, pp. 110-11.
6. *History of the Sixtieth Alabama Regiment*, p. 24.
7. Todd, pp. 385-86.
8. *Battles and Leaders*, III, 748-49.
9. Todd, p. 386.
10. Osborne, p. 267.
11. After the war, Poe said the assaulting troops were veterans and not demoralized by the wire barrier. Ducloux Scrapbook.
12. Burrage, p. 112; *Confederate Veteran*, XVIII (January 1910), 24.
13. *Confederate Veteran*, XVIII (October 1910), 468; *Battles and Leaders*, III, 749.
14. J. B. Kennedy, 100th Pennsylvania Volunteer Infantry, in a letter to a Knoxville newspaper (date deleted), in Ducloux Scrapbook.
15. *Confederate Veteran*, XVIII (October 1910), 468.
16. *Battles and Leaders*, III, 749.
17. *Confederate Veteran*, XXII (June 1914), 266.
18. *Battles and Leaders*, III, 749.
19. *Ibid.*

20. *Confederate Veteran*, XXI (December 1913), 585.
21. *Confederate Veteran*, XXXI (October 1923), 372.
22. *Confederate Veteran*, XXI (December 1913), 585.
23. Osborne, p. 168.
24. J. B. Kennedy in Ducloux Scrapbook (see note 14, this chapter).
25. *Ibid.* Lieutenant Benjamin was quite a boaster. Kennedy said that the story is exaggerated somewhat regarding the "cigar" episode, and that the fuses were actually lit by a burning stick previously prepared for such a purpose by Captain Baird of the 79th. Also see Todd, p. 389.
26. *Battles and Leaders*, III, 749.
27. *Ibid.*
28. Todd, p. 391.
29. *Battles and Leaders*, III, 743. The colors of these regiments were captured by the Federals.
30. *Confederate Veteran*, XVIII (June 1910), 24.
31. Todd, p. 397.
32. O. R., Ser. I, XXXI, Part I, 342-44.
33. *Confederate Veteran*, XXII (June 1914), 266.
34. O. R., Ser. I, XXXI, Part I, 528-29.
35. Osborne, pp. 268-69. Lieutenant Benjamin was in command of the defenses of Fort Sanders. The fort was located within the sector assigned to General Ferrero's division, and the general maintained his headquarters in a bomb-proof shelter within the fort. Benjamin had written many official reports in which he gave himself credit for devising fortifications and strategy which

confused the enemy, but only after he had convinced his superior officers of their own wrong thinking. In his official report to Burnside (O.R., Ser. I, XXXI, Part I, 342), Benjamin submitted a masterpiece of self-aggrandizement in which he belittled his own superior officers and other commands. He made the astounding claim that he placed temporary embankments in front of the embrasures of the bastion to trick the Confederates into assaulting the northwest salient and that they fell for his trick. (The Confederates had decided to attack that point even before the fort was completed.) Benjamin in his report said: "I put my pistol within six inches of a rebel's face and pulled the trigger three times. They were on the exterior crest of the parapet all the time. I claim credit mainly for building up the work, getting it properly garrisoned, and above all, for drawing the attack on the northwest salient. If the assault had been made anywhere else it would have succeeded. During the assault, I handled the troops, giving all orders and seeing to their execution. General Ferrero was in the little bomb proof, and I did not see him outside, nor know of his giving an order during the fight." Benjamin was a West Point graduate, and, while many of his classmates became general officers, he never advanced beyond a majority.

36. Longstreet, pp. 505-506.
37. *Ibid.,* pp. 506-507.
38. Sherman, II, 407.
39. Shaver, *History of the Sixtieth Alabama Regiment,* pp. 24-27.
40. *Battles and Leaders,* III, 743.
41. *Confederate Veteran,* XVIII (January 1910), 24.
42. *Confederate Veteran,* XVIII (October 1910), 468; XXII (June 1914), 266.
43. *Confederate Veteran,* XVIII (October 1910), 468.
44. *Battles and Leaders,* III, 750.
45. O. R., Ser. I, XXXI, Part III, 274.

26

"Now I Can Have a Good Snooze"

PORTER Alexander's signal guns had boomed forth their challenge at 6:00 A.M., November 29, 1863, while the national flag was being unfurled in the murky darkness at Fort Sanders to the music of "The Star-Spangled Banner." Startled by the thundering artillery, the people of Knoxville rushed to their west windows and watched the meteoric shells burst over the Union lines.[1]

In the defense positions all around Knoxville, Union soldiers listened anxiously as the cannonade pounded Fort Sanders. In their trenches to the south near Kingston Road, the men of the 36th Massachusetts Infantry fixed their straining eyes on the fort so dimly outlined in the gray dawn. As the cannon fire slackened, in its stead rose the well-known Rebel yell in the direction of the fort. Then followed the rattle of musketry, the roar of more cannon, and the screams of the wounded. Now suddenly the yells died away and then rose again. Now the roar of musketry and artillery was redoubled. Now, as the yells died away again, the men of the 36th heard three loud Union cheers, long-drawn-out and deep-throated: "Hurrah! Hurrah! Hurrah!"

Henry Burrage of the 36th wrote: "How those cheers thrilled our hearts, as we stood almost breathless at our posts in the trenches! They told us that the enemy had been repulsed, and that the victory was ours. Peering through the rising fog toward the fort, not a hundred yards away, oh, glorious sight!—we dimly saw that our flag was still there."[2]

As the sun broke through the misty fog and the explosions of shells were replaced by the cries of the wounded, the men of blue and gray looked at each other in stunned disbelief at the magnitude of the carnage. The flag of truce was gratefully received by both armies, and men who had stood toe to toe and fought until flesh could take no more now embraced one another in soldierly comradeship.

In the comparatively brief period of twenty minutes the attacking Confederate troops sustained 813 casualties—129 killed, 458 wounded, and 226 missing. Lieutenant Benjamin reported the Union losses in the fort as five killed and eight wounded.[3] The great disparity between the Confederate and the Union casualties resembled that between the losses of Sir Edward Pakenham's British troops and Andrew Jackson's Americans at the Battle of New Orleans in the War of 1812.

Edward Pollard, the Southern historian, writing in 1864, said that the Confederate assault "ranks with the most famous charges in military history. Never, excepting Gettysburg, was there in the history of the war a disaster adorned with the glory of such devoted courage as Longstreet's repulse at Knoxville."[4] Praising the Federal stand, General Burnside said: "The gallantry of this defence has not been excelled during the war."[5]

The ground between the fort and the defilade to the northwest was strewn with the dead and the dying. The ditch was filled with men, some piled on top of each other, the wounded underneath gasping for air. Ninety-eight bodies were hauled from a twenty-foot space around the northwest bastion. Sergeant Granberry, of the 20th Georgia, said that at the first sign of the truce the Federals "swarmed out of the fort and

Captain Orlando M. Poe and Colonel Orville E. Babcock on the ground north of Fort Sanders. Captain Poe supervised the building of the Union defensive works around Knoxville. Babcock, in 1865 as Grant's aide, delivered the surrender terms to General Lee at Appomattox Courthouse.

our men met and mingled with them between the fort and the picket lines where the dead and wounded lay. The federals claimed the wounded; but those who could walk paid no attention, but returned to our lines. Our dead were collected and we buried them in one grave."[6]

Colonel Hawkes, of the 21st Massachusetts, wrote in his diary on the 29th: "I went to the field this afternoon, and I never saw so many dead rebels on the same space. . . . During this time the hostile armies met each other on friendly terms. My 21st Massachusetts boys met some of the Palmetto sharpshooters when they caught a pig together, and killed and divided it equally." [7]

The men of the 79th New York Highlanders wandered between the lines looking for their old antagonists from the Virginia armies they had fought at Bull Run, South Mountain, Antietam, and now at Knoxville. They found one congenial Irishman fighting with a South Carolina regiment who exclaimed: "Yees Yankees is divils. If yees can't shoot us yees thry to break our necks over the damned wires." The Highlanders succeeded in smuggling some Confederate soldiers who said they were New Yorkers into the fort by gathering around them so they could not be seen by their own men and putting Yankee overcoats around them. During the truce, which was extended until 7:00 P.M., the pickets of both armies, without official sanction, agreed not to

Wartime sketch of terrain approaching Fort Sanders, as viewed from within the fort

fire on one another for the duration of the siege. As one Rebel put it to the Union pickets, "Say, Yanks, let's agree not to fire on each other's pickets, will ye. It don't do no kind a good and only worries both parties."[8]

Sergeant Granberry said that the Confederates secretly agreed to allow the sentinels at Fort Sanders to walk their posts unmolested, even though the targets were tempting. Nevertheless, in spite of the comradeship, there was great jealousy in Rebel hearts that cold Sunday morning. Sunday was inspection day for the Federals, and they were dressed in clean uniforms and polished shoes which contrasted sharply with their barefoot antagonists.

General Burnside generously allowed the Confederate army the use of his ambulances for the transport of the wounded. His own men as-

sisted the Rebel surgeons. Burnside's hospitals were mostly filled with captured Confederate wounded.

However, one soldier was cared for in a unique manner. Lieutenant Colonel Alfred O'Brien of Louisiana, serving with the 13th Mississippi Infantry, was nursed back to health by his sister, Mrs. William G. Brownlow, the wife of Knoxville's outstanding Union leader. But when the authorities offered him his freedom if he would take the oath of allegiance to the United States flag, O'Brien refused and was sent north to Camp Chase.[9]

The Confederate dead were hastily buried in a common shallow grave. One bitter Tennessean in the Union army kicked a wounded dog in the side and pushed him into the grave. "Let the sleeping dogs lie together," he exclaimed.[10] Not many days afterwards the bodies began protruding from the ground because of the heaving of the earth from the bitter cold and thawing. Some were being rooted out and eaten by hogs. S. T. Atkin, seeing this desecration, consulted with an anonymous friend, and together they contracted with James H. Renshaw, an undertaker, to make individual pine-box coffins for the soldiers at four dollars a corpse. Ninety-two bodies were removed from the battlefield grave and re-interred in the Confederate Cemetery on Bethel Avenue, along with 1,500 other Confederate soldiers already buried there.[11]

At 7:00 P.M., November 29, a single cannon's roar marked the end of the truce. The friends of day became the foes of night. The "victorious" Union army was once again besieged in Knoxville. The "defeated" Confederate army was still in a position to starve the Union army into surrender or to capture it by another assault.

When General Longstreet first learned of General Bragg's defeat at Missionary Ridge and his subsequent retreat to Ringgold, Georgia, he had ordered his baggage trains to move back from Knoxville in preparation for joining Bragg as soon as possible. Later reports indicated to him

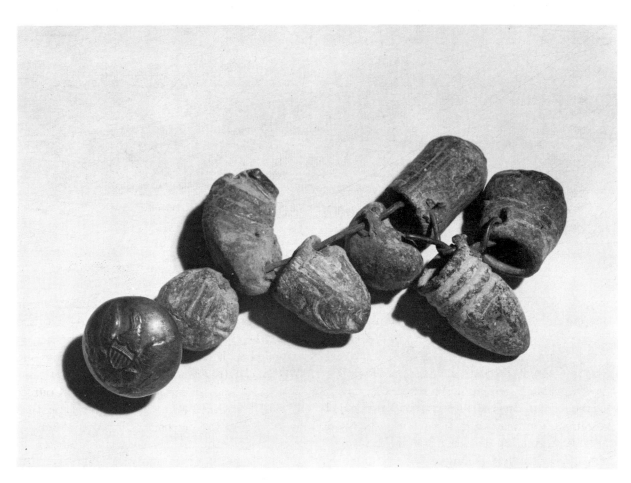

Relics of the battle. These seven Minié balls and a Union blouse button were collected from the battlefield at Fort Sanders by Sergeant Samuel G. Wright, Company E, 29th Massachusetts Infantry.

*Longstreet's barefoot troops huddling over a fire in an
East Tennessee cave*

that this move was impractical. General Grant
had cut off the roads to Georgia and dispatched
Major General Gordon Granger and General
Philip Sheridan with the Fourth U.S. Corps and
Major General William T. Sherman with the
Eleventh and Fifteenth Corps toward Knoxville
for the relief of Burnside. Longstreet then decided
to retreat northeastward from East Tennessee
into Virginia to rejoin Lee. But first he would
remain at Knoxville as long as possible to insure
that the Union relief columns would not turn
around and pursue the retreating Braxton Bragg.

For several days after the unsuccessful assault
on Fort Sanders, the Confederate troops kept up
the ruse of preparing further assaults. The Union
troops were forced to maintain constant watch-
fulness, and during the daylight hours they
strengthened their defenses. Skirmishers were
supplied with cotton balls soaked in turpentine,
which when thrown blazing into the air at night
would expose an attacking column. Coupled
locomotive wheels were poised on the slope, their
axles tied to the defenses with ropes. When the
ropes were cut, the wheels would roll rapidly
downhill and crash into an assaulting force. But
as the defenses grew stronger, the men grew
weaker, so that they frequently stole the rations
of corn intended for the horses.

From Chattanooga, General Grant sent a message to Burnside congratulating him on the te-

nacity with which he had held out against superior forces and informing him of the movements in progress for his relief. By Grant's order a copy of the dispatch was deliberately allowed to fall into enemy hands. In this way, Longstreet learned on December 1 of Sherman's advance toward Maryville and Knoxville. Longstreet now saw that the siege must be raised at once, and he made his preparations accordingly, but determined to remain only one day's march ahead of Sherman.[12]

At midnight of December 4, 1863, as the men in Fort Sanders were standing to arms, something of an unusual nature was observed going on in the Confederate camps. Lanterns were seen flitting about in the batteries. Night signals were at work. Above one fixed lantern near the ground, another lantern swung from side to side. The Union pickets all along the siege lines were doubled, and the troops in the fort were ordered to the parapets. The men in Fort Sanders made wild speculations. Some thought the Confederates were preparing one final assault,

others that they were retreating. At daylight, Captain Ames, Company B of the 36th Massachusetts, discovered that the Confederates were indeed gone. The siege of Knoxville was over.[13]

A single cannon was fired from Battery Noble to announce the end, and the order went up and down the line: "Stack arms! All but the camp guard may rest!"

The historian of the 29th Massachusetts recorded that "The termination of the siege was an important and joyful event to the whole nation; it was also a great crisis in the lives of the soldiers there, and what they said and did on this important occasion, our readers may be curious to know. The answer shows how utterly unromantic and prosaic were the Yankee soldiers who made so much history during the four years of the war. 'Thank God! Now I can have a good snooze,' said one, in no irreverent spirit. 'Captain, can I go down to the river and wash my shirt?' said another. 'Sergeant, has the company got any soap?' asked a third. Probably the thought of one-half of the men in Knoxville, at

Wooden Confederate canteen

Drum used in Longstreet's Corps at the siege of Knoxville. This well-preserved military drum is on display at Confederate Memorial Hall, Knoxville

that moment, was sleep, and of the others, a wash, either of clothes or person. A few officers of the staff, a few orderlies, and surgeons rode out to visit the deserted camp, while our pickets were thrown out to capture the stragglers. In the course of an hour the loiterers and laggards of the late besiegers began to come into our lines in crowds. Some of them had overslept, others had strayed away, and others still had lost heart and skulked in the woods."[14]

While the Union troops were thinking of soap and sleep, congratulations were pouring in from all quarters. From Maryville, fifteen miles south of Knoxville, General Sherman sent a message

to Burnside: "I am here and can bring 25,000 men into Knoxville, tomorrow, but Longstreet having retreated, I feel disposed to stop. . . . Accept my congratulations at your successful defense and your patient endurance."[15]

At a joint congressional session, it was voted that "The thanks of Congress be, and they hereby are, presented to Major General Ambrose E. Burnside, and through him to the officers and men who have fought under his command, for their gallantry, good conduct, and soldier-like endurance."[16]

On December 7, 1863, Abraham Lincoln signed the following proclamation: "Reliable information having been received that the insurgent force is retreating from East Tennessee, under circumstances, rendering it probable that the Union forces cannot hereafter be dislodged from that important position, and esteeming it to be of high national consequence, I recommend that all loyal people do, on receipt of this information, assemble at their high places of worship, and render special homage and gratitude to Almighty God for this great advancement of the National Course."[17]

At Knoxville on December 6, General Burnside issued an official order congratulating his troops. "The Army of the Ohio has nobly guarded the loyal region it redeemed from its oppressors, and rendered the heroic defense of Knoxville memorable in the annals of War."[18] In commemoration of the "grand result" of the Union defense, Burnside's order authorized his men to inscribe on their colors and guidons the comprehensive words,

"EAST TENNESSEE."

NOTES

1. Burrage, of the 36th Massachusetts (p. 110), said the attack commenced at 6:00 A.M. Captain Poe said the signal for the artillery fire sounded at 6:00 A.M. and the barrage continued for twenty minutes (*Battles and Leaders*, III, 743). Dr. Humes said the attack began at 6:30 (pp. 274-75). Most historians of the time merely recorded that the guns began firing at "the first sign of dawn."

2. Burrage, p. 111.

3. O. R., Ser. I, XXXI, Part I, 475, 341-43.

4. E. A. Pollard, *Southern History of the War*, III, 161-62.

5. Humes, p. 279.

6. *Confederate Veteran*, XVIII (January 1910), 24.

7. Walcott, p. 289.

8. Todd, pp. 398-99.

9. *Confederate Veteran*, X (September 1902), 414. Lieutenant Colonel O'Brien of the 13th Mississippi had hoisted himself into the fort by pulling on a Yankee cannon. After the battle he was in the fort alive, but wounded. His own superior in the 13th had fallen early in the encounter and had left him in charge of the assaulting column. When the Federals asked him if he knew anyone in Knoxville who would care for him, O'Brien replied: "I know one person, but I do not think she would want to receive me." Knoxville *News-Sentinel*, date deleted, Scrapbook of Mrs. Charles Wayland, Knoxville. Mrs. Brownlow, after the war's end, was always honored by the United Confederate Veterans for her efforts to restore franchise to Southern soldiers.

10. As told to Mrs. George Bearden of Knoxville by her father, who was a Union soldier and an eyewitness.

11. Creekmore, p. 106. The 1,500 Confederate dead, whose names, rank, and regiments were recorded by Mr. Renshaw, the coffinmaker for the L. C. Shepherd Undertaking Co., are buried in the cemetery. In addition to these known soldiers, 105 unknown Confederate soldiers killed in or near Fort Sanders were re-interred at Bethel. There are about 50 Union prisoners within the lot. Some of the soldiers' wives were later buried atop their husbands' coffins.

Mr. Shepherd's business was taken over by the E. B. Mann family, which still operates mortuaries in Knoxville.

The Ladies Memorial Association of Knoxville was founded in 1868 to collect the remains of the Confederate soldiers and to watch over and protect the graves. The Knox County Court allowed them custody of that portion of the public cemetery in which many had already been buried. In 1873 a deed was executed giving the ladies the cemetery. On May 21, 1891, the cornerstone of the monument was laid. The monument was unveiled on May 19, 1892. General Kirby Smith was the Grand Marshal. Former General William Bate, then a United States Senator, was the principal speaker at the ceremony. Annual services are held at the cemetery, located between Bethel and Vine avenues. The monument is 12 feet square at the base and stands 48 feet tall. At the top is a statue of a figure of a Confederate private as he stands at "Parade Rest," still defiantly facing north.

12. Burrage, p. 118.

13. *Ibid.*

14. Osborne, pp. 271, 272.

15. *Ibid.*, p. 273.

16. Burrage, p. 120. Longstreet was also thanked by the Confederate Congress. O. R., Ser. I, XXXI, Part I, 549.

17. Burrage, p. 120.

18. General Field Order No. 38, Hdqs. Army of the Ohio, Knoxville, December 11, 1863. (Copies of all general orders of the Army of the Ohio are in a bound volume, Lawson McGhee Library.)

The Aftermath:
Horseshoes for the Cold and Hungry

LONGSTREET pulled the last of his bare-foot troops from the siege lines around Knoxville on the night of December 4, 1863, and marched them in cold rain eighteen miles up the Holston valley to Blaine's Cross Roads. Safely beyond pursuit, the Confederate boys sang out "Carry Me Back To Ole Virginny," and the hills echoed the joy for miles around. The sick and wounded were abandoned to the mercy of the Federal army, but Longstreet was kind enough to detail some of his soldiers to remain behind with the men until they could be cared for by the Union surgeons.[1]

Longstreet retreated north toward Virginia to avoid battle with Sherman and the 25,000 troops he had brought for the relief of Knoxville. By the 9th, Longstreet was at Rogersville, sixty-five miles from Knoxville, and was reinforced by 4,000 troops under General Robert Ransom, who had come from Virginia too late to participate in the battle for Knoxville. Already Longstreet, who was called "Bull of the Woods" by his men, was planning further demonstrations against Knoxville. The stubborn general was never one to let defeat dampen his hopes.

On December 5, General Sherman reached Maryville, where he received notice from Burnside of Longstreet's retreat. Halting all of his army except General Gordon Granger's two divisions, Sherman rode into Knoxville on the morning of the 6th with Granger and their staff officers. The march from Chattanooga to Knoxville had been unpleasant for Sherman and his men. He had told Grant that he had a "horror" of East Tennessee and that the whole countryside should be pillaged and abandoned. Earlier he had written Halleck of his personal distaste for "the Union men of the South" whom he considered "afraid of shadows" and full of complaints when his men took a few fence rails for fires or corn for their horses. He said that the Unionists "stay at home, claiming all exemptions of peaceful citizens. I account them as nothing in this great game of war."[2]

His men had marched from the Mississippi River, fought a battle at Chattanooga, and made a forced march in bitter cold weather to Maryville. His soldiers were in no mood to bandy with civilians over local problems. They had come to relieve their soldier comrades from starvation. Sherman approached Knoxville from the south. He said that before crossing the Tennessee on the pontoon bridge, he looked across the river "and in a large pen on the Knoxville side I saw a fine lot of cattle, which did not look much like starvation. I found General Burnside and staff domiciled in a large, fine mansion, looking very comfortable, and in a few words he described to me the leading events of the previous few days, and said he had already given orders looking to the pursuit of Longstreet. I offered to join in the pursuit, though in fact my men were worn out, and suffering in that cold season and climate. Indeed, on our way up I personally was almost frozen, and had to beg leave to sleep in the house of a family at Athens."[3]

When Sherman arrived in Knoxville, the Union ladies of the town wanted to show their appreciation to him for delivering them from the siege. They formed a group, went to Burn-

Laurel Avenue and 17th Street today, approximate location of the northwest bastion of Fort Sanders

side's headquarters, and asked permission to give a dinner in Sherman's honor. "Old Burnie" thought it a splendid idea. The ladies went home and brought out their silver, china, crystal, and fine linens which had been hidden for two years and scoured the city and the French Broad country for the best foods they could find.

While the ladies were preparing the banquet, Burnside urged Sherman to assist him in the pursuit of Longstreet. He explained that, reinforced by Granger's two divisions of 10,000 men, he would be able to capture Longstreet or push him out of Tennessee. Granger felt that his men were in no condition for further fighting and objected strenuously. Sherman asked Burnside to make his request in writing. The generals then toured

the Knoxville defenses and examined Fort Sanders in detail.

Returning to Burnside's headquarters, the generals and their staff officers put on their finest uniforms and proceeded to the home of Perez Dickinson, where they sat down to a roast turkey dinner served in fine style. Burnside toasted Sherman for delivering Knoxville and asked him if he would make a speech. The host general soon perceived that he and the ladies had made a *faux pas*. Sherman, who had expected to find privation and hunger in Knoxville, was aghast at the sumptious feast. Instead of being pleased, he was wrathful. He said that he had never seen anything of this kind in his field experience. He had pressed his barefoot troops on a forced

Memorial to the 79th New York Highlander Regiment, at 16th Street and Clinch Avenue

march because Grant had assured him that the Knoxville garrison faced starvation. He made it clear that if he had known the true situation he would never have left Chattanooga. Burnside and the ladies were stunned. As Sherman and his men made a leisurely return to Chattanooga, they picked the countryside clean, probably in revenge even though many of the people were Unionists. He and Burnside never hit it off during the rest of the war.[4]

General Philip Sheridan, who had come with Granger, was not as dismayed as Sherman. In fact, the cavalryman was downright pleased with his assignment. From Maryville, Sheridan moved to Sevierville and established his headquarters. He spread his divisions out over the French Broad country between the Big Pigeon and the Little Pigeon rivers and soon had all the mills grinding out flour and meal. Surplus food was floated on flatboats to the troops at Knoxville. Sheridan was particularly impressed with the people, recording that "The intense loyalty of this part of Tennessee exceeded that of any other section I was in during the war."[5]

From Blaine's Cross Roads a rear-guard detachment of Longstreet's men made feints against Knoxville, causing Sheridan and his command to be recalled to help protect the city. Sheridan led his cavalry northeastward to Strawberry Plains near Blaine's Cross Roads, leaving behind 600 men without shoes and unfit for combat who were to await the arrival of a relief train coming from Chattanooga. When the ten-car freight train pulled into the Knoxville station, the ragged troops came down to meet it, fully expecting warm clothing, food, and ammunition. They were greeted with a monumental quartermaster error. As they opened each car door, they found nothing inside but horseshoes![6]

To further complicate the supply problem in Knoxville, Confederate guerrillas led by Captain Harvey Shannon of Goodlettsville, Tennessee, invented "infernal machines" designed to blow up Federal supply ships coming up the Tennessee River from Chattanooga. Shannon's men would

Confederate memorial marker placed by the United Daughters of the Confederacy on 17th Street near the site of the ditch at Fort Sanders

sneak past the Negro troops guarding the steamboats while they docked and steal pieces of wood used as fuel. They drilled holes, filled them with fine rifle powder, and then smuggled the wood back on board. One boat was sunk and another set on fire before the Federals caught on to what was happening.[7]

General Grant himself came to Knoxville and made arrangements to maintain rail connections between Chattanooga and Knoxville. He left Knoxville and inspected Cumberland Gap and the Wilderness Trail. During Grant's trip, the temperature dropped as low as 15 degrees below zero. The intense cold and the ruggedness of the country convinced Grant that no large army could be supplied through this area to drive into southwest Virginia. Georgia appeared a more inviting target.[8]

At his own request General Burnside was relieved from command at Knoxville and returned to his home. Burnside's successor, Major General John Foster, was unpopular with the Knoxville people and the Union soldiers. Sheridan said that after Sherman went back to Chattanooga "the operations in East Tennessee constituted a series of blunders lasting through the entire winter, a state of affairs doubtless due to the command of troops which was so frequently changed. . . . It had already been intimated that Burnside was to be relieved, and in consequence, he was inactive and apathetic, confining his operations to an aimless expedition to Blaine's Cross Roads, then withdrawing. General Foster superseded Burnside, but he was physically unfit, so the chief authority evolved on Parke. Parke transferred the command to Granger, who then unloaded it on me."[9]

Longstreet established his winter headquarters at Russellville, Tennessee, and made rail connections with Virginia. He seemed happy with his position. He said in his memoirs that "It would be difficult to find a country more inviting in agriculture and horticulture than East Tennessee, and its mineral resources are as interesting, but for those whose mission was strategic, its

geographical and topographical features were more striking. Our position at Bulls Gap was covered by a spur of mountains which shoots out from the south side of the Holston River towards the north bend of the Nolichucky, opening gaps that could be improved by the pick and shovel until the line between became unassailable. In a few days our line was strong enough, and we looked for the enemy to come and try our metal, until we learned that he was as badly crippled of the cavalry arm as we."[10]

Still determined to capture Knoxville, he requested 10,000 men from Virginia to reinforce his army. When General Robert E. Lee heard of Longstreet's request, he wrote to President Davis that he considered another assault on Knoxville unwise.

I have received the dispatch forwarded to me today from Genl Longstreet, requesting ten thousand men to insure the capture of Knoxville. I have no information of the practicability of the plan. I think it may be assumed that its defenses are stronger now than when it was last attacked & an attempt to capture it by assault would not only be hazardous but attended with great loss of life. To reduce it by approaches would require time &, it seems to me at this distance, render necessary an army sufficient to defeat a relieving force that, now the railroad to Chattanooga has been opened, could be quickly sent from Grant's troops. If a movement could be made to cut off supplies from Knoxville, it would draw out the garrison & this appears to me the wiser course.[11]

In March, 1864, General Longstreet went to Richmond where he conferred with President Davis, Secretary of War James Seddon, and Generals Lee and Bragg. A plan was devised whereby Longstreet would "isolate" Knoxville, and General Joe Johnston in command of the Army of Tennessee would unite with Longstreet for a drive into Middle Tennessee toward Nashville, forcing Grant and Sherman back into Kentucky. By letter, General Johnston rejected the plan, saying that merely to march through Kingston into Middle Tennessee would require all of his supplies, leaving no resources with which to capture Knoxville on the way. General Lee

Dedication of the Confederate Memorial in Knoxville, 1892

agreed with Johnston that the plan lacked merit. On April 7, Longstreet's command was ordered back to the Army of Northern Virginia. There would be no more important fighting in East Tennessee.

Sherman, in planning his drive into Georgia, cut out all civilian traffic on the railroads, a move which helped his army. He said that

of course it naturally raised a howl. Some of the poor Union people of East Tennessee appealed to President Lincoln, whose kind heart responded promptly to their request. He telegraphed me to know if I could not modify or repeal my orders; but I answered him that a great campaign was impending, on which the fate of a nation hung . . . our railroads had but a limited capacity, and could not provide for the necessities of the army and of the people too; that one or the other must quit. Mr. Lincoln seemed to acquiesce.[12]

Northern soldiers who could not always distinguish a loyal Tennessean from a Rebel added to the woes of the beleaguered area. Their countryside stripped bare by both armies, the people of East Tennessee discovered that friend and foe alike had robbed them. In January one of them plaintively wrote to the Knoxville commander, "If the army needs all we have, let us know, and we will leave the country. The soldiers are robbing smokehouses and taking supplies, even where your safeguard is shown. Deal with us as you please, but let us know the worst."[13]

Relief from hunger and scarcity of clothing came not from the liberating armies but from the citizens of the North. In January, 1864, Mr. Nathaniel G. Taylor, armed with letters of recommendation from Military Governor Andrew Johnson and President Lincoln, arrived in Philadelphia, Pennsylvania, to describe the wretched condition of the people ravaged by both armies. With the assistance of some kind women of Philadelphia, Taylor's mission grew to such proportions that the governors of Pennsylvania, Maine, Massachusetts, and New York formally aided in the establishment of "A Relief Association for East Tennessee."

William Cullen Bryant, the poet, took an active part in raising funds. Edward Everett, the famed orator who had delivered a two-hour speech at the dedication of the Gettysburg battlefield, spent the remainder of his life working for the Association, which raised $252,205.51. Into Mr. Everett's hands came a strange mixture of bequests. One poor woman sent seven cents, all she could afford. A man sent six English sovereigns, all he saved when he escaped from the burning ship "Lafayette," sunk by a Confederate raider.[14]

When the Civil War ended, many former Confederate sympathizers left Knoxville and East Tennessee for the friendlier climates of more typical Southern cities. Many of the Union people were disenchanted with the whole four years of struggle. There was little concerted effort to honor the heroes of either side. No great monuments were erected in Knoxville.

Knoxville never adopted the custom widespread in other Southern cities of naming streets, schools, and public and private buildings for Confederate heroes. It is notable that the infrequent examples of the naming of streets and buildings for Civil War leaders reflected the strong Union sentiment characteristic of this Southern town, the names of Admiral David Farragut, General William P. Sanders, and President Andrew Johnson being the most prevalent in this regard.

Knoxville presented no united front as either victor or vanquished. The people buried their past. Attempts to preserve Fort Sanders as a national monument failed because of public apathy.[15] Fort Dickerson remained remarkably intact for reasons of inaccessibility, but buried beneath a century of underbrush it was all but forgotten until recently rediscovered and restored.[16]

Confederate Memorial. This monument was erected in the cemetery on Bethel Avenue where the dead from the Knoxville battles were buried.

Now, after one hundred years have dimmed the passion and bitterness, most of us can look back, not in anger, but rather with humble pride in the epic deeds of both the Blue and Gray. However, except for Chickamauga, the struggle for isolated East Tennessee has been overshadowed by Shiloh, Fredericksburg, Vicksburg, and Gettysburg, and its story has been relegated largely to footnotes in history.

East Tennessee's part deserves a better fate in the annals of the Civil War. The loss of this region, so vital for its strategic position, its railroads, and its resources, was a major factor in the collapse of the Confederacy.

The roll-call of personages who took part in the conflict in this area is long and illustrious—Zollicoffer and Sanders, Burnside and Longstreet,[17] Alexander and Benjamin, Poe and Leadbetter, John Hunt Morgan, Forrest and Wheeler, Shackelford and Sheridan, Crittenden, Kirby Smith and Buckner, Sherman and Grant, and unnamed thousands in the ranks. Some of them fell in battle long ago. Now they are all gone; may they never be forgotten. The magnificent record of their valor in East Tennessee is an enduring portion of our heritage to save.

State Historical Marker IE 68 at the site of the assault on Fort Sanders

NOTES

1. *Confederate Veteran*, V (April 1897), 153.

2. Letter from Sherman to Halleck, September 17, 1863.

3. Sherman, I, 367.

4. *Ibid*, I, 368. Details of the banquet supplied by a letter from James W. Baker of Huntsville, Tennessee, whose grandfather had been a member of General Sanders' staff and had attended the affair.

5. Philip H. Sheridan, *Personal Memoirs*, I, 325.

6. C. C. Briant, *History of the Sixth Regiment Indiana Volunteer Infantry*, p. 114.

7. *Confederate Veteran*, XIII (October 1905), 458.

8. General Grant came to Knoxville on December 31, 1863. On January 1, he called on Judge Temple, and later went to Mrs. Brownlow's home to pay his respects. The general refused offers of wine and would not smoke his cigars in the presence of the ladies. At Mr. Temple's home Grant discussed the possibility of sending a Union army up the French Broad River into North Carolina, striking Lee from the rear. Grant was persuaded that such a move was practically impossible because of the mountainous terrain. Temple, p. 517.

9. Sheridan, pp. 325-26. Following the disaster at the famous "Petersburg mine," Burnside was relieved. He returned to Rhode Island and became Governor 1866-69 and United States Senator from 1875 until his death, September 3, 1881.

10. Longstreet, p. 542.

11. Lee to Davis, February 18, 1864.

12. Sherman, II, 10.

13. *Confederate Veteran*, XXXI (October 1923), 383. Some of the "loyal" population soon became disenchanted with the Union army and its behavior. First Lieutenant V. P. Mason of the 22nd Indiana Infantry was cashiered for dressing a woman in male attire and publicly riding with her so disguised at the rear of his regiment. On January 6, by General Order No. 6, General Foster ordered all colored persons between eighteen and forty-five, except those servants of loyal Unionists who preferred to remain with their masters, to be conscripted under General Davis Tilson, the chief of artillery. (Copies of all general orders of the Army of the Ohio are found in a bound volume in Lawson McGhee Library.)

14. Humes, pp. 310-33; 391-92.

15. On October 7, 8, and 9, 1890, Knoxville was host to 800 Union and 475 Confederate veterans who returned for a reunion at Fort Sanders. The celebration was initiated by Colonel Baird of the 79th New York Highlanders, and the program was directed by the Ed Maynard Chapter of the G. A. R. and the Fred Ault Chapter of the United Confederate Veterans. General R. N. Hood, President of the Third National Bank of Knoxville, gave the welcoming address, and General William H. Gibson of the Tenth Ohio Infantry responded. The main address was delivered by the Honorable J. W. Caldwell. General Longstreet came for the ceremonies, but having been wounded in the throat in the Wilderness Campaign was unable to speak publicly. Mr. E. A. Amgier of Atlanta read Longstreet's address.

For three days there were speeches, fireworks, rebel yells, Union "huzzahs," cannon fire, and parades. Many Union soldiers returned plundered articles. On the final day, 35,000 people observed a fireworks display at Fort Sanders, whose red clay embankments still stood intact.

16. The trenches of Fort Higley and some of those of Fort Stanley are still there in the forest because the hand of "progress" has not removed them.

17. President Grant appointed his old friend General Longstreet to a Federal job in New Orleans. Longstreet became a Republican, and was therefore considered a traitor by many Southerners. He spent considerable time in his remaining years defending his conduct at the Battle of Gettysburg. In 1880 he was made U. S. Ambassador to Turkey. It was not until the 1896 Confederate Reunion that there was noticeable cheering for Longstreet. In 1897 he married Helen Dortsch, who died in 1962, a hundred years after her husband's triumph at Fredericksburg.

Appendix A

The following forces and their commanding officers took part in the battle for Knoxville. Various symbols after the names of some of the officers designate casualties during the siege: k, killed; mw, mortally wounded; and w, wounded.

THE UNION ARMY AT THE SIEGE OF KNOXVILLE
November 17—December 4, 1863

ARMY OF THE OHIO

Major General Ambrose E. Burnside, Commanding
Major General John G. Parke, Second in Command
Brigadier General Samuel P. Carter, Provost Marshal
Captain Orlando Poe, Engineering Officer

NINTH ARMY CORPS
Brig. Gen. Robert B. Potter
    Escort: 6th Indiana Cavalry (4 companies)
    Col. James Biddle

FIRST DIVISION
Brig. Gen. Edward Ferrero

    First Brigade, Col. David Morrison
    36th Massachusetts, Maj. William E. Draper
    8th Michigan, Lt. Col. Ralph Ely
    79th New York, Capt. William S. Montgomery
    45th Pennsylvania, Lt. Col. Francis M. Hills

    Second Brigade, Col. Benjamin C. Christ
    29th Massachusetts, Col. Ebenezer W. Peirce,
      Major Chipman
    27th Michigan, Maj. William B. Wright
    46th New York, Capt. Alphons Serieri
    50th Pennsylvania, Maj. Edward Overton, Jr.

    Third Brigade, Col. William Humphrey
    2nd Michigan, Maj. Cornelius Byington (mw),
      Capt. John C. Ruehl
    17th Michigan, Lt. Col. Lorin L. Comstock (k),
      Capt. Frederick W. Swift
    20th Michigan, Maj. Byron M. Cutcheon
    100th Pennsylvania, Lt. Col. Matthew M. Dawson

Artillery
    34th New York, Capt. Jacob Roemer
    Co. D, 1st Rhode Island, Capt. William W. Buckley

SECOND DIVISION
Col. John F. Hartranft

    First Brigade, Col. Joshua K. Siegfried
    2nd Maryland, Col. Thomas B. Allard
    21st Massachusetts, Lt. Col. George P. Hawkes
    48th Pennsylvania, Maj. Joseph A. Gilmour

    Second Brigade, Lt. Col. Edwin Schall
    35th Massachusetts, Maj. Nathaniel Wales
    11th New Hampshire, Capt. Leander W. Cogswell
    51st Pennsylvania, Maj. William J. Bolton

Artillery
    Co. E, 2nd U. S. Artillery, unattached, Lt. Samuel N.
    Benjamin

TWENTY-THIRD ARMY CORPS
Brig. Gen. Mahlon D. Manson

    General Headquarters
    McLaughlin's Ohio Squadron Cavalry, Maj. Richard
    Rice
    Engineering Battalion, Capt. O. S. McClure

SECOND DIVISION
Brig. Gen. Julius White

    Second Brigade, Col. Marshall W. Chapin
    107th Illinois, Lt. Col. Francis H. Lowry
    13th Kentucky, Col. William E. Hobson

23rd Michigan, Maj. William W. Wheeler
111th Ohio, Maj. Isaac R. Sherwood
Illinois Battery, Capt. Edward C. Henshaw

THIRD DIVISION
Brig. Gen. Milo S. Hascall

First Brigade, Col. James W. Reilly
44th Ohio, Maj. Alpheus S. Moore
100th Ohio, Col. Patrick S. Slevin
104th Ohio, Lt. Col. Oscar W. Sterl
Co. D, 1st Ohio Artillery, Lt. William H. Pease

Second Brigade, Col. Daniel Cameron
65th Illinois, Lt. Col. William S. Stewart
24th Kentucky, Col. John S. Hunt
103rd Ohio, Capt. John T. Philpot
Indiana Battery, Capt. Hubbard T. Thomas

Reserve Artillery, Capt. Andrew J. Konkle
24th Indiana, Capt. Joseph A. Sims
19th Ohio, Capt. Joseph C. Shields

Provisional Brigade, Col. William A. Hoskins
12th Kentucky, Maj. Joseph M. Owens
8th Tennessee, Col. Felix A. Reeve
Tennessee Brigade, Col. John S. Casement

CAVALRY CORPS
Brig. Gen. James M. Shackelford

FIRST DIVISION
Brig. Gen. William P. Sanders (mw), Col. Frank Wolford

First Brigade, Col. Frank Wolford, Lt. Col. Silas Adams
1st Kentucky, Lt. Col. Silas Adams
11th Kentucky ————————————
12th Kentucky ————————————
Law's Howitzer Battery ———————

Second Brigade, Lt. Col. Emery S. Bond
112th Illinois Mounted Infantry, Maj. Tristram T. Dow
8th Michigan ——————————————
45th Ohio Mounted Infantry ——————————
15th Indiana Battery ——————————

Third Brigade, Col. Charles D. Pennebaker
11th Kentucky, Col. S. Palace Love
27th Kentucky, Lt. Col. John H. Ward

SECOND DIVISION

First Brigade, Col. Israel Garrard
2nd Ohio, Lt. Col. George A. Purington
7th Ohio ————————————
2nd Tennessee ——————————

In his official report General Burnside said: "Our force at this time [commencement of the siege of Knoxville] was about 12,000 effective men, exclusive of the new recruits of loyal Tennesseans." Total Union loss: killed, 92; wounded, 394; captured or missing, 207; TOTAL, 693.

THE CONFEDERATE ARMY AT THE SIEGE OF KNOXVILLE
November 17—December 4, 1863

Lieutenant General James Longstreet, Commanding
Lieutenant Colonel G. Moxley Sorrel, Adjutant
Brigadier General Danville Leadbetter, Engineering Officer
Dr. J. D. Cullen, Medical Director

McLaws' Division
Maj. Gen. Lafayette McLaws

Kershaw's Brigade, Brig. Gen. Joseph B. Kershaw
2nd South Carolina, Col. John D. Kennedy (w), Lt. Col. F. Gaillard
3rd South Carolina, Col. James D. Nance
7th South Carolina, Capt. E. J. Goggans
8th South Carolina, Col. J. W. Henagan, Capt. D. McIntyre
15th South Carolina, Maj. William M. Gist (k), Capt. J. B. Davis
3rd South Carolina Battalion, Lt. Col. W. G. Rice

Wofford's Brigade, Col. S. Z. Ruff (k), Lt. Col. N. L. Hutchins, Jr.
16th Georgia, Lt. Col. Henry P. Thomas (k)
18th Georgia, Capt. John A. Crawford
24th Georgia, Capt. N. J. Dortch
Cobb's (Georgia) Legion, Maj. William D. Conyers
Phillips (Georgia) Legion, Maj. Joseph Hamilton (w)
3rd Georgia Battalion Sharpshooters, Lt. Col. N. L. Hutchins, Jr.

Humphreys' Brigade, Brig. Gen. Benjamin G. Humphreys
13th Mississippi, Col. Kennon McElroy (k), Maj. G. L. Donald
17th Mississippi, Lt. Col. John C. Fiser (w)
18th Mississippi, Col. Thomas M. Griffin
21st Mississippi, Col. W. L. Brandon

Bryan's Brigade, Brig. Gen. Goode Bryan
10th Georgia, Lt. Col. Willis C. Holt
50th Georgia, Col. P. McGlashan
51st Georgia, Col. E. Ball
53rd Georgia, Col. James P. Simms (w)

Hood's Division
Brig. Gen. Micah Jenkins

Jenkins' Brigade, Col. John Bratton
1st South Carolina, Col. F. W. Kilpatrick
2nd South Carolina Rifles, Col. Thomas Thomson
5th South Carolina, Col. A. Coward
6th South Carolina ————————————
Hampton (S.C.) Legion, Col. M. W. Gary
Palmetto (S.C.) Sharpshooters, Col. Joseph Walker

Robertson's Brigade, Brig. Gen. Jerome B. Robertson
3rd Arkansas, Col. Van H. Manning
1st Texas, Col. A. T. Rainey
4th Texas, Col. J. C. G. Key
5th Texas, Col. R. M. Powell

Law's Brigade, Brig. Gen. E. McIver Law
4th Alabama, Col. P. D. Bowles
15th Alabama, Col. W. C. Oates
44th Alabama, Col. W. F. Perry
47th Alabama, Col. M. J. Bulger
48th Alabama, Col. James L. Sheffield

Anderson's Brigade, Brig. Gen. G. T. Anderson
7th Georgia, Col. W. W. White
8th Georgia, Col. John R. Towers
9th Georgia, Col. Benjamin Beck
11th Georgia, Col. F. H. Little
59th Georgia, Col. Jack Brown

Benning's Brigade, Brig. Gen. Henry L. Benning
2nd Georgia, Col. E. M. Butt
15th Georgia, Col. D. M. Du Bose
17th Georgia, Col. Wesley C. Hodges
20th Georgia, Col. J. D. Waddell

Artillery
Col. E. Porter Alexander

Leyden's Battalion, Maj. A. Leyden
Georgia Battery, Capt. Tyler M. Peeples
Georgia Battery, Capt. A. M. Wolihin
Georgia Battery, Capt. B. W. York

Alexander's Battalion, Maj. Frank Huger
Louisiana Battery, Capt. G. V. Moody
Virginia Battery, Capt. W. W. Fickling
Virginia Battery, Capt. Tyler C. Jordan
Virginia Battery, Capt. William W. Parker
Virginia Battery, Capt. Osmond B. Taylor
Virginia Battery, Capt. Pichigru Woolfolk, Jr.

Buckner's Division
Brig. Gen. Bushrod R. Johnson

Gracie's Brigade, Brig. Gen. Archibald Gracie, Jr.
41st Alabama, Lt. Col. T. G. Trimmier
43rd Alabama, Col. Y. M. Moody

59th Alabama, Lt. Col. J. D. McLennan
60th Alabama, Col. J. W. A. Sanford

Johnson's Brigade, Col. John S. Fulton
17th Tennessee, Lt. Col. W. W. Floyd
23rd Tennessee, Lt. Col. W. W. Floyd
25th Tennessee, Lt. Col. J. L. McEwen, Jr.
44th Tennessee, Lt. Col. J. L. McEwen, Jr.
63rd Tennessee, Maj. J. A. Aiken

CAVALRY CORPS
Maj. Gen. Joseph Wheeler, Maj. Gen. William T. Martin

DIVISION COMMANDERS
Maj. Gen. William T. Martin, Brig. Gen. F. C.
  Armstrong, Brig, Gen. John T. Morgan

BRIGADE COMMANDERS
Col. Thomas Harrison, Col. A. A. Russell, Col. C. C.
  Crews, Col. George G. Dibrell

TROOPS
Parts of the 4th, 8th, 9th, and 11th Tennessee
  1st, 2nd, 3rd, 4th, and 6th Georgia
  1st, 3rd, 4th, 7th, and 51st Alabama
  3rd Arkansas
  8th and 11th Texas

1st and 8th Confederate regiments
Wiggins' Battery

RANSOM'S CAVALRY

Jones' Brigade, Brig. Gen. William E. Jones
8th Virginia, Col. James M. Corns
21st Virginia ——————————
27th Virginia Battalion ——————————
34th Virginia Battalion, Col. V. A. Witcher
36th Virginia Battalion ——————————
37th Virginia Battalion

Giltner's Brigade, Col. H. L. Giltner
16th Georgia Battalion, Maj. E. Y. Clark
4th Kentucky, Maj. N. Parker
10th Kentucky, Lt. Col. Edwin Trimble
1st Tennessee, Col. James E. Carter
64th Virginia, Col. Campbell Slemp
Virginia Battery, Capt. William N. Lowry

Total Confederate strength probably numbered 20,000.
Total Confederate loss, exclusive of cavalry loss, which is
estimated at 250: killed, 182; wounded, 768; captured or
missing, 192; TOTAL, 1,142.

Appendix B

OPERATIONS IN EAST TENNESSEE
A Summary

Between the two great Confederate armies in Virginia and Tennessee lay a long stretch of country, principally covered by the Allegheny and Cumberland mountains. The only means of direct communication and transportation between these armies was the East Tennessee, Virginia and Georgia Railroad. Near this road were the great King's salt-works in Smyth County and the lead mines of Wythe County, Va. The farmlands along the route furnished the Confederacy with a large part of its provisions.

Because the mountainous terrain rendered the occupation of the country impracticable by a large army, numerous invasions by smaller forces, principally cavalry, were made in order to destroy the railroad and the salt-works.

On December 17, 1861, General Buell sent Colonel (afterward General and President) James A. Garfield against General Humphrey Marshall and his "Ragamuffin Regiment" of Kentuckians. In January the two forces skirmished at Paintsville, Kentucky. Garfield's men were recalled to fight in western Tennessee.

In December, 1862, General Samuel P. Carter of Tennessee and Colonel T. T. Garrard of Kentucky led a Union cavalry raid upon the railroad in East Tennessee and destroyed the bridges over the Holston and Watauga rivers. Marshall prevented them from capturing Bristol and pursued them to Jonesville.

In June, 1863, Colonel William Sanders led a Federal raid against Knoxville, but was repulsed as described in the narrative.

On September 7, 1863, about five hundred of Burnside's infantry advanced as far northeast as Telford's Depot in Washington County, Tennessee, but were driven back to Limestone Depot near Greeneville.

In October, 1863, General John Williams, commanding the Confederates in upper East Tennessee, was driven back from Blue Springs, near Bulls Gap, to Leesburg, Virginia.

In November, 1863, the Confederate forces crossed the Holston River at Kingsport and advanced to Big Creek.

From November, 1863, to April, 1864, upper East Tennessee was controlled for the Confederacy by Longstreet's corps. Until December, 1864, most Federal raids were made through eastern Kentucky.

In December, 1864, Federal General George Stoneman left Knoxville with a force of 4,000 cavalrymen and entered southwest Virginia, occupying Bristol and Abingdon. The salt-works were destroyed, and Stoneman withdrew.

March 20, 1865, General Stoneman, on instructions from Grant, left Knoxville and moved via Morristown and Bulls Gap to Boone, North Carolina, crossed into Virginia, and destroyed the railroad from Wytheville to Lynchburg.

Bibliography

Albaugh, William A., III, and Edward N. Simmons. *Confederate Arms*. Harrisburg: 1957.

Alexander, E. Porter. *Military Memoirs of a Confederate*. New York: 1907.

Amann, William F. *Personnel of the Civil War*. 2 vols. New York: 1961.

American Annual Cyclopaedia, 1861-1870. New York: 1862-71.

Baker, Sydney. "Sydney Baker Papers, 44th Ohio Volunteer Infantry." Ohio Historical Society, Columbus.

Basler, Roy, ed. *The Collected Works of Abraham Lincoln*. 8 vols. New Brunswick: 1953.

Battles and Leaders, see Johnson, Robert U., and C. C. Buel.

Black, Robert C., III. *The Railroads of the Confederacy*. Chapel Hill: 1952.

Blackford, Charles M., III. *Letters from Lee's Army*. New York: 1947.

Botkin, B. A. *A Treasury of Southern Folklore*. New York: 1949.

Brearley, Will H. *Recollections of the East Tennessee Campaign*. Detroit: 1871.

Briant, C. C. *History of the Sixth Regiment Indiana Volunteer Infantry*. Indianapolis: 1891.

Brown, Dee Alexander. *The Bold Cavaliers, Morgan's 2nd Kentucky Cavalry Raiders*. Philadelphia: 1959.

Brownlow, W. G., *Sketches of the Rise, Progress, and Decline of Secession*. Philadelphia: 1862.

Buffat, Elisa. "Some Recollections of My Childhood Days." Unpublished manuscript in McClung Collection, Lawson McGhee Library, Knoxville.

Burrage, Henry S. *History of the Thirty-Sixth Regiment, Massachusetts Volunteers*. Boston: 1884.

Campbell, Mary Emily Robertson. *The Attitude of Tennesseans Toward the Union, 1847-1861*. New York: 1961.

Carruth, Sumner. *History of the Thirty-Fifth Regiment, Massachusetts Volunteers*. Boston: 1884.

Carter, J. S. *History of the Fourth Regiment Tennessee Volunteer Cavalry*. Knoxville: 1902.

Catton, Bruce. *The Coming Fury*. New York: 1961.

Chesnut, Mary B. *A Diary from Dixie*. New York: 1905.

Cogswell, Leander W. *A History of the Eleventh New Hampshire Regiment*. Concord: 1891.

Confederate Veteran, 40 vols. Nashville: 1893-1932.

Creekmore, Betsey B. *Knoxville*. Knoxville: 1958.

Dana, Charles A. *Recollections of the Civil War*. New York: 1898.

Davidson, Donald. *The Tennessee*. 2 vols. New York: 1946, 1948.

Davis, Jefferson. *The Rise and Fall of the Confederate Government*. 2 vols. New York: 1881.

Deaderick, David. "The Diary of David Deaderick, 1827-1872." Unpublished manuscript in Lawson McGhee Library, Knoxville.

Dickert, D. Augustus. *History of Kershaw's Brigade.* Newberry: 1899.

Dowdey, Clifford, and Louis H. Manarin. *The Wartime Papers of R. E. Lee.* Boston: 1961.

Downey, Fairfax. *Storming of the Gateway, Chattanooga, 1863.* New York: 1960.

Duane, J. D. *Manual for Engineer Troops.* New York: 1862.

Ducloux, Charles. "Scrapbook." Lawson McGhee Library, Knoxville. "Miscellaneous Papers." Confederate Memorial Hall, Knoxville.

Duke, Basil. *History of Morgan's Cavalry,* Cincinnati: 1867.

————. *Reminiscences.* New York: 1911.

Eckel, Alexander. *The Fourth Tennessee Cavalry.* Knoxville: 1929.

Eckenrode, H. J., and Bryan Conrad. *James Longstreet: Lee's War Horse.* Chapel Hill: 1936.

Ellis, Daniel. *Thrilling Adventures of Daniel Ellis.* New York: 1867.

Everett, Edward. *Account of the Fund for the Relief of East Tennessee.* Boston: 1864.

Fink, Harold S., "The East Tennessee Campaign and the Battle of Knoxville in 1863." The East Tennessee Historical Society's *Publications,* No. 29 (1957).

Fiske, John. *The Mississippi Valley in the Civil War.* Boston: 1900.

Folmsbee, Stanley J. *East Tennessee University 1840-1879.* The University of Tennessee *Record,* Vol. 62, May 1959, No. 3.

————, Robert E. Corlew, and Enoch L. Mitchell. *History of Tennessee.* 2 vols. New York: 1960.

Freeman, Douglas Southall. *Lee's Lieutenants, A Study in Command.* 3 vols. New York: 1942-44.

Goodspeed Publishing Co. *History of Tennessee from the Earliest Time to the Present.* Nashville: 1886.

Grant, Ulysses S. *Personal Memoirs.* 2 vols. New York: 1886.

Green, William M. *Memoir of Rt. Rev. James Hervey Otey.* New York: 1885.

Guernsey, Alfred H., and Henry M. Alden. *Harper's Pictorial History of the Great Rebellion.* Chicago: 1868.

Hamer, Philip M. *Tennessee: A History.* 4 vols. New York: 1933.

Hamilton, William D. *Recollections of a Cavalryman of the Civil War After 50 Years.* Columbus: 1915.

Harper's Weekly. Vols. V-IX. New York: 1861-65.

Holland, Cecil F. *Morgan and His Raiders.* New York: 1943.

Horn, Stanley F. *The Army of Tennessee.* Indianapolis: 1941.

Hughes, James B., Jr. *Confederate Gun Makers, Armories, and Arsenals.* Southern Edition. N.p.: 1961.

Humes, Thomas W. *The Loyal Mountaineers of Tennessee.* Knoxville: 1888.

Johnson, Robert U., and Clarence Clough Buel, eds. *Battles and Leaders of the Civil War.* 4 vols. New York: 1887.

Johnson, Rossiter. *Campfires and Battlefields.* New York: 1960.

Johnston, Joseph E. *Narrative of Military Operations.* New York: 1874.

Jones, John B. *A Rebel War Clerk's Diary.* Philadelphia: 1866.

Kincaid, Robert L. *The Wilderness Road.* Indianapolis: 1947.

Knoxville *Daily Register.*

Knoxville *Journal.*

Knoxville *Journal and Tribune.*

Knoxville *News-Sentinel.*

Knoxville *Sentinel.*

Knoxville *Tribune.*

Knoxville *Whig.*

LaBree, Ben. *The Confederate Soldier in the Civil War.* Louisville: 1895.

Lasswell, Mary, ed. *Rags and Hopes: The Memoirs of Val C. Giles, Four Years with Hood's Brigade, Fourth - Texas Infantry, 1861-1865.* New York: 1961.

Longstreet, James. *From Manassas to Appomattox.* Philadelphia: 1896.

Lord, Francis A. *They Fought for the Union.* Harrisburg: 1960.

Lytle, Andrew H. *Bedford Forrest and His Critter Company.* New York: 1960.

McFarland, R. W. *The Surrender of Cumberland Gap, September 9, 1863.* Columbus: 1898.

McMurray, W. J. *History of the Twentieth Tennessee Regiment, Volunteer Infantry, C.S.A.* Nashville: 1904.

Marshall, Park. *A Life of William B. Bate.* Nashville: 1908.

Milhollen, Hirst D., James R. Johnson, and Alfred H. Bill. *Horsemen Blue and Gray.* New York: 1960.

Miller, Francis T., ed. *The Photographic History of the Civil War.* 10 vols. New York: 1912.

Montgomery, James S. *The Shaping of a Battle: Gettysburg.* Philadelphia: 1959.

Moore, Frank, *The Civil War in Song and Story.* New York: 1899.

Moore, John Trotwood, and A. P. Foster. *Tennessee: The Volunteer State, 1769–1923.* 4 vols. Chicago and Nashville: 1923.

Nelson, Thomas A. R. "Papers and Scrapbooks." Unpublished manuscripts in Lawson McGhee Library.

Noll, Arthur H. *General Kirby Smith.* Sewanee: 1907.

Osborne, William H. *The History of the Twenty-Ninth Regiment of Massachusetts Volunteer Infantry in the Late War of the Rebellion.* Boston: 1877.

Patton, James Welch. *Unionism and Reconstruction in Tennessee.* Chapel Hill: 1934.

Pittenger, William. *The Great Locomotive Chase.* Philadelphia: 1893.

Pollard, Edward A. *Southern History of the War.* 4 vols. New York: 1866.

Poore, Ben Perley. *The Life and Public Services of Ambrose E. Burnside, Soldier—Citizen—Statesman.* Providence: 1882.

Powell, Lyman P. *Historic Towns of the Southern States.* New York: 1900.

Reeve, Felix. *East Tennessee in the War of the Rebellion.* Washington: 1902.

Rothrock, Mary U., ed. *The French Broad-Holston Country.* Knoxville: 1946.

Rule, William. *Standard History of Knoxville, Tennessee.* Chicago: 1900.

Scott, Samuel W., and Samuel P. Angel. *History of the Thirteenth Regiment, Tennessee Volunteer Cavalry, U.S.A.* Philadelphia: 1903.

Scruggs, J. C. "Random Recollections of an East Tennessean." Knoxville: 1900. Unpublished manuscript borrowed from Richard Evans.

Seitz, Don. *Braxton Bragg, General of the Confederacy.* New York: 1923.

Seymour, Charles M., ed. *St. John's Church, Knoxville.* Kingsport: 1947.

Shaver, Lewellyn A. *A History of the Sixtieth Alabama Regiment, Gracie's Alabama Brigade.* Montgomery: 1867.

Sheridan, Philip H. *Personal Memoirs.* New York: 1888.

Sherman, William T. *Memoirs of General William T. Sherman.* 2 vols. New York: 1875.

Smith, Albert B. "Albert B. Smith Papers, Company U, 100th Ohio Volunteer Infantry." Unpublished manuscript in Ohio Historical Society, Columbus.

Sorrel, G. Moxley. *Recollections of a Confederate Staff Officer.* New York: 1905.

Southern Bivouac, The. 6 vols. Louisville: 1886-87.

Stickles, Arndt M. *Simon Bolivar Buckner.* Chapel Hill: 1940.

Temple, Oliver P. *East Tennessee and the Civil War.* Cincinnati: 1899.

Thompson, B. F. *History of the 112th Regiment of Illinois Volunteer Infantry.* Toulon, Illinois: 1885.

Todd, William. *The Seventy-Ninth Highlanders, New York Volunteers.* Albany: 1886.

Toney, Marcus B. *The Privations of a Private.* Nashville: 1905.

Tucker, Glenn. *Chickamauga, Bloody Battle in the West.* Indianapolis: 1961.

United Daughters of the Confederacy, files, in Confederate Memorial Hall, Knoxville.

Walcott, Charles F. *History of the Twenty-First Regiment, Massachusetts Volunteers.* Boston: 1882.

War of the Rebellion, Official Records of the Union and Confederate Armies, Series I, 128 vols. Washington: 1880-1901.

Watkins, Samuel R. *Company "Aytch"—First Tennessee Regiment.* Nashville: 1882.

Wiley, Bell I., and Hirst D. Milhollen. *They Who Fought Here.* New York: 1959.

Woodbury, Augustus. *Major General Ambrose E. Burnside and the Ninth Army Corps.* Providence: 1867.

Worsham, W. J. *Old Nineteenth Tennessee Regiment, C.S.A.* Knoxville: 1902.

Pictures and Sources

Index

Island No. 10, 44

Jacksboro, Tenn., 26, 32, 41, 46
Jackson, Abner, 11
Jackson, Dr., 149
Jackson, Gen. Thomas J., 70, 80, 99, 190
Jamestown, Tenn., 26, 29, 32, 41
Jefferson City, Tenn., 16
Jefferson County, Tenn., 164
Jenkins, Gen. Micah, 90, **92**, 103, 130, 132, 134, 138, 167, 173, 187, 188, 199, 203
Johnson, Andrew, 8, **10**, 11, 25, 36, 37, 39, 40, 44, 218, 219
Johnson, Gen. Bushrod, 91, **95**, 170, 187, 199, 202
Johnson, Gen. R. L., 60
Johnston, Gen. Albert S., 26, 41, 44
Johnston, Gen. Joseph E., 50, 55, 73, 75, 76, 80, 90, 217
Jomini, Baron Antoine H., 8
Jones, Reps, **52**
Jones, Gen. Samuel, 72, 97
Jones, Gen. William E., 175, 226
Jonesboro, Tenn., 24, 93
Jordan, Capt. Tyler C., 225

Kain, W. C., 55
Keelan, Edward, 32
Kennedy, J. B., 203
Kennedy, Col. John D., 141, **144**
Kennedy, Dr. John M., **52**
Kershaw, Gen. Joseph, 90, **92**, 140, 145, 185
Key, Col. J. C., 225
Kilpatrick, Col. F. W., 225
Kingsport, Tenn., 98, 227
Kingston, Tenn., 74, 77, 85, 86, 105, 110, 130, 168, 217
Knoxville Arsenal, 16
Knoxville College, **108-109**, 137, 156, 164
Knoxville *Register,* 17, 20, 32, 78
Knoxville *Whig,* 4, 21
Konkle, Capt. Andrew J., 224
Ku Klux Klan, 8

La Fayette, Ga., 83, 89
Lamar House, 54, 75, 147, 149
Lane, Gen. W. P., 21
Langford, Capt. N. C., 54
Law, Gen. E. McIver, 90, **92**, 132, 134, 164
Lawder, Maj. R. E., 144, 147, 149
Leadbetter, Gen. Danville, 76, 168, 173, 177, 180, 185, 220
Lebanon, Ky., 39, 58, 60
Ledbetter, Col., 35, 38
Lee, Clifton, 153
Lee, Gen. Robert E., 8, 39, 49, 56, 67, 69, 72, 73, 80, 82, 89, 90, 91, 96, 97, 183, 208, 217, 221
Lenoir City, Tenn., 77, 98, 105, 111, 126, 127, 134, 136, 138, 164
Lexington, Ky., 70
Lexington Rifles, 56
Leyden, Maj. A., 16, 103
Lincoln, Abraham, 7, 10, 20, 24, 26, 27, 32, 37, 39, 40, 44, 45, 56, 58, 74, 75, 77, 83, 85, 93, 110, 175, 212, 218
Little, Col. F. H., 225
Little Tennessee River, 8, 105, 164
London, Ky., 37, 71
Longstreet, Gen. James, 73, 74, 80, **82**, 89, 90, 91, 92, **96**, 97, 99, 102, 103, 104, 105, 110-11, 112, 113, 114, 119, 125, 126, 130, 132, 134, 136, 137, 138, 141, 151, 164, 167, 169, 173, 174, 175, 177, 183, 184, 185, **187**, 188, 192, 198, 199, 202, 203, 205, 208, 210, 213, 217, 220, 221
Longstreet, Mrs. James, 221
"Long Tom," 56, 69
Loudon, Tenn., 32, 77, 86, 97, 98, 103, 104, 105, 111, 114, 126, 130
Louisville, Ky., 37, 39, 59, 69, 70
Louisville, Tenn., 125
Louisville and Nashville Railroad, 60
Love, Col. S. Palace, 224
Lowry, Lt. Col. Francis H., 223
Lowry, Capt. William N., 226
Luttrell, James C., **165**
Luttrell, James C. III, 165
Luttrell, Samuel B., **165**

Mabry, Joseph A., 16, 18, 87
Mabry's Hill, 151, 153, 157, 173, 175
McAdoo, W. G., 18
McClellan, Gen. George, 32, 39, 40, 70, 73, 74, **77**
McClung, H. L., 55, 77, 78
McClung, Capt. P. M., 16
McClure, Capt. O. S., 223
McCown, Gen. John P., 55, 67, **72**
McDermott, S. A., **52**
McElroy, Col. Kennan, 198, 225
McEwen, Lt. Col. J. L., 226
McGhee, Charles M., 16
McGhee's Hill, 78
McGlashon, Col. P., 225
McLaws, Gen. Lafayette, **90**, 102, 103, 126, 130, 132, 134, 138, 140, 167, 184, 185, 187, 188, 199
McLennan, Lt. Col. J. D., 226
McMinn County, Tenn., 13, 21
McMullen, Stuart, **52**
McNutt, Dr. Newton, **52**
McNutt, Robert H., 164
Madrid Bend, 44
Mahoney, Sgt. Jeremiah, 199
Malvern Hill, 90
Manassas, Battle of, 90
Maney, Capt. Frank, 49
Manning, Sgt. Joseph, 199
Manning, Col. Van H., 225
Manson, Gen. Mahlon D., **96,** 157
Marietta, Ga., 61
Marshall, Gen. Humphrey, 70, 227
Martin, Rev. Joseph, 79
Martin, Gen. William T., 104, 166
Maryville, Tenn., 105, 113, 122, 130, 175, 210, 211, 213, 215
Mason, Lt. V. P., 221
Maury, Gen. Dabney H., 72
Maury, Matthew F., 8
Maxwell, A. L., 13
Maynard, Horace, **23**, 24, 25, 36, 37, 39, 40, 54, 111
Meade, Gen. George F., 80, 93
Melrose, **108-109, 119**, 151, **155, 156**
Memphis, Tenn., 138
Mill Springs, Ky., 39, 41, 43, 44, 49
Miller, M. M., 117
Minnich, J. W., 130
Missionary Ridge, 96, 110, 167, 174, 203, 208
Mitchel, John, 10, 25